DIPLOMAT BETWEEN WARS

HUGH R. WILSON

DIPLOMAT BETWEEN WARS

BY

HUGH R. WILSON

LONGMANS, GREEN AND CO.

NEW YORK · TORONTO

1941

DIPLOMAT BETWEEN WARS

COPYRIGHT · 1941

BY HUGH R. WILSON

First edition March 1941
Reprinted March 1941

To

KATE

PREFACE

Every man can and does, I think, divide his life into sections. As he grows older, however, the sections expand or contract like the pleats of an accordion played by the hands of time and experience. A few years ago I should have divided my life into three sections: the period before the Great War, the Great War itself, and the subsequent years. These sections seemed to me, as I looked back on them, of almost equal duration, although in point of time there was, of course, no comparison. The events of the past three years have been such as to alter radically my own view of my life in retrospect. The outlines of the various periods have become modified by the pressure of the tremendous events of the last few years. I still see my life as sharply defined in point of time and experience, but the lines of demarcation have shifted from those of three years ago.

Now, in the late months of 1940, I think of events and of my own relation to them still in three periods: that which preceded the entry of the United States into the World War in 1917, a twenty year period until the summer of 1937, and a succeeding period in which I took a more active and direct part in the policy of the United States.

Almost four years ago I wrote about the first or educational period of my existence. *The Education of a Diplomat* was published in 1938 and carried my account to the point of the declaration of war by the United States on Germany in April,

1917. This present volume, continuing the account until the early summer of 1937, constitutes, then, a sort of second chapter of the experiences of Hugh Wilson. When and if the third chapter will be written, I am not sure. Certainly the present does not seem to me to be the time for an account of that nature.

PART I

CHAPTER I

A few days ago I looked through my biography as published in the *State Department Register*, in order to give myself an inspiration as to how to begin this account. I find that it reads like an index to a volume of the National Geographic Society, showing that I served in posts in Latin America, the Far East, a number of points in Europe, and in Washington. In a man's account of his life, however, it matters less where he has been than what he has done ; and what he has done in turn, it seems to me, matters less, than what he has become. It is from this point of view that I shall try to present my story.

I entered the diplomatic service of the United States I cannot say fortuitously, but certainly it was lightheartedly. After several years in our family business in Chicago I came to the conclusion that I would sever my connection with business and study for the Foreign Service examinations. The way I say it sounds as if the conclusion was slow in developing. Such was not the case. I knew almost immediately that mercantile business was not the occupation which would give me the type of satisfaction that I wanted ; the fact that I remained in business for several years was partly owing to family consider- ations, partly to opposition I encountered to the idea of leaving it, and partly, I must confess, to inertia.

In the solid, enduring, and, we thought, everlasting world in which we lived before 1914, it did not seem a particularly serious adventure to enter the Foreign Service for a few years of experience and diversion. For I had always the thought in mind that the existence I had left behind me would remain forever unchanged, that I could return to it, take it up again where I had left it after the thirst for change had been slaked.

My studies in Paris at the Ecole Libre des Sciences Politiques were cut short by an offer to serve as private secretary to the American Minister in Lisbon. A few months of revolution, old-fashioned border raids, color, and bull fights preceded a visit to Washington in 1911, where I took my examinations and was accepted as a member of the diplomatic service.

Two years in Guatemala followed, years on which I look back still with affection, and with a certain amused aloofness at the young fellow who found himself such a big frog in a small puddle and who enjoyed himself with a zest and thoroughness that I would give much to recapture.

In August, 1914, I set sail from New York with Kate, my wife of three months, for Buenos Aires via London. War was declared while we were on the water and since there were no ships from England to Buenos Aires, I worked for some months in the Embassy at London. The year and a half in Buenos Aires was marred by Kate's serious illness and we hurried back to the United States to allow her to recuperate.

During vacation a telegram from Washington suddenly ordered me to Berlin. No one event of my existence has come with such stunning impact nor was more full of portent on the active years of my life. Berlin seemed then — in the spring of 1916 — to be in a state of siege by the whole world. News from there was scanty, information vague and contradictory. To proceed there under such conditions meant leaping into the unknown and the formidable.

I was a junior member of the Embassy staff in Berlin and there for a few months only ; nevertheless, events themselves and the work of that Embassy confirmed a conviction that the profession of diplomacy, which I had regarded up to that time more as a cheerful diversion than as a calling, had become for me something to which I could well devote my existence, a task that would call into play every atom of energy and intelligence I might possess.

President Wilson broke relations with the German Government on February 3, 1917, and the Embassy staff departed in a special train for Switzerland a week later. Scarcely was I settled in Switzerland, to which post I had been named, than a sudden order sent me to our Embassy in Vienna where I arrived just in time to repeat the experience of Berlin — packing up the files, burning the codes, and returning to Switzerland in a special train.

The President had declared war on April 6, 1917, the United States had entered the conflict, and my duty and inclination lay plain before me.

Everywhere one looked there was war. You could hear it and see it from Basle and its neighborhood, you could hear it again on the lower Engadine. The wall of war that ran from the North Sea to the Adriatic was interrupted only by the width of Switzerland. At that time, April, 1917, there was a period of relative quiet along the wall. Ominous mutters came from Russia, wild scenes in the Duma, Kerensky's assumption of power ; among the Allies, renewed hope of the rebuilding of a useful front in the East. The submarine was taking its toll of British shipping but its full menace was not yet realized. Major operations along the West front had ceased with the colossal effort and failure by Germany to capture Verdun. No serious change was in progress in the Dolomites between Italy and Austria-Hungary. An Allied force under the French General Franchet d'Esperey lay at Saloniki, maintaining a front but little else. The United States had declared war on Germany and a ripple of optimism stirred the tired forces of the Allies. In Germany there was complete skepticism as to the value to the Allies of American participation ; the High Command preferred to believe that we could make no contribution beyond what we had been offering already as neutrals. The Allies were stimulated and refreshed but they, too, when they talked in confidence, had little faith that an unorganized nation could do more than intensify its industrial contribution.

Such was the Europe I saw as I returned to Berne from Vienna. As I said, I had left Berlin with Ambassador Gerard in February, had remained in Berne a few weeks only, had been ordered to Vienna, and had shared again in the work of evacuating an Embassy on the break of relations. Thus, Berne and Switzerland were not entirely new to me, and I turned to my work with the advantage of having planned in advance exactly what had to be done in the event that the United States entered the war.

There were no limits to the scope of the Legation's work. As I look at our reports of more than twenty years ago, I see cables split into different sections : Germany, political ; Germany, economic ; Austria-Hungary in its varied nationalities ; the Polish question ; Bulgaria ; Turkey ; and so on. Switzerland was as well placed as any other neutral state as an observation post for Germany and German affairs, particularly South Germany. It was the only post from which to observe Austria-Hungary, Bulgaria, Poland, and occupied Rumania. It was almost the nearest point for observation of the distant land of Turkey. Many of these lands we in the staff did not know from personal observation, so we had to acquire detailed knowledge and all qualified personnel. Information meant following the press of various countries, interviewing travellers, émigrés, and neutral diplomats. It meant the establishment of secret services, it meant intercourse with deserters, with those ready to betray their countries for gain or through conviction.

A hundred other activities developed, some of them I shall discuss later as they came into being, but our essential job was information, more information and always information. Thrust into the flank of enemy Eastern and Central Europe, we had to keep our President informed of the progress of events through this wide area ; living in the nearest observation post to military events, we had to furnish our General Staff with what could be obtained on the organization, numbers, movements and plans of the enemy forces from the Baltic to Asia Minor.

As I set about these tasks with zeal and enthusiasm, I began to become aware from conversations in the Foreign Office and with other acquaintances, how much the Swiss disliked activities such as I was beginning and such as the other belligerent Legations had already developed into great organizations.

The Swiss Government was dominated by one overwhelming preoccupation, the preservation of their precarious neutrality. Under pressure from every direction, impelled by their own sympathies, they nevertheless had to maintain that most difficult of all attitudes, impartiality. They had rigid regulations against unneutral activities on the part of the belligerent diplomatic missions and agents. They enforced these regulations when they could, but realized that an enormous activity went on under cover of diplomatic immunity which they could not reach. They did not like it because they feared that some act of a belligerent on Swiss territory would jeopardize their neutral position and give pretext to a belligerent to carry the war onto their soil. The official attitude was one of unfailing and scrupulous neutrality; a word or gesture of a public man which showed even a trace of partiality brought about instant resentment and sometimes dismissal from office.

Shortly after my arrival the Swiss Federal Councillor Hoffmann had undertaken the transmission of overtures for a separate peace with Germany to Russia, through the Swiss Legation at Petrograd. When the facts came to light, such a storm of disapproval broke that he was swept from office.

Although the Swiss insisted on and obtained that scrupulous observance of neutrality on the part of their public officials which I have noted, the individual citizen was far from impartial in his sympathies. I have heard frequently, and have seen it written, that Switzerland was divided in its sympathies in accordance with its racial and language alignments. Along such lines, the Swiss would have been divided into something over seventy percent pro-German, the remaining portion pro-Ally. If such a division of sentiment had ever existed, it certainly had disappeared by the time I arrived in the country.

It seemed to me then, as I grew to know Switzerland and to

talk with men and women in different localities, that the sentiments of the country were less simple to approximate. The
Swiss in Vaux, Fribourg and Geneva, the French-speaking
portion, were fiercely pro-Ally ; they used a bellicose tone
that frequently embarrassed the Government and often led to
acrimonious discussion with the press in other cantons. The
Italian-speaking Swiss in Ticino were less bellicose but still
pro-Ally. The German Swiss, on the other hand, came closer
to an attitude of impartiality than any group with whom I
came into contact. They had only one desire, and a passionate
one, to stop the war. Like all sweeping assertions, this one
too needs qualification.

In Basle, Zürich, St. Gall, and other towns in Germanic
Switzerland, I knew numbers of college professors, bankers
and industrialists who, in spite of Germanic antecedents and
language, ardently hoped for an Allied victory, who were
persuaded that a defeat of Germany was essential to the well-
being of Europe and their own land. But wherever the citizen's sympathies lay, one and all were Swiss first and the consideration of their own interests and the maintenance of their
own territorial integrity was the fixed star of their navigation.
I am persuaded that they would have resisted an invasion from
either side with equal determination, and would have died to
the last soldier rather than allow either to violate their territory.

To the Swiss, neutrality was a legal conception ; they knew
that no law could bind their sympathies. They recognized at
the same time the danger of allowing their sympathies to be
translated into legal or Government action. The Government was obligated at all times to be meticulous in its attitude
and never to be betrayed into an act which could be con-

strued by one belligerent or the other as an act or speech of unneutrality. So correctly did they follow this procedure that the International Red Cross of Geneva could function at all times among the belligerents, and Swiss officers accompanied all armies in the field.

It is an old conception of neutrality, to regard it as a legal obligation and nothing which has anything to do with the heart, nevertheless it is a sound one. The citizen must write and speak as his sympathy dictates. A curtailment of this liberty is inconceivable among free men, but the Government, being the machinery for carrying out the law, has no such liberty and its administration is suspect, and rightly, if it or its members perform acts or make utterances which show partiality. We in the United States have departed widely from this ancient conception. I hope we are spared paying the penalty. Perhaps our distance from the conflict and the might of this nation permit us certain violations of this tradition which would spell disaster to a state neighbor to the conflict.

It may be worth while to examine the causes which brought about this realization among the Swiss of the necessity of curbing any expression of unneutral character by the Government or its agents. Probably the differences of race and language bring home to each citizen instinctively the danger of performing any public act which might split the nation along those natural lines of cleavage. The presence on every frontier at that time of a neighbor infinitely more powerful than themselves, had imbued every man and woman with the realization of the impossibility of survival if the Government should take sides. A long experience of neutrality in war had shown the efficacy of that policy in preserving their integrity and independence.

But back of all that lies the fact that Switzerland has a people instinctively prudent and intelligent. They have a homogeneity of political faith and experience which is lacking in many nations of greater homogeneity of race and speech Each boy and girl in school absorbs the doctrine of Swiss neutrality and realizes from his studies that his nation will go to war only for the purpose of national defense and that if there is a war it will be truly a war for existence and not one entered into by his Government "as an instrument of national policy."

They know they have an historic role to play in any war. They are the clearing-house of humanity in times when humanity is in abeyance. They keep alive the tradition of service to the wounded, of ameliorating the unhappy lot of the prisoner, of accepting and nursing to health the maimed and desperately sick who have fallen into enemy hands. They are the meeting-ground, the cockpit of the intellectual struggle that always accompanies the struggle on the field in modern warfare. It is well for us all to remember that the battle of principle and doctrine was just as acute more than twenty years ago as the present struggle in the spirit of ideology. The "war of nerves" went on then as well.

The American Minister to Switzerland, Pleasant A. Stovall, owner and editor of the *Savannah Press*, was a gentleman of integrity, courtesy and courage, but his knowledge of Europe was limited to his few years of residence in Switzerland and by his lack of any language other than his own. A political appointee, his interests lay in his own country and countrymen. Certainly Central and Eastern Europe to his mind were populated by the "enemy" and the thought of any distinction between them, of any differentiation between Czechs, Poles, Hungarians and Germans, was not only unimportant but was definitely dangerous — they were all "enemy" and all had to be defeated.

Such a state of mind was not so difficult to understand then as now. Maps showed the Empire of Austria-Hungary, it was all the same color. The frontier between Germany and Russia showed no break to indicate the existence of Poland. It required more study than the average American had given to political geography in those days to realize that the area of Austria-Hungary was made up of innumerable units with more or less determination for autonomy, to realize the urge of the disruptive forces of the ancient Empire. Certainly there was little understanding that the armies of the Empire held numberless men and officers who, through motives of patriotism to their own units, were willing to work for the destruction of the whole. Fortunately for our work, there was full understanding of these matters in the State Department and telegrams clamoring for information began to arrive. There was such ardent appreciation of what we could give that the Minister acquiesced in our attempts to set up an adequate organization to supply it.

So for this type of work we had to assess our own aptitudes among the staff of Secretaries. Fred Dolbeare and Allen Dulles had served in Vienna, I had served in Berlin. Information on Germany naturally fell to my lot. Dolbeare happened to be acquainted with a Mr. Perlowski residing in Montreux, who was the unofficial representative for Switzerland of the

Polish "Regency Council." It seemed to be indicated to appoint him the Polish expert for the Legation. His good judgment and intelligence soon made him master of his work.

This left a large field to cover — the races and politics of Austria-Hungary, the Balkans and Turkey — and to this complex and sizable territory, Allen Dulles was the only one on the spot to assign. Allen was a grandson of General Foster and a nephew of Mr. Lansing, and took his tradition seriously. He came to Berne on a visit from Vienna with a diplomatic pouch, and encountered Fred Dolbeare and myself, both considerably older in years and service. Now among Service men there is a sort of acknowledged rule that its members are worthy of confidence and that you can discuss things freely with them, even small pieces of gossip about your Chief and your Mission. This was not the case with Allen. He rebuffed us courteously but firmly, implying the bad taste which we had shown in questioning him in such an indiscreet manner. A few weeks later we all met again in Berne, this time all members of the Legation in that city. We then found that Allen had been seething with indignation at conditions in the Embassy at Vienna. He gave us full details once he found that we were worthy of his confidence. I called him into my office and told him that he was appointed expert of all of the places I had listed.

"Sir," said Allen (he had a Johnsonian habit of speech in those days), "how long have I to prepare myself?"

I replied, "Say a week or ten days. We have to get started; Washington is clamoring."

"I shall report on the subject in ten days," said Allen, bowed, and departed.

I did not lay eyes on him in the meantime, and he duly reported. He had spent the ten days in Geneva, Zürich and Basle, had become acquainted with the refugee representatives of the South Slavs, of the Czechs, with the Bulgarian Legation, with Hungarian malcontents. In a word, he had come as near accomplishing the fantastic assignment which I had given him in the ten days allotted as a human being could. Certainly from that moment on he was never at a loss as to the means of ascertaining any piece of information desired about his area.

We found it worked beautifully, this idea of creating experts instead of hunting around to find them. I have never met a prepared expert who went for his task with the same energy and determination as these lads on their assignments. I created another one. Some months after my arrival — the Minister had gone home and I was Chargé d'Affaires — I read in the Paris edition of the *New York Herald* of the arrival in Paris of an "Assistant to the American Minister in Berne" and of his imminent arrival in Switzerland. I had heard nothing of his assignment and being at the time thirty-two years old, the grisly picture arose in my mind of an elderly gentleman with a gray beard who would sit in my office and give me the benefit of his wisdom.

A day or two later his card was brought in ; it read "Franklin Day, Assistant to the American Minister," and confirmed my apprehension. The door opened and admitted a short stocky figure with a round face, huge horn spectacles, and the grin of a gamin, the whole making the impression of an engaging undergraduate. Franklin explained that he was little more, that he had tried for the Army and been refused because of defective eyesight. His father had been connected with the American Consulate in Berlin and the boy had been born in that city. He had spent the first fourteen years of his life there, with the result that German was as native a tongue to him as his own English.

As soon as he explained himself to me I knew that one difficulty was solved, the question of how to keep in touch with émigré Germans, get their news, and utilize their zeal against the Fatherland to the fullest extent. Let no one suppose that émigré Germans present a new problem for the present war. They were not so numerous then and there were not many Jews, but Switzerland held at that time a quantity of deserters and political refugees, mainly Socialists ; a large proportion of them offered their services to help against their country. Franklin became a bosom friend of this group and a number of them were of genuine assistance to us.

I had a letter from Franklin the other day, in which he recounted some of his memories of the war period in Switzerland. He said that his most vivid recollection was of the time when I had made a schedule of departures for American citizens in case of invasion of the country, and had taken measures for the safe and rapid departure of everybody on the Staff with the exception of one person, himself. When he had reproached me with this omission I had replied that his German was impeccable and that he could doubtless take care of himself. He said that he had then made the private reflection that my remark might be flattering but that his facility in the language was much more likely to get him shot as a spy.

CHAPTER II

I soon found that all of the belligerent Governments were making persistent and vigorous efforts to persuade the Swiss of the justice of their cause. Musicians and opera companies came from Germany, theatrical troupes from England, lecturers from France and Italy, money was available and poured out to influence the press though the Swiss writers, with their ancient tradition of independence, were not venal. Bookstores were opened or purchased for the cheap sale of French and Italian literature and propaganda. The Swiss were deluged with propaganda and it ran off their backs like water off a duck. The presentation of a case was old stuff, and the Swiss were hardly interested, they made their own interpretation of events, and I can assure you that the Swiss man or woman clings to his own interpretation. What impressed them were events themselves. I remember the wave of enthusiasm for the United States that ran over the country when we agreed to facilitate their supply of wheat. Mr. George Creel, of the Committee on Public Information, spent vast amounts of American money in supplying the Swiss press with accounts of our might and our effort and enthusiasm for the cause, not to mention our baseball scores, but the single act of facilitating the wheat supply had already won the Swiss and Mr. Creel, so far as Switzerland was concerned, was merely gilding the lily.

Mr. Creel's organization sent to Switzerland as its representative a beautiful black-haired woman from Newport, Rhode Island, Mrs. Norman Whitehouse. The political activity of women, especially of beautiful ones, was not so customary then as now, certainly not on the continent where her activities created no small sensation. One episode in particular was witnessed by one of our military officers in the French custom house at Pontarlier and when recounted by him ran over Europe like a flame. At that time, it was obligatory to bring all luggage from the train into the shed for examination at the French frontier when entering from Switzerland. The luggage of diplomats, even those not accredited to France, was normally exempt, and Mrs. Whitehouse had diplomatic status. Her irritation was natural when the inspector insisted that she open her bags and her protests were equally to be expected. Unfortunately, her French was of that variety which finishing schools confer so abundantly and by no means adequate to the emotion that flooded her. She used what argument she could, the inspector was unmoved. She bethought herself that perhaps she could impress him by the fact that she knew the President of the United States, so she played her last card. "*Je suis l'amie du Président Wilson,*" she declared. This phrase, of course, has a special meaning in French and no Frenchman could resist such a declaration. The inspector was transformed. "Pass then, madame. I will aid in putting your bags on the train."

The Swiss imperturbability to propaganda often recurred to me especially during the opening months of the Second World War. I have seen my country in a twitter of anxiety over propaganda. We were in a state of timidity where foreign literary men hesitated to make their annual lucrative tour of the United States lest they be accused of propaganda in their lectures, where the British Ambassador felt obliged to confine his comments to future peace and not to an immediate situation of more than passing interest. We scrutinized each item of news as to its propaganda origin as if all Government-inspired news were necessarily false. Now I am all in favor of impartial observation of news, and discrimination in its acceptance, but I see no reason for this extraordinary apprehension in regard to anything that may have a tinge of partiality, or the backing of Government authority. Of course they are prejudiced, of course the reports from the opponents must be checked against each other, but why are we afraid of them? I have talked to many people about this unexpected development among us and usually am told that the experience of the years preceding our entry into the Great War shows that we are peculiarly susceptible to propaganda and that our present apprehension is lest, beguiled by the siren call, we succumb again to the voices and follow them into war.

There is another sort of apprehension that to me is even more difficult to understand. It is that apprehension which expresses itself mainly in our columnists and in the Dies Committee, a fear lest foreign propaganda, Fascist, Communist or anti-Semitic, should so corrupt us as to shake our faith in our institutions and drive us into the adoption of one or the other of the foreign inventions. If our faith is deep-rooted, if we really prefer the American way of life, surely there is something slightly absurd and perhaps childish in our fear of the effect upon us of a few foreigners and their doctrines. If our faith in our own way is not profound, and if we are really searching a fundamental change, then surely the effect of the foreign voices will not materially modify the situation.

I believe that our faith in our institutions is rooted profoundly deep in our consciousness, that while every thinking man recognizes all is not for the best in America, nevertheless he knows that in comparison with other countries we are exceptionally fortunate. We know that the changes that must be brought about, can be brought about by our own unaided efforts, by our own methods, and without the abolition of the Bill of Rights and the constitutional guaranties. The Swiss have been and are today deluged with propaganda, they take it with a shrug, they know that their institutions have been chosen because they fit their type of thought and are the free choice of their people. They have deeper worries than the ungrounded one that their citizens are going to rush off to pursue foreign gods. Let us put an end to chasing phantoms and turn our efforts to what is wrong with us and remedy it ourselves. If we can find those things and rectify them, no one in America will be in a state of nerves about propaganda from abroad.

As to our being beguiled into war, that is a larger subject. Suffice it to say at this moment that I do not believe the temper of the American people is now such that they will enter the war on other grounds than those of their own considered decision that such a course is in their best interest. What is said from abroad or by foreigners here will have little to do with it. The contrast in America between now and twenty-five years ago is striking. Then we were ignorant of matters abroad, today we are doing our own thinking and interpreting.

One day shortly after my arrival in Berne two cards were brought to me in my office — "Dr. Field, Zürich," and "Professor George Herron, Geneva." The two gentlemen who followed the cards were an oddly contrasting couple. Dr. Field was a Quaker, a burly man, with bushy gray hair and beard, heavy gray eyebrows behind which lay the gentlest, bluest, most candid pair of eyes that I ever saw on an adult man. They were the eyes of an unsophisticated and lovable child. Professor Herron was thin and awkward, his gestures were somewhat like those of Arthur Twining Hadley, President of Yale when I was a student there. His voice was resonant and his speech abundant. I subsequently learned that he had the fervor of a fanatic and that whether in enthusiasm or invective he carried the conviction of sincerity of an Old Testament prophet. He, too, wore a beard — but pointed and straggly ; his sparse gray hair was unkempt. These two men, unlike in character and appearance, were united in the depth of their conviction as to the righteousness of the Allied cause, in their reverence for the President of the United States, for his wisdom and character, for the promise, of which he was then showing the first indications, of leading the world into new relationships between men and men and States and States.

In the conversation which followed it became clear that these two men had unique relationships with university and liberal elements in Germany and Austria-Hungary. Both had produced books widely read in Germany. Dr. Field was a graduate of a German university and spoke the language flawlessly. Professor Herron had been a professor of a university in Kansas, a Socialist in his relation to internal politics, but at the moment finding his economic theories less interesting than the course of the war, and the clash which he saw between rival conceptions of human relationships. He watched and wrote of the course of events from his house in Geneva. Never having met President Wilson, he had fallen under the spell of his personality and he wrote and spoke of him as someone from another world. They told me of the conversations they were having both in Zürich and Geneva with friends and acquaintances from the Central Empires, conversations full of genuine information on the trend of thought and even on political events in that portion of the world. It was obvious that these men would be a mine of information in our work, and that the thing to do was to organize to get it.

So I said, "Why don't you write down these matters, or let me send you a stenographer after your conversations so I can have a current idea of what is being said to you?" They glanced at each other and smiled.

"Oh, we do keep a record and we have a report here that we were about to ask you to send in the diplomatic pouch to Mr. Sharp." At that time, William G. Sharp was the American Ambassador to Paris. I inquired why they were sending it to Mr. Sharp when we were here and could consult with ease and plan out the course of conversations. They replied that they had not felt that the members of the Legation at Berne were interested in this sort of material and in any case they had heard that the attitude of the Legation was so hostile to any Americans talking to men from enemy countries that they had not been willing to broach the matter. I remember saying, "If you can find any man more interested in such conversations anywhere than myself, then send him in and I will resign in his favor. Furthermore, if anyone, American or Ally, becomes a nuisance to you because you have talked to people of enemy nationality, send them to me, I should be happy to talk to them."

From that moment, we were continuously at work together, and I know of no other persons who were so valuable and of so continuous and self-sacrificing usefulness. I was often reproached, both during the war and after, as it became known through Central Europe that these men were talking to the enemy, for having "selected" two such men, and non-official men, to do work of such a delicate and confidential character. The answer was easy : they were there ; Germans and Austrians and Hungarians had already been visiting them. The lines were all laid, all I had to do was to utilize them. The Germans would not have come to an official, they would have got into trouble at home ; as a result, they came to the men they knew and trusted. In war you don't "select" your tools, you make use of what lies at hand.

CHAPTER III

I had heard that a Czech national named Osusky who lived in Geneva was an intelligent individual, so the next time I was in that city I called on him. Osusky has become well known to numerous Americans in the past twenty years as Czechoslovak Minister to Paris. At that time I encountered a robust individual, burning with a patriotic desire to obtain the freedom of his land from Austrian domination. His breadth of information on what was taking place in the Dual Monarchy was astonishing, his comment was intelligent and without what we have learned to call in recent years, wishful thinking. I remember I asked him what nationality he had at that time and he replied airily, "Oh, we are of many and all. Let me introduce you to a compatriot of yours." We went through a door into another office where a man was working. Osusky said, "Mr. Wilson, let me present Captain Voska of the American Army."

It was only gradually that I became aware of the magnitude of the work that the Czechs were carrying on. They had an organized information service that furnished reports in businesslike form, economic, military and political. It gave advice on conditions not only in Bohemia, but also from the various theaters of war where Czechs were serving. It was astonishingly accurate.

It was Osusky who told me I ought to see the Chief of their organization, an ex-professor from the University of Prague,

Benes by name. So the next time I went to Paris I climbed
three flights of steps to a room under a Mansard and found
Benes seated at a table working, the table and the floor piled
deep with papers and books. As I think of Benes at that, the
first of many meetings we had throughout the years, it does
not seem to me he has changed greatly. I got the same impression then that I got in New Haven in 1939 when he was getting an L.L.D. from Yale, where I last talked with him. Benes
is a man of tireless energy, great penetration and undeviable
sincerity ; he was giving himself then, as he gave himself during
the succeeding twenty odd years in unstinted generosity to his
country. Whether his purpose and resolution matched his
other qualities, each must judge from Benes' later history.

I persuaded Fred Dolbeare to take me to Montreux to make
the acquaintance of his Polish friend, Perlowski. We sat on
a terrace and looked over lake and mountain while I began
to get my first insight into the mind and aspirations of the
Poles. Perlowski, later to become Polish Ambassador to
Madrid, was a man of exceptional charm. He spoke numerous languages with meticulous accuracy and pronunciation.
Tall and slender, beautifully dressed, a drooping blond moustache, he was the Polish gentleman of fiction. Himself a classi-
cist, he had a fund of citation and anecdote from the literature
of all countries.

It was at that interview that I first heard the famous story
about the Polish student. Perlowski attributed it to Heine.
Perlowski was expounding the devotion of Poles the world
over to the fate of their nation, how the preoccupation of Polish freedom colored their whole existence. He told the story
and it sets off the Polish attitude toward the universe so ad-

mirably that I shall repeat it even if you have heard it before. Here it is : a prize was offered in the University of Paris for an essay on *The Elephant*. As the prize was of some magnitude there were numerous competitors, among others, an Englishman, a Frenchman, a German, a Pole. The Englishman set out to Africa with a case of rifles, killed a lot of elephants, returned to Paris and presented a book called *Hunting the Elephant*. The German plunged into the public library and did not emerge for months, when he did it was to produce a book in 3 volumes called *The Elephant — His Habits and Habitat — a Hand-book for Those Who Know, or Desire to Know, the Elephant*. The French student, on the contrary, waited until the last moment. Then he strolled out to the zoo, watched the animals with some amusement while he smoked a cigarette, noted some of their peculiar social manners, returned to his desk and wrote a delightful paper entitled *l'Eléfant et ses amours*. The last competitor, a Polish student, climbed the five flights to his attic, he was poor like all Polish students and, of course, lived in an attic, seated himself at his table, picked up his pen and wrote the title for his essay, *The Elephant and the Polish Question*.

I mentioned before that Perlowski represented the Regency Council in Warsaw. I subsequently learned that the Poles under the various flags of Austria-Hungary, Germany and Russia had widely different conceptions as to the future of Poland. They were united, however, in their fanatical devotion to their land, and to that end were helping the Allies to defeat Germany, the land they all felt the most dangerous to their hope for freedom.

There was not a General Staff in the three Empires that did

not include Polish officers, there was not a legislative body or,
I would almost dare to say, not a Government, that did not
have influential Polish members.   Nevertheless it is safe to say,
I think, that there was not a Pole in the three Empires who was
not a man of divided loyalties, and who did not hope in his
heart, not necessarily for the defeat of the nation for which he
was fighting, but certainly for a sufficient weakening to permit
the recrudescence of Poland.   I know of no race in whom the
fire of patriotism burns higher, nor among whom the thought
of country is so persistent and dominant.

While I am discussing the special and fanatical devotion
of the Poles to their race and country let me give an appealing
example. Again the exponent was Perlowski. When hostilities were over, when the Germans had laid down their arms
and evacuated Poland, I remarked to Perlowski, "Now that
fighting is over, and the necessity for secrecy is not so overwhelming, I want to ask you a question that I would not have
asked you during hostilities but on which you may, perhaps, be
willing now to satisfy my curiosity.   How did you deliver to
me so regularly, so comprehensively, the views of the Regency
Council ?   They often sent information for which they would
have been shot as spies if it had become known, yet they got it
to you through the censorship, and regularly and even in what
was obviously the phraseology of Warsaw and not of yourself.   Do you mind telling me ?"

Perlowski replied, "Yes, now the battle is over I shall tell you
and I shall tell you not because the method was clever, not
merely to satisfy your curiosity, though your collaboration
and friendship justify such satisfaction, but to show you the
spirit of Poland even among its children.   You know that the

Rockfeller Foundation has arranged to bring to Switzerland, and this country has been receiving, a few score of Polish children every fortnight. This country receives them hospitably, feeds them up and sends them back to their parents in Poland. Well, every two weeks my friends in Warsaw select one of the children — usually a little girl because they are often cleverer than the little boys — who is set the task of memorizing a paper. Sometimes the paper is five to six pages in length. She is instructed that on the arrival of the children's train at Zürich, she is to watch out on the platform for a tall blond gentleman, wearing a red carnation — who will be myself — whom she is to approach, take by the hand and repeat what she has memorized. She is told that she is working for Poland and that if she talks of her mission to anyone other than the gentleman who meets her at the station, it will injure Poland. Never once did the little girl fail, never once did she betray us. She knew she was working for Poland and it was enough."

The Poles have a gallantry in adversity, a hopefulness and enthusiasm in the most hopeless periods that wins them affection. They are showing it now in their overwhelming affliction. A Frenchman once said to me, "The Poles are the world's best martyrs." It is true. They have had, alas, centuries of experience in the role.

The Catholic Church had then and probably has now the best information service in Europe. We had no representative at the Vatican and our Embassy at Rome did not have the relations with the Blacks or clerical society which would give them access to the knowledge of the Church representatives. It was not easy for any of us in Berne to establish the type of confidence necessary with the Papal Nuncio and his staff.

The General of the Jesuits was residing during the war at Einsiedeln in Switzerland, but he too seemed inaccessible.   It was
only by accident that this difficulty was solved and a Pole came
to the rescue.   One of the members of the American Embassy
at Paris had given a letter of introduction to me to his Polish
friend, Horodyski, who, duly presenting it, was brought to one
of the afternoon meetings of the staff.   During the course of
the conversation he mentioned that he had just been to call on
the General of the Jesuits, and gave a most interesting account
of the General's views of what was taking place in Central
Europe.   From that time on, Horodyski made periodic trips
to Einsiedeln and never failed to return to Paris via Berne to
give me an account of his visit.   He would also frequently
stop en route to Einsiedeln in order to discuss the subjects that
it might be desirable to bring up.

It needs no flight of imagination to recognize the accumula-
tion of information that is gathered into the hands of the high
dignitaries of the Church.   Through its representatives the
Church has access to the thoughts of men in every chancery
in Europe and in remote villages in every country.   An admirably equipped and trained service of their diplomatic staff
collects and correlates this news.   The Church has a unique
vision into the bewildering complexity of the seething European turmoil.   Ever since that experience I have been an advocate of sending an American representative to the Vatican.   I
could not understand the state of mind which led us to miss the
unique opportunity for information which the post offered.
It has taken another European war to bring an American President to the decision to take this eminently practical step.   Mr.
Myron Taylor was sent to Rome as Mr. Roosevelt's unofficial

representative to the Pope. I know that material is in the Vatican which any government needs to form opinions and policies on European matters. I know that in this critical period the Government of the United States needs all this type of material it can get. I had earnestly hoped that Mr. Taylor had the European background which would enable him to assess and evaluate it. Unfortunately, he has been obliged by ill health to return home.

We developed a habit which combined business with pleasure. Every afternoon we met at five o'clock for tea. The big dining room of the Legation served for a board meeting where we all talked of what had happened during the day, where we checked every item we had collected against the knowledge of the others. I encouraged the others to invite to this meeting anyone they encountered of interest who was willing to tell his story to the whole staff.

I have memories of the guests spreading their maps on the great table while we all crowded around to absorb what was elucidated. Comnène — later Minister for Foreign Affairs of Rumania — was frequently there, black brief-case under his arm from which he would extract documents to prove the claims of Rumania to Bessarabia and Transylvania. His country had been overrun by von Mackensen's forces the year before but he never faltered in his conviction that it would be restored and triumphantly greater.

Except for this daily meeting we had only one other fixed gathering. Each week we all met on Friday afternoon to assemble the weekly report to the Department. This consisted of press, our own commentary, and occasionally reports of conversations which we had not considered of sufficient urgency to cable separately, and so were summarized for incorporation in the regular weekly message. The *Foreign Relations of the United States* reproduces many of these reports and their pages stir forgotten memories. I would usually dictate but any of the six or seven listeners was free to comment, interrupt or criticize. It may seem a clumsy way to work, but experience showed that the result was much more vivid and cohesive than when we attempted to write up individual sections and circulate them for comment.

During the course of the war, through some anomaly of policy, the relations between the United States and Bulgaria were never severed, and we kept a Consul General, Dominic Murphy, in Sofia throughout. This in spite of the fact that Bulgaria was associated with the Central Powers and the United States with the Allies. American thought and civilization were important in Bulgaria, many of the leaders in that country, both in politics and in civil life, were graduates of Roberts College in Constantinople; they spoke English and had the highest respect for the American way of life. One Bulgarian especially, Theodore Shipkoff, a businessman of large interests, was constantly coming to Switzerland and reporting conditions to us. The Bulgarian Legation itself was a useful source of information and we were able even to send cipher messages through its code to our representative in Sofia and to get replies. Practically all the information about Turkey that reached the American side came from this source, although I have no doubt that the British and French had built up their own Arab sources in Syria for espionage purposes.

To me one of the least interesting phases of the activity of a belligerent mission in a neutral country is the endless manhunt for spies, "counter-espionage," the activity is called. This, of course, was the principal business of the Passport Bureau of the Legation, although in the last year of the war this work was taken over, much to my gratification, by the Military Attaché and his staff. It never interested me profoundly because I had the conviction that the energy devoted to it was out of all proportion to the results achieved. The dangerous spy, it seemed to me, was never the little fellow on the payroll — what he was in a position to get could not be of high importance. The dangerous man was the spy by conviction, the man who, in a high place, risked his life to give information to the enemies of the country he was serving, and did it because his patriotic interest drove him to such service. Such men were the Poles, Alsatians or Czechs in positions of genuine importance in the Central Powers who felt that the destruction of the Empire was the only means of achieving the independence of their peoples.

So, as I say, I took little interest in the Passport Bureau though occasionally its officers would bring me a case for discussion. One incident of this nature remains in my mind. The Chief of the Passport Bureau came to my office and said to me, "I have a fellow in my room applying for a visa to France. His credentials are in perfect order, so is his passport. He is an American by his talk and a correspondent of the *New York Herald* by name of Cyril Brown. The only thing I don't like about him is that he doesn't talk like a newspaperman and I know a lot of them."

Now Cyril Brown had been correspondent in Berlin while I was there and I knew him well.

"Send him up," I said. "I know Cyril Brown and would like to greet him and talk to him. I think you must be mistaken about there being anything fishy about him, but in any case don't tell him I know Cyril Brown."

The man came up, he was a total stranger. I struggled hard to control my excitement and told him that we needed a couple of days to arrange for a visa to France. He had better go away, I said, and come back in two days, and in the meantime to leave his passport. On his departure we examined the passport ; as far as we could see, it was perfect in watermark, engraving, in practically every detail. However, the seal varied from an original by a fraction of an inch in diameter and this was sufficient to establish forgery, coupled with the fact that I knew the genuine Cyril Brown. To make assurance doubly sure, I wired the Legation at Copenhagen and ascertained that Cyril Brown was there and had his passport bearing the same number as the forgery. Our "Cyril Brown" duly returned, we gave him a visa, and he departed for France. At Pontarlier, the French control officers, who had been appraised by us of his arrival, took him from the train and he spent the rest of the war in a French prison.

CHAPTER IV

It is far from my intention to attempt to write the history of Europe for the years 1917–1918, this has been done frequently and competently. Nevertheless, my work during those years was so intimately associated with the struggle on all sides of Switzerland that I feel obliged to make a very brief review of some of the leading events so that later, when I attempt to picture some of the incidents in which we participated, they will be appreciated better by reason of a refreshed memory. Anyone who feels his memory sufficiently vivid, may skip the following paragraphs.

The winter of 1916–1917 had been the hardest the German people had had to endure ; Rumania was conquered too late for Germany to get the benefit of Rumanian harvests, heavy fighting in the East through the autumn had prevented much provisioning from Poland, and the blockade had reduced stocks in Germany to a minimum. Toward the middle of April, strikes against food conditions had broken out in Leipsig, Berlin, and in other great German centers. However, in spite of the tightened blockade brought about by the entry of the United States into the war, by the autumn of 1917 the situation was appreciably better in Germany because of their own harvest, food from Rumania and relaxation of fighting in the East. In July, however, the pressure had become enough to encourage the peace elements to such a point that the Reichstag passed a resolution on July 6, urging peace without annexations or indemnities. The resolution had been offered by Matthias Erzberger, leader of the Center or Catholic party, and became known as the Erzberger resolution.

In the meantime Russia was breaking up. A final desperate attempt was made by moderate elements to carry on the war in alliance with the Allies, an effort which culminated in the final great offensive under General Brusilov early in July. But back at home, in Petrograd, Moscow, and other towns strikes were prevalent, disorder everywhere and the overwhelming desire to stop the fighting at any cost gradually became apparent. Arthur Henderson went to Russia from England, Senator Root from the United States, Albert Thomas from France, to rally the failing will to fight. Their efforts were useless. In October, Kerensky fell and the Soviet offered peace terms. A few weeks of internal struggle and the Soviets had met the Germans at Brest-Litovsk and Russia was out of the war.

Continuous fighting took place on the West front through 1917 but no major changes of position occurred. The submarine menace rose to its peak through the summer and made the most serious threat to Great Britain which occurred during the war. The Italian-Austrian front had been more active. On October 24 a tremendous offensive of the Austrians, aided by shock troops from Germany, broke the Italian line at Caporetto; for weeks the assault continued but the Italians finally held on the lower Piave.

During the summer the American Army set up its General Staff, first in Paris and later in Chaumont. American troops landed in France after this in constantly increasing numbers, their power and numbers to some extent offsetting the discouragement of the defection of Russia.

The early months of 1918 were characterized by ominous threats of a great German offensive in the spring. Scarcely had the treaty of Brest-Litovsk been signed, March 3, when the Germans transferred the bulk of their Eastern Army and hurled their forces against the British, March 21, in the West, breaking the line and penetrating by the middle of June to within a few miles of Paris. American troops were flung into line at Amiens and made an heroic resistance at the Bois de Belleau near Paris. Then came the turning point of the war, the final German offensive of July 15, which was not only checked but turned into an Allied advance by Foch's masterly strategy. From then on the Allied advance was continuous.

Bulgaria surrendered on September 30 to the Allied forces under the French General Franchet d'Esperey, who had advanced from the Saloniki base. On October 4, Germany issued a plea for an armistice. Austria-Hungary signed an armistice on November 4, and Germany on November 11, 1918. And that is the end of my historical summary.

To return to my story — the long period of unchanging position on the West front through the summer and autumn of 1917, coupled with increasing shortage of food and growing apprehension as to the final result of the war gave rise to a number of attempts on the part of Germany's allies to find a way out of the struggle, whether through general peace or a separate peace for their nation.

The Austro-Hungarians began the effort with the Allies.

Count Mensdorff, the former Austrian Ambassador to London, approached the British through Philip Kerr, the late Lord Lothian, British Ambassador to Washington ; the French were approached through Prince Sixtus of Bourbon-Parma. Both of the efforts were unavailing ; they were neither definite enough nor well enough hidden from the Germans who in each case managed to intervene to stop the conversations.

A number of Austrians got in touch with us, mostly indirectly, and began to give us an insight into the ideas of the new Emperor Karl. My government was sufficiently interested to authorize me to notify the Emperor through a confidential channel that in the event he made a separate peace he could count on American financial assistance.

The most colorful and far-reaching of these negotiations were carried out by Professor Herron with Professor Lammasch of Vienna. The latter was a venerable figure, well-known to students of international law throughout the world. He had been tutor to Emperor Karl and had exercised, and continued to exercise, great influence over the mind of the Emperor. I did not know Professor Lammasch personally, but I knew that he was a man of unquestioned integrity, so that when Professor Herron told me late in January of 1918 that Lammasch desired to see him and had sent word that he had a most important message to deliver, I was ready to credit the faith of such an emissary.

The moment was one of the most tense from the point of view of diplomatic negotiation and intrigue. Switzerland was full of rumors, every important figure from the Allied countries or from the Central Powers was watched sedulously by the emissaries of the enemy. Certainly the Allied representatives, and, we feared, the Germans, had heard rumors of a meeting between Herron and Lammasch. A man resembling Professor Herron was assaulted and badly beaten near Herron's house in Geneva a few days before the meeting was scheduled. His pockets were rifled but no money was stolen, hence it seemed probable that Professor Herron had been the intended victim of the assault.

Thus it was in surroundings worthy of an Oppenheim novel that we made arrangements for the meeting. Herron came to Berne and stayed with his father-in-law, reporting to me on the evening before the meeting of his preliminary communications. The meeting was to take place in the house of Herr von Muehlon in Gümligen, a village a few miles from Berne. My car called for Herron ; the driver was an interned British sergeant, within the car were the American Military Attaché and his aide. All of these men were armed, and the blinds of the car were drawn to prevent recognition. They delivered Herron at von Muehlon's house and called for him some hours later when the interview had been terminated.

In the interview, Lammasch reminded Herron that Count Czernin, the Austro-Hungarian Prime Minister, had just made an important speech hinting at the possibility of peace. Lammasch stated candidly that Czernin was not to be trusted and that the Emperor had himself forced Czernin to make the declaration. The Emperor had expected to forward the speech officially to President Wilson, in spite of the state of war existing between the United States and Austria-Hungary. The German Embassy at Vienna, however, had intervened and had prevented transmission of the message.

Lammasch went on to explain that the Emperor was a man

of general liberal tendencies ; as tutor, he knew intimately his mind and heart.   The Emperor desired to effect a great change in the constitution of the Dual Monarchy, he desired to set up autonomous racial bodies unified under the throne of the Haps-burgs.   At the same time he ardently desired to regain the friendship of America and to be free from Prussian hegemony. This project, Professor Lammasch stated, could not be ac-complished without aid from outside.   The Emperor knew himself to be too weak to undertake such a project and risk invasion by Germany unless he were assured of assistance.

The plan which Lammasch urged on Herron was as follows : President Wilson would make a public address of some kind recognizing the speech of Czernin as intimating a readiness on the part of Austria-Hungary to make peace.   The Emperor would then write to the Pope at Rome, and give the letter pub-licity, setting forth his desire for the formation of a federated state of Austria-Hungary along autonomous and racial lines. He would urge in this letter general disarmament and a society of nations as proposed by President Wilson.   He would sug-gest the establishment of a Peace Congress to adopt these general principles rather than specific details since, he argued, the formation of such a society would make frontiers less im-portant and would facilitate the drawing of them along lines of self-determination.

As to Austria-Hungary itself, Lammasch suggested the for-mation of the Yugoslavs, Croatians, Slavonians, Bosnians, Herzegovinians, Dalmatians into one state, the Poles in another, the Austrians in another, Transylvania and the Magyars to form separate states, and the Italians within the Empire to unite into a single province.

The suggestion of Professor Lammasch was of considerable interest to the Government of the United States. The President duly made reference to Count Czernin's speech. We never ascertained exactly what happened in Austria-Hungary since subsequent events, including the great offensive of March, 1918, overwhelmed all efforts toward a separate peace. Certainly Professor Lammasch, after becoming Premier in the last stages of the Hapsburg dynasty, made an attempt in the Herrenhaus to introduce the type of autonomy in the Empire that he had preached to Herron. The attempt was followed by one of those stormy scenes in which inkwells as missiles take the place of verbal argument. The whole attempt, alas, was made too late and too half-heartedly for success.

I reported to Washington in considerable detail the series of conferences between Herron and Lammasch. The report is too voluminous for incorporation, but has been published by the State Department, *Foreign Relations of the United States, 1918, Supplement I, Volume I, February 8, 1918, Page 82.* While an unsuccessful attempt at negotiation has no profound historical value, nevertheless the document is, I find, of deep interest in revealing not only the characters of two unusually remarkable men — Herron and Lammasch — but also as an exposition of the thought and philosophy prevailing at that time. I find as I read it that it is difficult to cast myself back into the mood of that time. Ideals were living and vivid. Faith in humanity, faith in miracles, were actual and living forces which motivated acts.

Toward the latter part of November of the preceding year, 1917, an evening of heavy snow and storm, a member of the Austro-Hungarian Legation — a Hungarian whom I had known before we entered the war — telephoned me at the Hotel Bellevue where I was living. He said he could not talk to me while I was in the hotel for fear of eavesdroppers, and implored me to go to a public telephone outside and call him at the number he gave me. I did so, taking Dolbeare with me as a witness to my end at least of the conversation. My friend explained that Count Michael Károlyi, a magnate of Budapest, and a member of one of Hungary's most famous families, wanted to talk to me as he had something of the greatest interest to say to the American Government. He added that Károlyi did not want to come to the Legation for fear of being spotted by his own people, and could we not meet in the house of our mutual friend who was talking to me at that moment.

I replied that if Károlyi wanted to see me, the initiative was his and not mine, therefore I would see him in the American Legation or nowhere. I added that I had no wish to embarrass him and to that end suggested he meet Dolbeare and me at the Legation at eleven that night. In the snowstorm there was no chance of anyone being abroad, and I guaranteed that there would be no one in the Chancery but ourselves and that we would be there ten minutes ahead of time to let him in. I could hear my Hungarian friend consulting Károlyi, then he accepted the suggestion in his name.

Fred Dolbeare and I watched through the blinding snow for the lights of his cab, then let in the tall muffled figure. We entered my office and I could see my visitor, a lean bronzed face, with a battered nose and a pair of burning and fanatical eyes.

Count Károlyi sketched his own situation in his country.

He stated that he had consistently maintained an independent position and had striven for democratic ideals in opposition to any scheme of German domination, as typified in the Mittel-Europa project. He was a member of the Hungarian Parliament, and while his immediate following was small he stated that his influence among the people was enormous and that this influence was recognized by the Government, by the fact that they consulted him on all important measures.

He added that for Austria-Hungary the future was indeed black, whether in the event of a German victory, a drawn fight, or a German defeat. In any one of these cases Austria, he said, would be ruined : because in the event of a German victory, it would be dominated by Germany ; in the event of a drawn battle, it would still be dominated by Germany ; in the event of a German defeat, it would be classed with the Germans and would have to pay the greatest penalty in forfeiture of land and citizens.

Károlyi felt that very probably within a short time Count Czernin would be overthrown and he (Károlyi) would be summoned to form an Austro-Hungarian cabinet. If he accepted this position, it would mean that he did so with certain specific purposes in mind on which we could count. If Károlyi became Premier, he proposed that the Entente should offer a peace conference on the basis of relinquishment of occupied territories and a discussion of the debatable territories such as the Italian Irredenta, Alsace-Lorraine, Poland, et cetera ; the Austrians would then declare to the Germans that they could no longer fight, and must send delegates to the conference. Germany in that event would be obliged to send delegates in order not to be isolated.

In the meantime, Károlyi proposed a secret agreement to be arranged between Austria-Hungary and the Entente on the following basis : That the Entente would guarantee that Austria-Hungary would not be heavily penalized territorially, that the brunt of the penalties would fall on Germany and that Austria-Hungary would receive financial backing and raw materials to reconstruct her economic life. In return for these pledges, Austria-Hungary would support the claims of the Entente on the debatable land. Thus the Entente and Austria-Hungary would isolate Germany and throw the burden of the payment of the war upon her.*

This was the same Károlyi who assumed power in Hungary on the break-up of the Empire following the Armistice and threw himself on the mercy of the Allies, relying on the declarations of President Wilson and claiming the application of the Fourteen Points to Hungary's fate. In the spring of 1919 he learned of the frontiers that had been drawn for Hungary at the Paris Peace Conference, frontiers which mutilated the ancient kingdom and even separated large numbers of Hungarians from their country. He turned over his country without further ado to Bela Kuhn and his Communist followers, and departed, while the land went through a reign of terror. He has subsequently been regarded as a traitor by his countrymen ; among the other accusations against him was that he had intercourse with the enemies of his land during the war and was preparing an act of treachery. Even twenty years after the event I regretted to see my despatch published in *Foreign Relations* by my Government, as the reputation of the

* My report to Washington on this subject is published in the form of a telegram dated November 26, 1917, *Foreign Relations of the United States, 1917, Supplement II, Volume I.*

man in his own land and while he was still living should not have been besmirched by any publication of ours of a step which he took in confidence and in reliance upon our guarding that confidence.

All of these efforts for a separate peace and others from Bulgaria foundered on the indomitable determination of the Germans to continue the struggle, and each effort as it came to light brought threats of German intervention against which the Allies and the United States were powerless to guarantee Germany's allies. Each nation that contemplated making a separate peace found itself faced with the probability not only of German intervention but also of becoming a battlefield for the Allied and German forces, and all withdrew aghast at the prospect.

During the months of the negotiations the Czechs in Paris, London and Washington had been insisting tirelessly that all idea of detaching any of its allies from Germany was illusion, that the foreign policy of all these lands was integrated and under German control, that Germany was tolerating the approaches with the idea of holding off Allied attack until Russia was liquidated. The idea may well have been illusory for the reasons I have given in the preceding paragraph. I do not believe, however, that at that time the foreign policy of all these nations was integrated and I still believe that these were serious efforts on their part to get out of the struggle.

The Czechs had every reason to battle against separate peace, only the complete destruction of the Hapsburg sovereignty would give them that complete independence on which they had set their hearts. To this end, Mr. Masaryk had been urging the President in Washington incessantly to declare war on

Austria-Hungary, a measure that the President remained unwilling to take as long as there was the faintest hope of separating the enemies.

But when it became obvious that the Western Powers were faced with the prospect of another great offensive by Germany, the United States declared war on Austria-Hungary on December 7, 1917. The Czechs continued to push for the recognition of their independence, an act which would have meant adopting as a peace aim the destruction of the Empire, and finally succeeded in obtaining that recognition in 1918, from the Allies on August 13, and from the United States September 3. I remember when the telegram came to our Legation announcing the recognition, the Secretary who brought it said as he handed it to me, "*Delenda est Austriaca.*"

Much criticism has been levelled at the Allied and Associated Powers for having broken up the Austro-Hungarian Empire and substituted therefor a number of small states, which at once set up tariff barriers and other restraints on trade that made their economic life precarious. The very size of these states, it was stated, made them an easy prey to Germany since they were unable to adopt a unified policy of resistance. It is certainly true that had a federation been possible, a federation with free trade and a unified foreign policy, the history of the past few years might well have been different. But it is hardly fair to make this the basis of criticism of the Peace Conference. Until just before the great German offensive of March, 1918, the Allies and the United States bent every effort to making a separate peace for a federated Austria-Hungary, and it was only when these efforts broke down that they adopted as a war measure, to cause disruption of the enemy, the policy of encouraging the units of the Empire in their aspiration to independence.

Furthermore, during these months the peoples of the various parts of the Empire had become ever more determined on their independence, to a degree that within a few days of the end of the fighting, local and independent governments had been set up in each unit, governments which entered office without bloodshed and, broadly speaking, with the consent of the governed. It would have taken an Allied Army of occupation to have upset this tendency, and probably the use of force to maintain the Empire. The peoples of the Allies and the United States were in no frame of mind at that time to set up Humpty-Dumpty again. So what the peace conference did was to recognize a fact already existing. The peace conference committed too many faults to add one that it did not merit.

CHAPTER V

We worked at high pressure through those years. My trips around the country, and I made them repeatedly, were for the purpose of meeting our Consuls, representatives of enemy nations and factions. They were nearly all hurried and carried out under pressure of time. But I remember one trip where I took a vacation of a couple of days with Ellis Dresel to climb from Kandersteg to the Rhone Valley over the Gemmi Pass. It was superb weather, the sky of deepest blue, and the mountains sharply outlined with deep gray rock and glacier. I learned in those days what the mountains can do to a troubled spirit. They were so vast, so enduring and so friendly. One could not think of war, all the daily tempest seemed ephemeral, it was as if a kindly hand had smoothed out the world's troubles. In subsequent years when I had learned to ski, I had the same experience repeatedly. The mountains have a healing power which I have never known to fail. You can always bring back from them aching muscles and peace of mind.

That reminds me that I saw men skiing for the first time during this period. I had gone to Mürren to see a British officer who was interned there, and found the whole camp assiduously practising the sport and talking of little else than slalom races and speed tests. They had imported skis from Norway, the first that were brought into Switzerland. Ten years later the sport had spread like wildfire and every Swiss had become a skier. The internment of British officers brought a new sport and enormous additional revenue to the country.

On a ridge back from the Lake of Geneva and not far from the city of that name, stands the eighteenth century château Garengo which belonged to Ernest Schelling and his wife Lucy. Ernest was a pianist and composer of genuine talent, a pupil of Paderewski's and a son in affection to that great genius. Ernest had received a major's commission in our Army and was Assistant to the Military Attaché at Berne. A man of unusual charm, he delighted in children and indeed there remained through his life something childlike and ingenuous about him. His humor even was youthful. Lucy was, I think, the most continuously amusing woman I have known. Occasionally biting, her humor played on every subject. A story teller of inexhaustible repertoire, she and Ernest together kept the table at Garengo in an uproar of mirth. The house was a museum of beautiful objects but Lucy had that virtue so rare in collectors, of making her house comfortable as well as beautiful. The occasional week-ends we could spend there were refreshment and solace, I gained an enduring affection for Garengo and its owners.

During the first weeks of October, 1917, frequent reports of heavy troop movements reached us from Austria-Hungary, together with stories of German "storm-troops" and heavy mobile howitzers crossing the Tyrol to the south. Nevertheless the bulletin of October 24, the first news of the Italian disaster at Caporetto, came as a thunderclap, none of us had had any conception that a sudden break through the mountain line was a possibility. For days the Austrian troops rolled on ; Italian reinforcements, British and French detachments were brought into line hurriedly and a front was eventually stabilized resting on the lower Piave. Those were days of intense anxiety throughout the world, but especially in Switzerland. An Austrian occupation of the Lombardy plain, and it looked as if this might well become a reality, meant Germanic forces on three sides of Switzerland. Under those circumstances, the temptation to straighten the front for an attack on France by marching through Switzerland would have been over-whelming to the German General Staff, at any rate so we felt. We took all preparatory steps for an evacuation, allotted seats in available motors, planned out routes, and were ready to move our people at a moment's notice. This moment, I be-lieve, was the high point of danger to Swiss neutrality but the Italian line held and the danger diminished.

Scarcely had this anxiety abated when a new one arose, one which did not menace the position of Switzerland but caused consternation to Allied sympathizers. Russia quit fighting. News trickled through slowly, but late in November we learned that Kerensky was overthrown by Lenin and was in flight from the country. Massacres followed in Moscow and Petrograd, troops laid down their arms and fraternized with the Germans.

On December 2, negotiations began at Brest-Litovsk, and the real propaganda battle of the war was under way. It is curious how little attention historians have paid to these discus-sions, their methods and results. Wheeler-Bennet has done it in his *Forgotten Peace*, but I know of no other writer who has treated it adequately. I won't attempt to do so, it would take a volume to present properly this meeting, even though its tangible results disappeared a year later. To me in Switzer-land, the amazing thing about the discussions was the way in which the Bolsheviks had discarded all rules that in the past had governed international dealings.

Instead of negotiating with von Kuhlmann and General Hoffmann, they harangued the world. They hit below the belt, they scolded and held up to ridicule. Trotsky had published already the Russian secret treaties with the Allies, now the Germans found they were opposed by negotiators who relied on public declamation and vituperation, who, representing a beaten nation, nevertheless were carrying the war over the heads of the German officials to the German people. It was startling and upsetting, but at the same time it was grimly amusing.

That meeting twenty-three years ago marked the beginning of the type of diplomacy which has become increasingly characteristic of our era, a diplomacy of vituperation by radio, of international mud-slinging. It marked the end of the scrupulous courtesy which had been the rule of international intercourse, a courtesy which endured until the guns began to go off. It marked the end of international good manners, and the beginning of guttersnipe phraseology to replace the age-old courtesy of the tradition of chivalry. Italy and Germany adopted the precedent and bad manners of Lenin, even Western Europe was infected, and in the United States our public men, even some in the Government, thought it a proper thing to vilify governments and persons with whom we maintained diplomatic relations. I know it is hard to have the self-control not to answer insult by insult, but I know as well that to do so breeds war, and that by doing so we put ourselves on the level of those who insult us.

Since this is a personal catalogue of events, I must include mention of one of overwhelming importance to Kate and myself. Our son was born on March 12, 1918. On the eve of the last great German offensive, in the midst of the anxiety aroused by knowledge that the offensive was in preparation, the birth of the child diverted thoughts for the moment to the age-old interests of mankind. He was christened in the lovely little British-American Church of Berne, we held a reception afterward, a breath of normal living and normal rejoicing in the grimness of those times.

March 21 was cold, gray and wet. I was talking in my office during the afternoon when I was interrupted by the telephone, it was a friend on the Swiss Telegraph Agency who read me the German communiqué at that moment received. It read about as follows : "Our troops have broken the British line and penetrated thirty kilometers. We have taken fifteen thousand prisoners, two hundred guns. Our long range guns are shelling the fortified city of Paris." It was devastating, not only the military success, but long range guns shelling Paris ! We had not then heard of the Big Bertha, with its sixty-kilometer range, and the shelling of Paris meant to our minds the presence of Germans in the very outskirts of the capital.

Around eight o'clock that evening I returned to the Hotel Bellevue. Now at that time the Swiss General Staff was quartered in the Bellevue, all the officers messed together in a private dining room, in the company of Switzerland's one officer of general rank, General Wille. The General was short and rotund, absent-minded in appearance, with sleepy blinking eyes. His uniform was gray, his face was gray, his hair was gray. He looked like a little gray gnome. The Swiss officers lived a life apart from the rest of us in the hotel, they found it easier to maintain their attitude of aloof neutrality by keeping to themselves. Nevertheless I had met the General on a number of occasions and had once or twice talked to him at some length. So when I saw him already in the elevator as I stepped in, I nodded and said *"Guten abend, Herr General."*

To my amazement he turned to me with a delighted smile, clapped me on the shoulder and exclaimed in German, "Have you heard the latest news? We have taken twenty thousand prisoners and two hundred guns. We are bombarding Paris. *Kolossal!"*

Here he clapped me again on the back and chuckled. At that moment the door opened at my floor and I stepped out in a daze. I had known that General Wille had married a von Bismarck, I had assumed that in his heart he preferred the German to the Allied cause, but he had never been accused of partiality, and I was stunned that he should address the American Chargé d'Affaires in such terms. He had identified himself with the German victory by the use of "we" — *"Wir haben,"* he had said. I paced my room in a fury, forcing myself to consider coolly what form of protest I should make, when footsteps came running down the hall, and the General's Aide, white of face, burst in my door without knocking.

"Mr. Wilson, what a terrible thing. You know that the General does not see very well. You probably don't know but it's a fact that you are not unlike Alfred von Hohenlohe in appearance. So when you entered the lift and greeted the General in German, he took you for Prince von Hohenlohe of the Austrian Legation and was being diplomatic."

The thought of the General's "diplomacy" was too much for me, I fell into a chair convulsed with laughter, the Aide gave me a startled look, began to grin and was soon in the same helpless state as myself. Needless to say, after this exhibition I could never make a protest.

The tremendous offensive rolled on, irresistible as an immense flow of lava from a volcano, overwhelming and consuming all opposition in its path, or so it seemed then. Bapaume, Noyon, Montdidier, fell after furious fighting. Marshall Foch became Commander-in-Chief of the Allied forces on April 14. In the same month the Americans entered the line in force for the first time near Amiens. A brief pause was followed by another furious assault in the end of May, the enemy crossed the Aisne, captured Soissons, came to the Marne and were halted in violent battle around Château-Thierry, where the Americans fought magnificently. In the first days of June a further German advance was checked at the Bois de Belleau, and the line remained relatively inactive until July 15. As Pickett's charge at Gettysburg represented the high tide of the rebellion, so the fighting at the Bois de Belleau marked the high tide of German victory. But the German ebb was faster.

During this period my business frequently took me to Paris in connection with the information work of our General Staff. This work was under the direction of General Denis Nolan, who at that period was at Chaumont, the headquarters of the American Expeditionary Force. General Nolan won my deep respect. A rugged American figure, he arrived in France in August, 1917, with the first skeleton of a General Staff and I had seen him in Paris shortly thereafter. In that first interview he was completely ignorant of European affairs, but in succeeding months his knowledge increased unbelievably to a point that by the period, in 1918, of which I write, you found no further need for explanations, you gave him facts; he knew where to fit them in and how to assimilate them.

Hugh Gibson was then assigned to the Embassy at Paris as First Secretary, but was serving as the principal liaison officer for the State Department with G-2 and General Nolan, Hugh and Walter Lippmann shared a flat on the top of a house in the rue de la Pompe. It was there I usually stayed on my visits. It was a long way to walk to the rue de la Pompe and taxis were hard to come by. I usually arrived with tired feet and so found the four flights of stairs doubly long. Hugh has been for years one of my closest friends; since I discuss his work at length in a later chapter, I shall not describe him here.

We went out to Chaumont, Hugh and I, about July 10, had our talk with General Nolan and were then invited to visit the front as it was only a short distance away. Several vivid impressions remain of that visit. We were led through a wood out to a point where we could see across a small ravine the skyline of Lucie-le-Bocage, a tiny village of stone cottages standing on a narrow ridge. German shells were falling amid the houses. From where we lay it was a scene from a stage, witnessed, we felt, in complete security. That feeling of security vanished when the officer accompanying us gave us a lecture on how to tell by the sound what shells were likely to fall close and then led us on the run across an open field to another woods. Here we were deafened by the unholy racket of a battery of six-inch guns.

The officer in charge greeted us with a broad grin on a face radiating good humor, and spoke with a southern accent that

was warming in those conditions.   He was "Pa" Watson, now
Military Aide to the President.   Thence we went to listen to
an examination of some German prisoners where we encountered General de Chambrun and gossiped about Washington,
where he had served as Military Attaché to the French Embassy.

I remember that our civilian clothes came in for a lot of comment.   Every detachment we met passed some observation
on our attire.   In one village toward evening two drunken
doughboys came down the street arm-in-arm.   They saw us,
halted in their tracks, we heard one say, "Jeez, two dudes with
a cane, let's beat it !"   Act followed speech, they departed on
the run.

There had been some discussion earlier, and it continued on
this visit, as to whether Hugh and I should take commissions,
get into uniform and join directly the work of army headquarters.   We felt, however, that in civilian clothes and with
diplomatic status there was nobody in Europe whom we could
not approach on an equal footing, that if we got into uniform
our relatively lowly rank would put an end to such access,
and we would probably find ourselves translating newspapers
for the General Staff at Chaumont.   We obviously were totally untrained for genuine military work, so we eventually decided to remain as we were, diplomatic secretaries without
uniform.

We returned to Paris on July 14 and spent that night in the
flat on the rue de la Pompe.   The Big Bertha was still dropping
occasional shells in the city, but late at night more formidable
sounds became audible, the uninterrupted rumble of big guns.
We hurried to the roof and saw the summer sky illuminated by

a thousand Fourth-of-July celebrations, the last battle of the Marne had begun. For two days the Germans attacked, on the eighteenth the sound of guns was intensified, Foch had begun his counter-attack and the turning point in the war had occurred. Subsequently an officer in the French G-2 told me that a German officer of Alsatian origin, a member of the German General Staff, had revealed to the French the plans of the last German attack, that Foch had allowed the Germans to advance to a position where he could assault them on both flanks. I have never been able to confirm this story, but whether or not Foch had knowledge of the German plans, his assault was overwhelming, the Germans were halted and driven back, and for the Allies the tide of victory had set in.

From time to time, it was urgent to communicate with the Embassy at Paris. There was no international telephone system during the war, so I would cross by boat from Lausanne to Evian, on the French side of Lake Geneva, and put in a call to Paris from the French customhouse. I had finished such a call one day and came out onto the station platform in time to see one of the most pathetic sights it was ever my fortune to witness. A train was pulling in slowly, the opening bars of the *Marseillaise*, slightly off tune, blared from a trumpet played by a lone *chasseur Alpin*, clad in tattered beret and worn uniform.

From every door of the train there poured onto the platform a ragged assembly of humanity, old men and old women looking like scarecrows, all singing the *Marseillaise* while tears poured down their wrinkled cheeks. They fell into line behind the trumpeter, marched into the station, singing, waving their arms, their wet faces transfigured by joy at treading again the soil of France. They were *repatriés*, citizens of Northern France, for years under German domination, and now returned through Switzerland to the motherland as their usefulness for labor had passed. Superfluous individuals, coming back to a land in which they must be supported by charity, with nothing to hope for but existence ; their rapture at returning home brought tears to my eyes and a lump in my throat.

During these months culminating in the Armistice, the figure of President Wilson became progressively greater throughout Europe. To the continental mind, something incredible was happening. Not only was the power of the United States appearing for the first time on the European field, it was proving day by day capable of efforts which had been considered impossible. The magnitude of our undertaking had something dazzling through its very size. The swift overcoming of transportation difficulties, the mobilization of industry, the deep emotional movement among our people, were awesome. Added to that, a leader began to emerge who voiced the hope of millions of suffering and dispirited people for a better world, and who even, they thought, showed the practical way to the realization of hope.

That leader began to be acclaimed as something more than human, a godlike man of infinite wisdom, rising in a new land, speaking English like Milton, and shining with the radiance of the immensity of America. He was the peoples' statesman, no other land had a figure to be venerated. President Wilson, wrapped in the mysticism of a prophet, became an object of veneration to millions of simple people, not only among the Allies, but in enemy countries as well.

I belonged to those simple people ; I could recognize the political potency of the President's declarations, I could appraise the slow weakening of the will to resistance which his doctrines began to bring about in enemy countries. I could even advise as to the best means in his speeches of weakening that resistance. Nevertheless, I was caught up in that glow of hope and faith. I believed genuinely that the breakdown of the Central Powers would be followed by something revolutionary in history, by a peace of conciliation and harmonious co-operation among the States.

I quickly sensed a resistance to the President's doctrines, particularly among the French, this I could understand, but to my dismay I began to sense it as well among Americans. A fantastic episode took place at a French frontier station. One of our army officers was held up, in spite of protests and diplomatic status, searched carefully, delayed twenty-four hours by the French authorities before being released to continue his trip to Paris. The officer happened to be a determined individual with a number of French friends in high quarters. He made a nuisance of himself to such a degree that he was finally told the reason for the delay.

Here is the explanation given him. It appears that the Allied Military Police co-operated with the French by furnishing confidential information concerning citizens of their countries who might be in France or who were likely to travel there. This information was handed in on cards, a white card for those citizens with a clean bill of health, a pink one for doubtful cases. It appears that the French frontier officials had unearthed from their files, a pink card dealing with the officer in question and furnished them by the American military authorities. In explanation of American suspicion regarding this

American officer, the card had this annotation : "Believes in President Wilson's doctrines." To believe in President Wilson, at that time, was to find oneself considered slightly "pro-German" by officials and military men. Nevertheless millions of men and women in Allied countries were slightly "pro-German" by this standard. I could sense the hostility, the instinctive mistrust of the realist for the visionary, but in this case I felt that the President's authority was so immense, that he could prevail at the decisive moment.

I have spoken of the contact maintained informally with the Bulgarian Legation in Berne. It caused me no undue surprise to receive a telephone call on September 21, 1918, from the Bulgarian Minister asking if he could come and speak to me urgently. I remember thinking that it would be interesting to get his views as to the extent of the victories claimed by the French press to have been gained over the Bulgarian forces by General Franchet d'Esperey in his advance from Saloniki to Usküb. The Minister was ushered into my room and, without a word, handed me a paper, herewith reproduced, signed by our representative in Sofia and reporting that Bulgaria had demanded an armistice. This was the first break in the resistance of the Central Powers, the first genuine sign of the end. We had felt throughout the orderly retirement of the German forces, that victory could be achieved eventually, but few of us had dreamed that it was within our immediate grasp. I rushed a cable to Washington and until September 25, when the Bulgarian offer was finally made public, I remember walking about in a daze, thinking that the immensity of the news which I was concealing must be visible to the casual observer.

On October 4, I was just leaving the office for lunch when

Pour le Secrétaire d'Etat
Lansing
à Washington

Le Gouvernement Bulgare
est décidé à demander la
cessation des hostilités avec
l'Entente sur son invitation.
Je pars ce soir pour le front
de Macédoine, où des délégués
du Gouvernement Bulgare
demanderont la conclusion
d'un armistice. Le soin de
régler les conflits dans la
Péninsule balkanique est
laissé au Congrès International

qui aura à conclure la paix
générale. Le Gouvernement
Bulgare sollicite les dé-
marches énergiques des États
Unis d'Amérique en vue
de mettre fin à l'effusion
de sang.

Murphy

the Swiss Telegraph Agency called to state that they had picked up a wireless message from Prince Max of Baden, who had become Chancellor of Germany, addressed to President Wilson, and proposing peace. The Minister, Mr. Stovall, I knew was lunching at the French Embassy. I drove there and found a large party seated at the table. I remember summoning Mr. Stovall and giving him the news, whereupon he took me into the dining room and bade me announce it to the table in French. A cheer broke out from the guests, a cheer interrupted by sobs of relief and joy.

The next month resistance collapsed and events moved with bewildering and kaleidoscopic rapidity. On October 17, telegrams came from Prague and Agram announcing the formation, respectively, of an independent Czechoslovak Republic and an independent State of Yugoslavia. On October 27, Colonel House arrived in Paris with Joe Grew, who had been designated Secretary General of the American delegation to the Peace Conference. Already, this far in advance of the conference, the Colonel had moved in with his General Staff. On October 30, Turkey signed an armistice with the Allied Powers. On November 3, after a terrific rout and slaughter of retreating forces, Austria-Hungary signed an armistice with Italy. On November 5 came an item of news hardly noticed in Europe, the elections of the United States had returned a Republican majority to Congress.

Even Americans abroad, to say nothing of foreigners, failed for months to recognize the significance of this news or to appreciate that President Wilson no longer had the backing of his own country, at least in its political bodies. But for its importance to the history of the world, scarcely any of the events that took place in this fateful month were of equal importance with this political news from the United States. On November 9, the Kaiser abdicated, and on November 11, 5 A. M., the final act of that phase of the tragedy, the Armistice was signed by the German and Allied delegates.

Here I am going to pause for a moment of digression from the narrative. I have read again recently in Washington the reports of the Legation at Berne, including my own. As the months of war progressed the reports show a change, a shift of emphasis. In the early months they are reports of events, pure and simple. Slowly they become comment and interpretation. Then begins advice and counsel. The report of events continues, the comment and counsel increase in maturity and authority. It is as if we in the Legation ourselves matured during this period, one might say that a group of routine Foreign Service officers became men of action and authority under pressure of events.

Such a change could not have been the development of one man alone. In a staff of that size, where each one played his indispensable part, each member must have made this progress. Perhaps it was that the peculiarly close relationship among all the men associated in this work enabled us to develop as a unit. There was a unity, a singleness of purpose, a devotion to our business, that I never saw equalled by any other group. At the risk of the charge of self-approval, I am going to add that Walter Lippmann wrote shortly after the Peace Conference a discussion of the inadequacy of our diplomatic representation in Europe throughout the war. After revealing the lack of proper information from the various missions he said : (I am quoting from memory only) "There was one shining exception. In Berne a group of the very best young men in the Service made themselves a center for information and advice of the highest order." Even if the praise was exaggerated, as no doubt it was, it was highly gratifying to the young men concerned.

CHAPTER VI

Shortly after his arrival, Colonel House telegraphed me to proceed at once to Paris to apprise him of the present situation in Central Europe and to discuss with him any thoughts I might have as to methods under which the American delegation to the Peace Conference should carry out its work. I arrived in Paris on the evening of November 10, telephoned Joe Grew at Colonel House's headquarters, and made an appointment to see the Colonel at nine o'clock the following morning. Barely had I presented myself at the Colonel's residence, shaken him by the hand, and started to talk, when the telephone in his office jingled.

Colonel House picked it up, handed it to me, saying, "He's talking French ; what is it all about ?"

I took the receiver.

A harsh voice crackled, *"Voici le Président du Conseil Clémenceau."* He continued, "The Armistice has been signed at five A. M. The Germans accept all terms. The war is over. Announcement of the Armistice will be made at eleven A. M. by the firing of twenty-one guns at the Place des Invalides. *Vive la France !"*

I turned slowly to Colonel House, gave him the message and said, "Colonel House, I take it that this is one day for nobody to do any work."

"I agree," said the Colonel.

I rushed into Joe Grew's room. I remember his office was a

cabinet de toilette with a mosaic bath and full length mirrors. I told Joe the news and found him in enthusiastic accord as to any further work. We decided that the place to see this coming show was the Place de la Concorde, and hastened toward the door. In the corridor we encountered Reggie Foster in the uniform of a second lieutenant, attached to the Colonel's mission. Without even telling him the news we seized him and hurried him out with us and took up our position in the Place de la Concorde.

The rumor had gotten around that an event of stupendous importance was in the making. As the hour of eleven approached, tens of thousands of French men and women packed into the Place de la Concorde. The throng was so immense that it was impossible to move, every face tense with expectation, awaiting the announcement they knew was coming. Punctually at eleven o'clock the measured booming of the guns began. Speakers from the balconies along the rue de Rivoli made the announcement through megaphones, but with the sound of the guns the public had no need of the spoken word.

The guns fell silent. The crowd neither moved nor spoke. They didn't seem to breathe. I don't know how long this lasted; it seemed an eternity before a voice somewhere near us began softly the *Marseillaise*. The music swept over the crowd, from a soft reverent tone it took on the blare and stridency of triumph. People sang with transfigured faces, tears raining down their cheeks. With the end of the song, silence for a moment again; suddenly it was as if everyone went crazy. Everybody embraced his neighbors, everybody yelled, everybody continued singing the *Marseillaise*, by this time in every key and with no coherence.

The three of us spent the next hours, I was about to say roaming the streets, but that word brings no adequate picture. It is too debonair and casual.   We pushed our way, rather, through the streets of Paris.   We had a hard time keeping Reggie Foster with us as this handsome young man in uniform had to be kissed by a vast number of women in every block. Joe and I felt a real sense of grievance.   Toward evening, still in the same mood of exaltation, we fought our way into the Café de Paris and even got seats at a table.   Heaven knows how.   It must have been the result of tremendous bribery.

I remember that Charlie McCauley, in a resplendent brigadier's uniform, was also at the table, and in the geniality of the evening the very junior Lieutenant Foster had the satisfaction of telling a Brigadier General what he thought of the administration of the American Expeditionary Forces.   We left the Café de Paris with the Brigadier and the Lieutenant arm in arm, followed by two members of the orchestra, the clarinet and the piccolo players, and proceeded in this fashion to the Place de l'Opéra and the boulevards — an unforgettable day !

I was awakened in the cold gray dawn, and it was a cold gray dawn after the festivities of Armistice Day, by a telephone message from the Legation in Berne telling me that a general strike had broken out in Switzerland, that all public services, railroads, trams, and industry of all kinds were at a standstill.   They added that there was genuine apprehension due to the Communist character of the demonstration, and that I should get back as soon as possible.   I replied that I would take the morning train and in view of the strike on the railroads it would be wise to send my car to Bellegarde, in France, and I would then motor from there to Berne.

I found my car waiting in Bellegarde, and as we drove into Geneva the change from the day before was profound. I had left a nation triumphantly rejoicing in victory. I entered a city still and hushed, heavy with apprehension, a city and a nation that lay as if under a medieval interdiction.

A cordon of troops, a regiment of Fribourg, was thrown around the section at Berne which comprises the federal buildings. I learned that the Federal Council had taken up residence in the Bellevue Hotel within this cordon, and were there directing the operation of precautionary measures. The Government had stationed in the various cities regiments from other cantons so that the danger of fraternizing with Communist elements was minimized. The Swiss Army had been under mobilization, in any case, for the past four years and plenty of troops were available.

Darkness fell early on this drizzling November day. Toward six o'clock in the evening I went out into the Marktplatz, a large square in front of the federal palace. This square was dimly lit, lined by the French-speaking troops, but within the hollow square which they formed, Communist orators were inciting the crowd to revolutionary activities. An ugly temper prevailed. People were jeering against the Government and taunting the soldiers. The soldiers, on the other hand, looked inexpressibly bored. From the canton of Fribourg, they spoke only French, and the insults from the Bernese citizens fell on deaf ears. It was cold and dreary standing on guard for long hours.

To while away this period of boredom, a little group of soldiers struck up the Fribourg national song. It has a good swing to it and is well known by every citizen of Berne. Gradually, like expanding ripples on a pond, the tune was taken up by wider and wider circles of the crowd, and before the end of the second verse practically the whole crowd in the Platz was singing lustily.

A brief pause followed the end of the song and then, as it were, spontaneously, the Swiss National Anthem began to roll out, the troops singing with the people. The song ceased. Cheers broke out and suddenly the yell, "Down with the Communists !" Speakers were hauled off the platform and disappeared in the seething swarm of burghers. A man with the voice of a Danton leapt on the platform and shouted to the crowd, "Let's go down to the Bellevue and show our loyalty to the Federal Council." The crowd responded with a mighty roar and set out in the direction of the Bellevue.

I ran ahead at all speed, showed my pass to the sentry and entered the Bellevue. There I found in the lobby Federal Councillors Motta and Schulthess, both of whom I knew intimately. They were in deep collaboration with the General of the Armies, and, since they were discussing precautionary measures to be taken in view of the uproar that they heard approaching from the Marktplatz, they were somewhat resentful when I broke in on them. The attitude quickly changed, however, when I began explaining breathlessly what had taken place in the square and that the Communist gathering had turned into a patriotic demonstration. The Federal Councillors rushed onto the balcony of the hotel, I with them. The crowd came down the streets singing, laughing and cheering.

A pandemonium of rejoicing took place under the balcony. Eventually it was still, and Giuseppe Motta made a golden speech, one of the most beautiful I ever listened to, as he poured out his faith in the patriotism of the Swiss people.

This dramatic scene marked the end of the general strike. News of what had happened in Berne brought rejoicing and courage to the citizenry of Zürich, Geneva, Lausanne, Basle, and other cities of the country. As I remember it, by noon of the succeeding day the strike was broken, the men were back at work.

For the next few months I lived a somewhat bewildering existence. I alternated between the Crillon Hotel in Paris, the seat of the American delegation to the Peace Conference, and my office in Berne. My bag was always packed and I never knew at what moment a telephone call might put me on the train in one direction or the other.

The work at Berne changed, radically. The various commissions at Paris began to send their own representatives and investigators to the far corners of Europe. While we continued to forward such information as we could about events, we dealt more with those persons who for political reasons were unable to get to Paris.

The whole world wanted to go to Paris. It seemed as if everybody in every country had an idea in his or her mind that he or she wanted to lay before President Wilson. Many of the simple folk felt that all that had to be done to solve their difficulties was to speak to President Wilson for five minutes, at the end of which time he would wave a magic wand and injustice would be righted.

Hundreds of them came to my office to explain why they

wanted to see the President. A group appeared one day clad in the Tyrolean Sunday costume. The mayor of a small village in South Tyrol, bare knees, leather breeches, green hat with a feather, was accompanied by three women — a school teacher, a nurse, and I have forgotten the profession of the other. As they entered my room the mayor bowed from the waist, while the ladies curtsied. The mayor, as spokesman, set forth the case. He set it forth in rolling periods, so that it was easy to see that days had been spent in the preparation of this address. He explained that he, an old man, was the only male in the village, barring young boys, that many of the men, of course, had died, but that others were in prison camps in Russia and in Italy.

Their desire was twofold : first, would the President please speak to the Italians and Russians and ask them to send their men back ; and, second, could they please stay in a country where German was spoken and not become a part of Italy. At the close of his address, the mayor lifted his rucksack from the floor where he had deposited it and pulled from it a sheet of parchment, beautifully scrolled and illuminated in the margin. This was the petition that they desired to lay before President Wilson.

I was touched. The faith of these simple people was rather pathetic when one thought of the maelstrom in Paris and the little likelihood that anyone in position of authority could ever be induced even to look at their paper, the fruit of their hours of study and anxious thought.

I tried to soften the blow as much as I could, I said, "You know the President is an extremely busy man and when he gets down to his office in the morning he finds papers on his desk a foot thick. It is impossible for him to read all the things that come to him or to deal with the individual desires of small groups of people. He must deal in the large and on general plans."

One of the women rose, curtsied again, and said, "But don't you know somebody who is close to the President?"

I replied that I probably did.

She continued, "Well, couldn't you write him and tell him to steal into the President's office five minutes before the President comes down to his desk, take our paper out of the heap and put it on top of the pile?"

Another visit that I had remains in my recollection, although I have forgotten the name of the visitor. A short gentleman in a silk hat and a black frock coat, with round ruddy cheeks, a beaming smile, and glistening black hair one day came in and announced that he was a Prince of Daghestan. He had been commissioned by the rulers of the Republic of Daghestan to call on President Wilson in order to impress upon him the desires of the people of his country for an independent existence and their fears lest they be incorporated within the Soviet Union. I told him that I would have to send his application for a visa to the French authorities in Paris for their decision, and that he would have to wait some days in Berne for an answer. Whereupon the Prince of Daghestan rose, shook me by the hand, accompanied me to the door.

As I threw it open for his departure, I saw standing on the threshold a huge figure with its arms folded, clothed in long baggy trousers with soft leather boots, a leopard skin over his blouse and a girdle about his waist to which was attached a formidable curved scimitar. The Prince said something in an unknown tongue to the figure and the figure bowed deeply to me.

I said to the Prince, "Do you mind my asking whether this rather formidable person is a bodyguard, or a valet, or both?"

"Neither the one nor the other, or maybe a mixture of both," replied the Prince. "You see, my Government realizes that when its representatives go abroad into great cities, they have had little experience with the temptations of civilization, so we have the habit of detailing a simple peasant of unquestioned loyalty to accompany them and be responsible for their behavior abroad. Also," he added, "he is responsible for the success of my mission."

"How do you mean?" I asked.

"Well, it is very simple. He knows that my mission is to see the President of the United States in Paris. If I fail in my mission he knows what his duty is and he will perform it."

"With the scimitar?" I asked.

"Yes," said he.

Now the worst of this story is that in the frantic life that we led in those months I never ascertained, although I tried to do so subsequently, whether the Prince of Daghestan got to Paris and, if not, whether his countryman did his duty.

In the days immediately following the Armistice I received surprising visits from members of enemy Legations. I remember the start it gave me when the Counselor of the Austro-Hungarian Legation walked into my office with a beaming smile and remarked that we were now allies since he was a Pole from Galicia. That Austro-Hungarian Legation seemed to have held within its walls representatives of most of the disruptive forces within the Empire. There was even one representative of a world-famous family as Germanic as the Teutonic Knights, who announced himself to be a Czech and, therefore, on the side of victory. I had been dealing constantly for months on end with subversive forces within the Dual Monarchy, but I don't think I realized until after the Armistice that members of the ruling caste would find it so simple to align themselves on the side of victory.

The Socialists of Europe were the first to gather in a genuinely international meeting. The Second International summoned a convention at Berne shortly after the Armistice, and it marked the meeting of such contrasting figures as Kurt Eisner, Bolshevist Prime Minister of Bavaria ; Grumbach of Alsatia, Arthur Henderson and Ramsay MacDonald, the latter eventually Nationalist Prime Minister of Great Britain. Organized labor in the United States had been invited to send delegates, but Samuel Gompers had declined in a scorching telegram arraigning the whole lot of Second Internationalists as a group of Bolshevists.

Listening to the debates in this conference, it was curious to reflect, with Gompers' telegram in mind, how generally the Socialist speakers from Europe were the advocates of orderly society, conciliation by the peoples, forgetfulness of the hatreds of the war. Firebrands there were, such as Eisner, but they were few. The overwhelming impression was of the widespread conservatism of Socialist groups in Europe. The policies of conciliation which they advocated were, alas, far in advance of the policies practised by their governments.

I began to think then, and have clung to the same idea through succeeding years, that the only health for Europe lay in the hope of coalition governments for all great states : the

Conservatives to run internal affairs — re-establishment of credit, resumption of peacetime production, and so on — and the Socialists with their ideas of conciliation to handle foreign relations.   Alas, there never seemed to be a proper combination.   The Socialists in power meant internal disintegration, the Conservatives in power meant rigid nationalism in the foreign field.

You might have thought that President Wilson was one of the leading exponents of Socialism if you listened to the tributes paid to him and to the doctrines which he advocated.   The meeting was held in a period in which the Bolsheviks were struggling only too successfully in the Eastern Baltic area, when Spartacist riots were a daily occurrence in Berlin, when Bavaria had gone Communist, and when every state in Eastern Europe trembled with the threat of this menace.   To the majority of the speakers of the Second International the Communist threat was a greater one than the war itself and their opposition to it was marked and emphatic.

Bill Bullitt came over from the American delegation in Paris to attend the sessions of the Second International.   This visit of Bill's was the foundation of a friendship between us of long duration.   It was the first time I had seen him, so to speak, in action, and it was extraordinary to see this youth on terms of intimate relationship with so many of the leading figures of Europe.   His French was fluent and colloquial and these older men treated him on terms of affectionate understanding.

My trips to Paris were usually sudden and brief, but on certain occasions I stayed long enough to gain something of an insight as to how the delegation was working and what progress the Peace Conference was making.   On one occasion I served as secretary to the American delegation, but a more interesting experience was when I replaced Bullitt during his absence in Russia on an expedition which has since become historical. My task consisted of rising at a very early hour in the morning, assimilating the news from the French press and the incoming telegrams before breakfast, then catching the various members of the American delegation while dressing, shaving, or breakfasting, and giving them a rapid oral summary of the day's events.

My most dominant recollection of that particular period is of conversations which I had on these occasions with General Tasker Bliss. I considered then, and I still believe, that General Bliss had the deepest appreciation of the situation in Europe and of the necessities not only of the moment but of the future. His reflection was thorough-going, his deductions were profound. Unfortunately, he was not the type of man to do battle for his ideas. He would reduce his thoughts to paper and consider his duty done when the paper was circulated. A study of his papers today serves to fortify the assertions I have just been writing and confirms the regret that General Bliss was not able temperamentally to convince others of the soundness of his views. In the hurly-burly of such a gathering it is the persistently vocal man who makes his views prevail. The man who does not know when he is beaten, provided he has ideas, is the man whose ideas are accepted.

Even to a young man like myself the meetings of the American delegation had an element of futility. During the period that I attended I never saw either the President or Colonel House in a session. Mr. Lansing would preside, General Bliss and Mr. Henry White would attend. A number of items would be on the agenda but, fresh as I was to the work, I could see that the items were of secondary importance. My understanding of what went on in the Conference lay in the brief talks that I had with Colonel House either when presenting the day's news or in some accidental meeting later.

It was early in my visits to Paris that forebodings began to arise as to the future of Europe under the treaty which seemed to be in the making. A thousand little incidents awakened apprehension. I remember encountering an old friend at that time serving in the financial section of the American delegation engaged in discussion of reparations. We greeted each other and he said, "It is a case of dog eat dog. I wish we had known it in advance."

Another time I travelled in the métro, the Paris subway. Across from me were seated two men, members of Parliament, I gathered, from their conversation. One was explaining to the other the danger to France which lay in the acceptance of the President's conceptions of peace, or any yielding to him. The other was equally convinced, and as I left the train I heard him say, *"Faut se méfier du Président,"* in other words, "We have got to be on our guard against the President."

These were straws only but everything that I heard in the delegation of the results of the struggle and clash of idealism versus realism brought more and more certainty to my mind that except for window-dressing the cause of idealism was lost. I was not alone in this feeling of disillusion. In the delegation itself and in other delegations, men were swallowing the bitter draught of disillusion. Harold Nicolson — I think it is in *Peacemaking, 1919* — gives a poignant account of his despair at the course the negotiations took. Many of us who cared deeply and went through this experience were never quite the same men afterward. We had lost something, perhaps something that every man loses in his maturity, the ability to believe in miracles, the belief that sudden and radical adjustments are possible, a certain faith in the wisdom of human beings. Perhaps, as I say, every man has some experience sooner or later in his life similar to that which we young fellows experienced at Paris. However general the experience may be, it is none the less a sad one.

I found myself blaming the President bitterly in my heart. I blamed him for creating hopes and then shattering them. I blamed him for what I thought was the lack of struggle he was making to carry through his convictions. I know now that I was at fault in assessing this blame. I seem to feel that the stature of President Wilson becomes ever greater through the passing of years, but the greatness of the President lay in his lofty ideals and the beauty and force of the language with which he presented them. It lay in the breadth of his imagination and in his moral courage to assert his faith. The world will never be quite the same as it was before the speeches of Woodrow Wilson. We have had a glimpse and a vision of what the world may become when human beings are wise enough and unselfish enough to give reality to such a dream.

It was when President Wilson entered into personal struggle with such redoubtable opponents as Lloyd George and Clémenceau that his limitations became apparent. He simply did not have the qualifications to deal with men of this stamp. His greatness lay in thought and not in action. I cite Harold Nicolson again in *Peacemaking*, 1919. Nicolson measures his impressions recorded in a diary of that time against his judgments formed twenty years later, and his strictures on the President are more severe after the lapse of time than they were at the moment.   I have had an evolution of thought in the opposite direction.   The bitterness that I felt twenty years ago has disappeared.   The greatness of the President is a certainty in my mind.   His limitations lay in his inability to handle men, but there are no limitations to the measure of the man as philosopher and statesman.

In Clémenceau and Lloyd George, Mr. Wilson was dealing with two intellects radically different from his own, at the same time more ruthless and more subtle.   He was negotiating with men of a profounder political experience and instinct, a better grasp of what humanity is capable of accomplishing.   His wide knowledge was no match for this instinct.   Clémenceau is quoted as making a profound comparison between his two colleagues.   He said : "Wilson knows everything and understands nothing ; Lloyd George knows nothing and understands everything."

The story of the frontiers fixed for Hungary by the boundary commission of the Peace Conference trickled through to Switzerland and rapidly came into circulation in Hungary itself.   In bitterness and disgust at what he considered treachery to a promise, Károlyi, as I have explained in detail in Chapter IV, abandoned the country and left it to the tender mercies of Bela Kuhn and his Communist followers.   I felt that my forebodings were justified and I telephoned Colonel House that I would like to come to Paris and see him.

I poured out to him all the disillusion and despair which filled me.   I told him how the beaten nations of Europe were going to regard us as faithless to our promises.   I said it was plain to me that the President could not prevail, that the cause was lost, that the League of Nations embodied in such a document as the Versailles Treaty could not be an instrument of justice. I said that in engaging in such a Treaty, we were merely involving the United States in another war, or series of wars. I ended by begging him to prevail on the President to pack his trunks and go home, take the American delegation with him, and let the Europeans work out their own solution for their own problem.

I can see him now, that kind little gray man with his wise eyes, as he listened to me without speaking. When I finished breathless he said, very quietly, "Come back at half-past three. I haven't time to go into this with you now but I want to talk to you at length. We will take a drive in the Bois de Boulogne and talk it over."

At half-past three we climbed into one of the gray army Cadillacs, so common a sight on Paris streets in those days, and departed for the Bois.

Colonel House said that during intervals throughout the day he had been thinking over my outburst of the morning and he had several observations to make to me. The most important was that he appreciated my state of mind, but that I must not be under the misapprehension that the President and he felt that all was for the best, in the best of all possible worlds. They both knew the course that events were taking, and the President had weighed matters carefully and had come to the conclusion that if he could attain only part of his objective it was better to do so than to sacrifice everything by going home. Colonel House added that the President knew well the risk he was running for his personal reputation, that he was willing to make a sacrifice of that reputation if through the sacrifice a better future could be offered to humanity.

I was a young man and defeated by this reply. It seemed to me that if the President had weighed all these things and had still determined upon his course, then there was nothing further for me to say, but I confessed then that I was not convinced by the reasons he offered. Nothing that has happened in the past twenty years has changed my mind and, indeed, countless things that have happened in the past twenty years have convinced me that it would have been better for the American delegation to depart at that time. Indeed, as I look back on it, I think that I spoke more wisely than I knew because I had no conception then of the development of opposition to the President in the United States. I have said before that with the press of events we in Europe paid little or no attention to the Republican opposition elected to Congress. I did not dream then of the battle that would develop against the Treaty or of the grounds on which this struggle would be fought. Had I had that foresight I would have been even more insistent in presenting my point of view. In any case, I have always held Colonel House in affectionate gratitude for his candor and the trust that he put in me at that time.

I have no intention of trying to analyze the faults and virtues of the Treaty of Versailles, a subject that has been treated not only exhaustively but *ad nauseam*. However, I think now the document itself was a much better document than I considered it in 1919. Examined historically, it compares favorably with many peace treaties, but its faults were glaring and obvious twenty years ago, as they are today, and not the least of these faults was that it was written by gentlemen who were publicly pledged to the application and implementing of the Fourteen Points of President Wilson.

The joy in Allied and neutral countries that followed the Armistice was clouded by the dreadful epidemic of what we called at the time Spanish influenza. Countless died in every country from the ravages of this disease. I came near being one of its victims, a sudden attack threatened to turn into pneumonia. It was staved off by heroic treatment which left me weak and depressed. In the early weeks of 1919 I fainted several times on the streets of Berne and had to be carried home. Toward the end of March the doctor came to see me and insisted that I apply for leave and get a rest. I had been frightened myself at my own condition, I was under the disillusion in regard to the Treaty which I have mentioned, I had been three years absent from the United States and was longing to be there again. I obtained a leave of absence and sailed with my family from Liverpool in April 1919.

CHAPTER VII

The S.S. *Adriatic* was transporting few passengers as it was repatriating some thousands of Canadian troops. It made a leisurely passage to Halifax, and I had a lot of time to think and to consider my position. The years that had just past, in spite of the breakdown of hopes for a better international order, had given me the most engrossing experience of my lifetime. I had been fascinated both by the work and by the problems of Central Europe. This area, small from the American point of view, gave such striking contrasts in race, religion, historical background and ambitions, that it offered more than a life study.

The work itself confirmed me in a conviction that had been slow in forming, that diplomacy was the task which I wanted to continue. After these years, I knew that I had found my profession, and would devote my life to it. I had had a measure of success, I had earned the good opinion of the senior men in the Department of State, and had grounds to hope that I could choose to some extent the type of work that I wanted. I wanted to see the United States, live an American life for a while and be refreshed thereby, and then return to Central Europe.

New York was dazzling. The rush of motors was unbelievable to a person fresh from Europe. It is odd to think that at that time I had never seen a self-starter except in the army Cadillacs brought over with the American Expeditionary

Force. The people were happy. The women on the street were all so beautiful and smart that they made one blink. The war was over, personal suffering had not come near the mass of our people. New York seemed to have become for all time the financial center of the world and the American people were convinced that a long era of prosperity would follow the cessation of hostilities. They were angry, it is true, about what had happened while they were occupied with their jobs during the war. While their backs were turned, so to speak, a group of reformers had passed the Prohibition Bill and New York certainly was deeply resentful. However this bill had not yet gone into effect and my friends were busily engaged in laying up stocks for the future and, incidentally, taking abundant advantage of the existence of bars destined to disappear.

My wife and I found ourselves caught up in New York by a number of parents of American women married to persons in Central Europe — Germans, Austrians, Poles, and others — and our rooms at the hotel became a sort of information center for these people, desirous of news of their daughters from whom they had been unable to hear for years. I remember that we had considerable difficulty in convincing the parents of some of these women that the war was over and that they would not be betraying their country by sending money and clothing to daughters in distress in Germany.

We set out to find a house for the summer, since I had been ordered by the doctors not to start work for some months. We eventually located a small house that suited our purposes charmingly situated on one of the Shinnecock Hills at the end of Long Island. That summer remains a delightful recollection. The hills were brilliant with heather, the sand was daz-

zlingly white, and the sea in the Sound a deep Mediterranean
blue.   I played golf at the National Golf Course which I still
think of as the most satisfactory course in any land.   In these
surroundings energy and health came back rapidly.

Generally speaking, the people of the United States were too
relieved that the war was over, that victory had been won, to
trouble themselves a great deal about the type of settlement
which was being made at Paris, but, week by week as the
summer advanced, mutters of the approaching storm that was
to break over the ratification of the Versailles Treaty in the
Senate became ever more audible.   I found myself in a difficult position when conversation turned on these matters.   I
resented the Treaty of Versailles but I did not resent the League
of Nations.   Generally speaking, the people that I encountered
paid no attention to the Treaty of Versailles but were deeply
resentful of the League of Nations.   I was in the Government
service, had shared to some extent in the work at Paris, so I had
to be cautious in my conversations on these topics.

I remember particularly in this connection a dinner at the
house of Mr. Patrick Murphy at Southampton, adjacent to
Shinnecock.   Mr. Murphy was one of the most brilliant speakers of his generation.   As an after dinner speaker, his reputation rivaled that of Mr. Chauncey Depew.   His conversation
sparkled with wit and irony.   It was not, however, until I
reached his table that I realized that he had passed on these
gifts to his children.   There were no other guests for the evening but we did not rise from the table until after twelve
o'clock.   During most of the period we had been discussing
the negotiations at Paris.   I had endeavored to tell them what
was happening, within the limitations I felt imposed on me and

without giving my own views on the results. As we rose, I remember Mr. Murphy said, "This has been a charming evening. What we have gotten from Mr. Wilson has been light without heat."

As the debate in the Senate developed subsequently it became still more apparent that the opposition attack on the Treaty was to be leveled at the League of Nations. As I think back over those debates it seems to me that Senator Borah was the only one to evaluate properly the effects of the Treaty and to have any conception of the high probability that was indicated therein of a renewal of the war within our lifetime. Senator Lodge, Senator McCormick, and other bitter opponents concentrated on what they considered the weak points of the League of Nations. Great emphasis was laid upon the voting power of the British Empire which, with its independent dominions, could clearly out-vote the United States.

It was not realized at the time that votes had nothing to do with the acceptance of measures in either the League Council or Assembly, that measures had to be passed by unanimity and that the veto of any one power not party to the dispute was decisive. Indeed, in the long years that I watched the operations of the League, I cannot recall to mind an instance in which a large majority was even considered a factor. Unless there was unanimity on a measure among the Great States, that measure fell to the ground. But this legalistic argument carried heavy weight in American opinion. Senator Borah's analyses of events, however, were those of a scholar and statesman. In the light of the past twenty-odd years, he seemed inspired with the gift of prophecy.

We journeyed to Washington in the autumn where I had been assigned to work in the State Department. Some of the excitement of the war years in Washington had subsided but the city was filled to overflowing, vast numbers of additional Government employees were still in office, and everyone was bent on having a riotously good time. In these crowded conditions it was difficult to find a place to live and extremely expensive particularly as I, in company with most Americans back from Europe, had been spending money lavishly in the endeavor to make up for the deprivations of the preceding years. We finally moved into a small flat on Sixteenth Street but had been there only a day when we recognized that we had made a mistake. It was noisy and crowded and after the tranquillity of Switzerland, was hard to bear.

We were sitting, depressed, in our salon the second evening when the proprietor of the building, Mrs. John R. Williams, or "Ma" Williams as she is widely and affectionately known, came in to see how we were getting along. We told her. Without further ado she packed us into a motor car and took us out to see a house that she also owned on S Street, remarking that she should have known better than to plant us in the flat and that she was determined to make us happy. She did. The house was charming, and we took it forthwith.

I found in the State Department that all the world and his wife, particularly the latter, wanted to come back to Washington to work after the war. Every diplomatic officer apparently shared the feeling that it was time to come home again and enjoy the United States. So in my conversations with Bill Phillips, the Assistant Secretary of State, and Frank Polk, the Under Secretary, I found much to my disappointment that

I couldn't find a task which dealt with any phase of the European situation and was obliged to take an assignment in the Latin American Division, as it was then called. The Chief of the Division was Dr. Leo S. Rowe, who subsequently became Director of the Pan American Union and has served for many years in that capacity. Dr. Rowe as a chief was thoughtfulness itself but I never became deeply interested in the work I was doing in this division.

I remember one particular task wherein I was engaged in endeavoring to work out a plan of mediation for a dispute between Honduras and Guatemala over the frontier in the neighborhood of the Caribbean coast. It aroused some interest in my mind in that I had hunted wild pigs in the neighborhood of the Motagua River, and I tackled the problem with some vigor. The matter was not settled when I subsequently left Washington and I noted during succeeding visits home over a score of years that in some phase or other the Latin American Division was still working on the same problem.

It wasn't a fair test of the State Department, my first experience there. The President had fallen sick on his western trip in behalf of the League of Nations and was lying in the White House, a stricken man. Requests for his decision were delayed almost indefinitely. Occasionally papers would be returned signed "W.W.," his initials, more often replies would come that the President was unable to consider this matter for the time being. We all knew that relations between the President and Mr. Lansing were strained. It was an open secret that the Secretary of State had no access to the President and an open secret as well that the President had become resentful of the Secretary's attitude.

Furthermore, a Republican majority had been elected to the House of Representatives in 1918, Republican opposition in the Senate was threatening to destroy the President's work, and a political tide seemed to have set in that would put the Democratic Party out of office in 1920. All these factors combined to make life in the State Department highly unsatisfactory and strengthened my determination to get out of it as soon as possible and return to Central Europe where my interest lay.

In mentioning Secretary Lansing, I am reminded of the day, February 13, 1920, when the morning papers carried a letter from the President to the Secretary of State accepting the resignation of the latter and couched in such terms that it amounted to an abrupt dismissal. In Washington certainly sympathy lay with the Secretary of State. Mr. Lansing had been accustomed to lunch at the Metropolitan Club, always sitting by himself at a small table by a window. On this day he appeared as usual at the club, entered the room and walked to his accustomed table, looking neither to the right nor the left. Spontaneously the members at lunch rose to their feet and applauded him.

I have always felt a certain regret that Mr. Lansing felt it necessary to explain the episode of his dismissal in a book which was issued shortly thereafter. It seemed to me then, and it still seems to me, that he had the American public on his side so fully that the book was superfluous as a justification and, indeed, I have heard it said that the book itself was a better justification of the President's attitude than could have been prepared by the President. Years after he resigned, my wife and I came to know Mr. and Mrs. Lansing more intimately. He and Kate shared a passion for mystery stories, which they were constantly exchanging. We all shared a passion for the theater and often attended performances together. He was humorous, he was gay, he was wise. He mellowed, it seemed to me, after leaving office and enjoyed his life and his friends thoroughly.

The Treaty was defeated in spite of efforts, sincere or not, on the part of opposition senators to evolve amendments which would make it acceptable. The Treaty was defeated, I am convinced, rather on a clash of personalities between Senator Lodge and the President than on any overwhelming desire on the part of the American public to defeat it. It is true that the subsequent political campaign of the Republican Party was predicated on the mandate given by the American people against the League of Nations, but I have always been skeptical of the actuality of that mandate or of its being given consciously by our people.

Those who love hypothetical discussion will continue to debate whether history might have been radically different had the United States accepted the Treaty together with the League Covenant. There is no proof for any contention and I am frank to say that I do not know whether history would have been different. I shall also be frank enough to add that I very much doubt if it would have been different. I shall endeavor to explain why when I come to the chapters dealing with my connection with the League of Nations.

In the meantime the Treaty of Versailles had been signed and ratified by the other signatories as well as by the German Reichstag sitting in Weimar. The Allied Powers agreed to re-establish their diplomatic missions in Berlin in January, 1920. The United States and Germany were still in a technical state of war since the Senate had rejected the Peace Treaty and the question arose as to whether American representatives should proceed to Berlin with the Allies and, if so, of what type the representation should be. Since it was generally recognized that our relations with Germany through the reconstruction of that country would be too important to ignore, it was readily decided that a representative should be sent.

More difficult was the decision as to the type of representation. By this time Frank Polk had returned from Paris, where he had been acting head of the American delegation at the time of the signature of the Treaty. He had been impressed by the ability of Ellis Loring Dresel and of the latter's knowledge of affairs and personalities in Germany. Dresel had worked with me in Berne in 1917 and 1918 and we had become close friends. It was at his suggestion, if I remember correctly, that the President eventually determined to send Dresel as Commissioner to Berlin. A happier choice could not have been made. Dresel was born in Boston of a German father and a Boston mother. His knowledge of German was wide, his love of music had often brought him to the country before the war, and his service for three years in the American Embassy at Berlin before we entered the war had given him a wide knowledge of people in prominent positions in that country. His service in the peace delegation at Paris had earned him the confidence and respect of Allied statesmen and of the President and Secretary of State of the United States.

He proceeded to Berlin, then, early in January and took with him Fred Dolbeare and Allen Dulles. No sooner had they arrived at the post than I began to be bombarded with letters and telegrams from each and every member urging me to come over. I replied that I would like to but that having besieged the Department for assignment in Washington only a few months before, I was reluctant now to initiate a petition for a change. Dresel was nothing if not thorough. He ceased his urging of me and trained his guns on the Secretary, the Under Secretary, the Assistant Secretaries, and such senators and representatives as he knew, and within a month Mr. Polk summoned me to his office and asked me whether I would like to proceed to Berlin as Counselor of Embassy.

I replied, I think, without hesitation. After my experience in Washington under the circumstances which I have sketched, there was no doubt in my mind that to watch the struggle of that formidable people to get back to normal would be infinitely more interesting than discussions over the frontiers of Central America. I had become immersed in Central Europe. I recognized how much this area had been disrupted by the establishment of new States and I wanted to see how it would work. Kate and I decided that she would remain in Washington a few months with our son until I could report from Berlin as to living accommodations, since we still had only the vaguest notions of what the war had done to Germany. I set out again for Berlin in March with eager anticipation.

CHAPTER VIII

It was during this period in Berlin that the impulse first came to me to write for publication. Fred Dolbeare and I conceived a somewhat grandiose idea of making a comparison between the effects on Germany of the Thirty Year War and the War of 1914–1918. I had voluminous notes and collected material. My sudden transfer to Japan in the succeeding year put an end to our joint project and all the papers were destroyed when my house was burned in Tokyo following the great earthquake of 1923.

When I come to the task of writing these chapters I deeply regret the loss of these notes since I must rely largely upon my memory, and one's memory of what took place twenty years ago is tricky, at best. I particularly regret the loss of the notes since this period was one of the most engrossing of my lifetime. The spectacle of the mighty and resourceful German people endeavoring to pull themselves out of the morass brought about by their own exhaustion and the impositions of the Peace Treaty was one which could not but fill the observer with profound interest.

Passing through Paris early in March, 1920, I found the papers full of ominous news from Germany. The Kapp Putsch had broken out. Reactionary soldiers returning from the Baltic provinces had seized the capital almost bloodlessly, had established headquarters in the Wilhelmplatz directly opposite the American Embassy building. The trade-union organizations of Germany had declared a general strike in retaliation, and except for international train service the nation's activities were paralyzed. Kapp had surrendered under this pressure and the strike had been declared off on the very eve of my departure for Berlin.

Such was the Germany that I entered as the train pulled into Aachen on a gray March morning in 1920. The Reichswehr troops in field-gray uniform and steel helmets poured into the train as we entered the Ruhr. Their officer told me that Communist elements had taken advantage of the general strike to provoke disorders in the Ruhr district, that they, the Reichswehr, had arrived on the scene only the day before and were guarding the passage of trains through the disaffected area. In Berlin I found the Wilhelmplatz still a tangle of barbwire and marred by placements for machine guns. Kapp had set up his headquarters in the Leopold Palais on the square and access to it had been barred except to bearers of passes issued by the Kapp headquarters.

The old Embassy building, No. 7 Wilhelmplatz, offered living accommodation for practically all of our staff. Commissioner Dresel, Dolbeare, Dulles, Reggie Foster and myself all lived within its somewhat dingy walls. It was not until Kate arrived some weeks later that we made the old place livable and attractive. During our entire stay the roof used to leak copiously under heavy rains or melting snows. We tried repeatedly but in vain to get money from the Government to make repairs. So whenever we were honored by the presence at our table of senators or congressmen we used to pray for rain with the expectation that we could rush out tinpans to place under the leak in the dining-room ceiling and thus give a vivid impression to our guests of the need for repairs.

The shabbiness of Berlin in that period had to be seen to be believed. Even when I had left approximately three years before, in the middle of the war, and in a period of intense suffering, the aspect of the city had presented nothing comparable to the present dilapidation. Everything needed a coat of paint, everything needed cleaning out. It was the only time that I ever saw this capital of a scrupulously cleanly people littered with newspapers and dirt. Berlin had been through not only a war but a series of internal convulsions. Beginning in October, 1918, through the Kapp Putsch and beyond, Spartacist riots, reactionary purges, even assassinations, had been prevalent.

Even after my arrival a year and a half after the cessation of hostilities, fighting occasionally took place in the streets, but it was a peculiar type of rioting. The Berlin public never lost its orderly appearance. Rioting seemed to be strictly circumscribed and there appeared to be rules of the game which the rioters themselves respected. Men who had been in Berlin earlier than I told me of the shelling with heavy guns of the section at Neukölm, the workmen's section of Berlin. The shelling had been ordered by Gustav Noske, a Socialist. He was commonly spoken of by the German population after this event as "murderer Noske." They told me that even during the shelling, observers could watch the gun crews at work with impunity provided they stayed a respectable distance from the batteries.

I myself have seen fighting on one street with machine guns and rifles blazing away at each other. A few hundred yards away the streets presented their orderly and normal appearance, the crowds went about their business. If you wanted to see the fighting you peered around the corner without apprehension that you would be attacked from the rear. I have seen disturbances in a number of places in my life, but Berlin was unique in being able to carry out its disturbances in a sort of orderly disorder. I saw another example of this. Some weeks after my arrival, a crowd of Spartacists — Communists as we call them now — staged a tremendous demonstration in the Wilhelmplatz, in front of the Chancery building, protesting against something or other. The square was checkered by little patches of grass and flowers with low railings to warn trespassers. The Spartacist crowd, thousands strong, was vituperative and angry, yet, as I watched from my window, I failed to see any man cross the iron railing or step on the grass.

Through these months one learned to acquire the deepest respect for the German Army. In some cases it was the Reichswehr that would maintain order. In other cases it was volunteer soldiers back from the front who fell instinctively into orderly company formation and turned out to quell disorder. To those of us who lived through this experience, the sight of the German Army brought not only thoughts of might and power but thoughts as well of order amid disorder, of security from danger, of patriotism and devotion to the land, and of determination that Germany should not fall prey to disruptive forces.

I had returned to Germany, leaving my family in Washington, as I stated before. I had done this partly to ascertain whether normal conditions of living could be found in Berlin and partly because I wanted to sense how deeply ran the feelings of hostility against foreigners among the German people. If this hostility was deep I would hesitate to bring my family over. My anxiety on this score was certainly groundless. The German people felt no enmity to any foreigner, they felt plenty toward various sections of their own population, but the foreigners were all brothers.

I have never seen a people of a great nation who so ardently and vociferously desired peace, friendship and affection. There was something almost touching about the German inability to understand the hatred of the outside world. To the simple warrior Germanic spirit, it was inconceivable to hate a nation which had fought a good fight for four years against overwhelming odds. They simply could not understand why the rest of the world continued to brand them as "Boches" and "Huns," once the fighting had ceased. There was distress among the Germans at the terms of the Treaty of Versailles. At the same time there was widespread and almost pathetic belief that somehow or other a better international order had been created, that the rest of the states would disarm, that as soon as Germany's pacific spirit was recognized the economic bonds of the Treaty would be lifted.

When I talked outside Germany of the spirit that prevailed in Germany during 1920 my hearers usually declared that the Germans must be inspired by a "lively sense of gratitude for favors to come." It was something more than this, but to try to convey what it was I would have to enter into a realm uncongenial to me, namely, that of broad assertion and undemonstrable hypothesis. Nevertheless the attitude of the Germans at that time and their capacity for such emotion are so important to the future of the world that I shall make the attempt.

I have seen the Germans in war and triumph, I have seen the Germans in defeat and humiliation, I have seen the Ger-

mans in the pride of the Third Reich, and the same characteristic has always been evident. They deviate more from the
normal than the other races of Western Europe. The French
and Italians are restrained by their irony, experience and humor from any appreciable deviation from the normal pattern
of living and their conduct has developed through centuries of
civilization. The Anglo-Saxon, with fewer centuries of civilization behind him, with perhaps more humor and less irony,
fluctuates in a greater degree than the Latin from what we may
conceive to be our normal Anglo-Saxon pattern of conduct.
I need only cite such fluctuations as our crusading spirit in the
Great War, our Prohibition Act, our readiness to set up strange
gods and curious religions.

We do fluctuate from the normal, but our fluctuation is
restrained by something that is anchored, something solid in
character and tradition. Not so the Germans. Their enthusiasm in the pursuit of the abnormal knows no bounds. I
have seen them the world's most pacifist nation, I have seen
them the world's most bellicose. I have heard the *Weltanschauung* of universal brotherhood preached with the utmost
sincerity by the fathers or uncles of men who today with equal
sincerity and passionate devotion, preach the doctrine of *Blut
und Boden*.

The German people are sincere in these faiths. There is
a restlessness, a necessity for faith that the older races cannot
comprehend. There is a violence in the expression thereof
that to the older races often approximates the ludicrous, but
this manifold possibility in the character of the German race
must be recognized abroad. It is the essential factor, it seems
to me, in dealing with these people. It is absurd, I submit, to

attempt to distinguish between Nazis and Germans, just as it was absurd to attempt to distinguish between "military circles" and the "German people" as we attempted to do twenty years ago.   This volatile and highly spiritual people are capable of the sublime in sacrifice and of incredible limits of ruthlessness. Somehow the means must be found to bring out among them those characteristics which will make them good neighbors among the peoples of the world.   Unless some way is found to accomplish this, the future of Europe is black indeed.

I had reached those conclusions regarding the Germans long before the present madness swept over that country.   But the very madness and ruthlessness of the present seems not incompatible with my hypothesis, and indeed tends to confirm it.

The Germans, then, in 1920, wanted to be friends with the world, but particularly they wanted to make friends with the Americans.   Curiously enough, the warrior instinct again showed in this respect.   One of the sources of this almost pathetic friendship was their desire to express the admiration they felt for the stupendous effort of the United States in 1917 and 1918, for the magnificent spirit and dash of our soldiers, and for the philosophy preached by our President.

I remember a curious incident where I drove with Dresel in an open gray army Cadillac in the streets of Berlin.   We turned a corner and suddenly found ourselves in a band of excited extremists.   They were demonstrating in front of a police station where some of their comrades had been carried under arrest.   They jumped on our running-boards, sticks in hand, and demanded who we were.   We explained that we were members of the American Commission and pointed to the large letters "U.S.A." painted on the side of the motor.   The crowd immediately began to cheer. Two of them stayed on the running-board, several of them dashed ahead to clear a path for us, and we heard the men on the running-board bellowing, "Stand aside, can't you ? Look at the letters on this car — U.S.A. That stands for *Unabhängige Sozialistische Arbeiter* (Independent Socialist Workers). The United States is in favor of the Spartacists !"

This spontaneous and evident desire for friendship was, alas, of short duration. The first signs of deterioration became apparent in connection with the disorders in the Ruhr district, where the "Red" elements among the workmen had seized the opportunity of the Kapp Putsch to attempt a counter-revolution. The German Government sent Reichswehr troops into the area of disturbance as soon as they had dealt with Kapp and his followers. The number of troops which the Government had a right to maintain in the area was limited by the Treaty of Versailles, nevertheless, it seemed reasonable to the British and American Governments that the Germans should have adequate forces on hand to quell the disturbance.

The French Government, on the other hand, lodged a protest with the German Government and advanced their troops of occupation over the bridgeheads into Frankfort, in other words, into unoccupied German territory. The American Ambassador in Great Britain, Mr. John W. Davis, reported in a telegram to Washington, dated April 7, that he had learned from Lord Curzon that "the French Government's action in sending troops across the Rhine was taken not only without the British Government's knowledge and consent but contrary to advice that had been given previously and their repeated refusals to sanction such a move."

This episode was followed by the stationing by the French of Senegalese and other black troops in the French-occupied portion of the Rhineland. A flame of resentment against France arose throughout Germany. Repeated episodes continued to inflame public opinion and the final destruction of the friendly attitude in Germany toward France was brought about by the occupation of the Ruhr, in 1923, as a result of a technical default on reparations.

It is interesting to reflect that as early as this the conflict became evident between British and French policy in respect to Germany. The Kapp Putsch occurred in March, 1920. The Treaty went into effect January first of that year. Three months later, then, the breach began between British and French policy in respect to the application of the Treaty of Versailles. The French had, of course, been bitterly disappointed both in the Treaty itself and in the subsequent refusal of Great Britain and the United States to implement the treaty of guaranty, on the basis of which the French had reluctantly accepted the Versailles Treaty. The French had been disappointed in their failure to obtain the left bank of the Rhine as their strategic frontier and the virtue that was left in the Treaty, in their eyes, lay in the possibility through its terms of holding Germany in a position of such weakness from a military standpoint that the possibility of an attack on France would be impossible.

Furthermore, and largely to replace the defunct treaty of guaranty, the French began to build up their fabric of alliances throughout Central Europe, rapidly bringing Poland and Czechoslovakia into their sphere. It was necessary from their viewpoint that the threat be always maintained of an unimpeded French advance into German territory in case Germany became aggressive toward her eastern neighbors, friends and allies of France. The terms of the Treaty of Versailles, then, that appealed to France were its military clauses and those were the very terms which gave to France in some degree that feeling of "security" on which they have been so insistent during the twenty post-war years and about which I shall write more fully later.

The British, on the other hand, ended the Great War with a feeling of complete security. It is ironic to reflect now on the satisfaction with which British statesmen and public regarded the future of the continent. To them the resurgence of Germany and its ability to threaten again the channel ports was beyond comprehension in those first post-war years. They were much more interested then in the economic clauses of the Treaty. Their most insistent desire was to see again a prosperous Germany, if possible a contented Germany, a Germany which would become again one of Great Britain's greatest customers.

I do not know to what extent the old balance of power conception played a role in this attitude of Great Britain but there were certain evidences in those early years that influential sections of the British Government were impatient of too complete a control of the continent by the French Army. Among certain sections of the Foreign Office and of the Government it may well have been that the desire for the re-establishment of Germany's prosperity was coupled with the desire to see some sort of a counter-balance to French power and authority on the continent.

In any case, the conflict of policy early made itself evident

and continued despite brief intervals of harmony, notably in
the period of Briand, Stresemann and Austen Chamberlain,
until the sudden turn of British policy in the spring of 1939,
when the unexpected guaranty of Poland aligned the British
with traditional French policy.

In my account of these early years of the Peace Treaty, it
seems unnecessary to elaborate here in further detail the conflict of policy which dominated the European scene for almost
a score of years.   I have just read a book by Arnold Wolfers,
of Yale University, called *Britain and France between Two
Wars* which gives an admirable account of the course of the
conflict.

It has become trite to say that either the British or French
policy might have worked.   It has become trite to say that
the only certainty lay in the fact that a combination of the
two policies was bound to fail.   Perhaps a ruthless determination to prevent the rise of Germany might have given us a
longer period of peace.   Perhaps a policy of conciliation and
encouragement to a struggling German democracy might
have given us a longer period of peace.   As I say, however,
the only certainty is that a policy of alternate conciliation and
threat, conciliation that came too late and threat that was ineffective, has rendered inevitable the Germany that we see
today.   That statement is too simple.   Policy alone did not
render modern Germany inevitable : economic distress from
1930 to 1933 was probably as potent a factor as policy.

CHAPTER IX

I had left Germany during the worst winter of the war, 1916–1917. When I returned the evidences of the hardship and suffering were visible and prevalent. The blockade, it is often forgotten, persisted many months after Germany had laid down her arms, so that in 1920 the traces of undernourishment and children's diseases, especially rickets, were found on every hand. The whole life of the nation was saddened and dull. German money was rapidly losing its value and even when food became abundant it was difficult for those on fixed salaries to purchase sufficient for themselves and their families. There was almost no entertainment. Families of fortune made little ostentation during those days of general penury. The Junkers had retired to their land and sulked in their tents through an era which they hated.

In striking contrast to this scene was the life of foreigners in Germany during this period. With the depreciation of the mark, everything was cheap. With the end of the war in victory for them everything was hilarious and life in leisure times was a mad scramble for amusement. We certainly were numerous enough to furnish our own amusement. All of the embassies had big staffs, all entertained lavishly, and the Allied Governments maintained commissions of control comprising hundreds of foreign officers and their wives. Allied uniforms were common on the streets of Berlin. I remember a dignified British admiral who purchased for himself a sort of a scooter with a motor in it. He became a common sight as he rolled down the Linden uniformed in gold braid, cocked hat over his ruddy countenance, moving solemnly through traffic propelled by his one-cylinder scooter. It was a bizarre sight even to apathetic Germans.

I remember the first dinner that was given at the French Embassy in the Pariserplatz. Most of the staff of the American Commission had been invited as well as a number of the German Government people with their wives. At that time there was a predominantly Socialist control of the Government, and, whereas the party leaders themselves did not seem so out of place amid the tapestries and Sèvres porcelain of the Embassy, their wives, in their best Sunday gowns, were difficult to reconcile with the splendor. There was music in the ballroom after dinner and the German wives clustered together, shy and apprehensive. The French Ambassador hurried over to the members of the American Commission and told us we had to dance with them and make it go. We took a deep breath and we did.

Dinners at the British Embassy were altogether easier. Lord D'Abernon himself spoke fluent German and had a genius for putting people at their ease. His wife, tall and blonde, was one of the loveliest women I have ever seen, but it was the Ambassador who was gifted with the ability to make his guests mingle freely and enjoy themselves. One of the features of dinner at the British Embassy was punctuality. You were invited for an eight o'clock dinner; at eight five the Ambassador gave his arm to the lady of senior rank and the company marched out to the table. Many a time I have seen careless juniors enter the room after the party was seated, covered with confusion and stammering their apologies.

Lord D'Abernon arrived in Berlin only a short time before I left so that I never came to know him intimately, much to my regret. His memoirs and history itself have accorded him a high place among successful ambassadors. Certainly the little I saw of him leads me to agree with this estimate. He was intelligent, eager to learn, patient, but decided. His work with Stresemann in initiating and bringing about the Locarno negotiations marks one of the few efforts of genuine intelligence shown in the field of diplomacy through this score of years.

I do not think that any of the authors of the Treaties of Locarno could have been expected to foresee the disasters which followed so rapidly after they were consummated. At that time no one, I submit, could have foreseen the wild inflation, the sudden panic, the despair of Germany, the access of Hitler, and the entry into force of a régime to which the pledged word had ceased to be binding. D'Abernon, Briand, Stresemann, Austen Chamberlain, were still men of the nineteenth century — men who felt that a nation's pledge was a solemn and stable thing. Their united effort marked a high point in the attempt to build a better world. No single subsequent event did more than interrupt temporarily the trend of events toward disaster.

Living in the Embassy with Dresel and the other members of the staff we found extraordinarily interesting. My wife kept house, our little boy lived with us, otherwise it was a bachelor establishment. We had guests for luncheon and dinner continuously — Germans of all categories, from generals on the Kaiser's staff to leaders of the radical Socialist Party and representatives of the trade unions. Rudolf Breitscheid, leader of the Independent Socialist Party in the Reichstag, the most radical of all groups save the Communists, was a frequent guest. Once our chef served plovers' eggs, a novel dish to the Americans present. It was Breitscheid, Socialist leader, who demonstrated to the bourgeoisie how to eat this delicacy.

Travellers were continuous. It was still somewhat of an adventure to visit Germany and the people who came usually arrived with the desire to learn and to study. I remember the advent into my office one day of a good-looking blonde-haired woman with an engaging personality, wearing a khaki suit with boots laced to the knees. She explained that she was Mrs. Philip Snowden, that her husband was a Labor member of the British Parliament and that she had just been on an expedition to Soviet Russia with a number of other members of the Labor Party. She told me of the expectation with which they had visited that land of applied socialism and of the horror and disillusion with which they had left it. She also stated that she had visited the British Embassy — this was before the arrival of Lord D'Abernon — but had received scant attention there since it was assumed that she and her like were too radical in their views.

Her story was of absorbing interest and it fell at a time when there was genuine danger in Germany of the spread of Bolshevist ideas. We not only brought her to dine with a number of the trade unionist leaders but we suggested to them, and they arranged for Mrs. Snowden, a tour of Germany in which she spoke of the experiences that she and her companions had encountered in Russia. The trade-unionist people were enthusiastic and declared that this tour had a most beneficial effect on their followers.

Another English visitor to the Embassy was an old friend of Ellis Dresel, Geoffrey Drage. Drage had been a Conservative member of Parliament when quite a young man but was beaten for his seat before the war in a Labor district in London by that very Philip Snowden whom I mentioned above and who subsequently became an unusually able Chancellor of the Exchequer. Drage had attended Heidelberg and had been a member of the Saxebourisse, one of the most famous *kneipe* or dueling clubs. He had the widest acquaintance in German university circles and even among eminent men in the Army. He knew Central Europe intimately and had written a first class book about the Danube states. He was one of those Englishmen so prevalent a generation ago who would set forth with a case of rifles, shoot on the estates of their friends all over the globe and come home and write admirable books of their experiences.

Drage gave me some advice that proved useful. He said, "If you want to learn about a thing, write a book about it."

I didn't start writing books about it but I started making voluminous reports on innumerable phases of German life. I found that Drage's advice was sound and that the obligation to write about a thing made one study it intensively. There were few American correspondents in Germany those days, few serious students of the many sociological and economic phenomena which these abnormal post-war years brought into being.

For example, the Germans instituted what they called a "Wirtschaftsrat," or economic council, on which they laid great hopes and which, had it been accorded genuine powers, might have introduced a new and salutary factor into government.   It was a council to study and report on pending and possible legislation respecting economic matters and was selected from among industrialists, trade unionists, bankers, professional men, and consumers.   The philosophy behind it — and the Germans always had to have a philosophy behind anything — was that the political organization represented adequately geographic sections and units of the population.   The economic council was supposed, on the other hand, to represent the interests of the various strata of society divided in accordance with their profession or occupation.

We made also comprehensive studies and voluminous reports on the co-operative movements.   These were old organizations in Germanic life and, indeed, in some cases it was possible to trace their descent from the medieval guilds, but the post-war period gave a fresh impetus to this movement which became wide-spread and flourishing in communal endeavors to cope with the currency and economic difficulties of the period.

This was an era of social instability, an era of the threat of Communist uprising, an era of fluid relations between capital and labor.   The most serious threat to orderly existence lay in the general strike with the resultant breakdown of normal supplies of food, water, light, and the resultant suffering to populations which had no part in the struggle.

Some genius in German life set up an institution called the "Technische Nothilfe" which might be translated as technical emergency aid. Thousands of young men throughout the nation volunteered their services and were enrolled in the Nothilfe. All of these young men had their special tasks assigned to them in case of call. Some entered the waterworks and maintained the supply, some worked in the gas and electric production plants, some worked as firemen on locomotives to bring supplies into the city. The leaders of the Nothilfe were able to gain the co-operation of the strikers themselves in many instances, using the plea that the maintenance of supplies and provisions prevented suffering among the strikers' families as well as among the rest of the population.

I followed the operation of the Technische Nothilfe in several cities in which general strikes had been declared — Bremen, Dusseldorf and Stuttgart. I remember reporting that this organization represented a striking effort of a patriotic and self-reliant youth to maintain order in the nation.

The formal report prepared on the subject of the Technische Nothilfe is too voluminous for insertion, but it had a subsequent history. Mr. Drage was in Berlin when I was writing it and became much interested in the report. When Great Britain was threatened with a general strike in 1923, Drage was appointed a member of a Royal Commission to draw up plans in anticipation of a strike, plans destined to maintain public supply and public life. He cabled me to Tokyo about the report and I was able to have a copy of it delivered to him in reasonable time in London. He subsequently wrote me that the Government's plans for dealing with the strike had been largely influenced by this report on how the German people had handled a similar problem.

One of the first things a diplomat must assess in a foreign country is the ultimate source of power. In Germany in those early years it did not lie in the Reichstag, split into innumerable parties, it did not lie in the shattered remnants of the Army, not yet fully converted into the admirable Reichswehr that it ultimately became. Besides, the Army had had a tradition of not taking an active part in politics; though the tradition had been broken by General Ludendorff, the General Staff was quick to return to it after the war.

The one stable and disciplined force in this tumultuous scene was the trade unions. A general strike had put an end to the Kapp Putsch, the threat of a general strike prevented the passage of French troops to the relief of Warsaw under the Bolshevist attack. The latent power of the trade unions was decisive. Furthermore, its leaders were all members of the majority Socialist Party, so that their political influence could be felt in current affairs through the influence of this, the largest party in the Reichstag. The trade unions were consolidated with headquarters in Berlin known as the "Gewerkschaftsbund," or Trade Union Federation. The leaders of the Federation welcomed our visits, they knew so little of foreign countries and foreign affairs that they were glad to turn to us for counsel in those troubled times and they proved the most useful of the many sources of information available to us.

In the first year of diplomatic relations with Germany none of the Great Powers had yet sent ambassadors, they were all represented by chargés d'affaires. The Japanese were represented by Debuchi, subsequently Ambassador to Washington, a rotund, cheerful figure of considerable acumen. De

Saint-Quentin, the French Chargé, had preceded me in the Ecole Libre des Sciences Politiques at Paris by a couple of years and was still described there in my time as "*le jeune homme le plus correct*." The United States knows him as Ambassador to Washington and he still merits the description. Dependable, staunch, and painstaking, he remains as correct as ever. Lord Kilmarnock of Great Britain was a dry figure but a competent workman. He retired after leaving Berlin, having inherited the title of Earl of Erroll.

In the Foreign Office our most frequent associate was von Haniel von Haimhausen, at that time Secretary of State, the equivalent of our Under Secretary in the State Department. Haniel was one of the few Germans left after the war who had the appetite for enjoyment, his duel-scarred face could wrinkle with merriment, his knowledge and consumption of food and drink were wide and deep. He had the habit of dropping in at the Embassy for a cocktail after a day's work; our gin was imported from London and unobtainable elsewhere in Berlin.

The head of the Russian section of the Foreign Office, von Maltzan, was a man of great political intelligence. I used to sit with him by the hour discoursing on Germany's future. He had read and absorbed enormously and was a convinced believer in close relations with Russia at a time when that belief was decidedly unpopular. He was mainly responsible for the Treaty of Rapallo in 1922 which sent cold chills down the spines of the Allies for the first time since the war. Von Maltzan also became Ambassador to Washington — it is curious how many of our group came to this post later—and met his death in an airplane crash in Bavaria when home on a vacation.

This account would be incomplete without an attempt to picture the exceptional position held by Ellis Dresel and his usefulness both to his country and to Germany. There was no circle of German life that he did not penetrate ; he had close friends, men who depended on his common sense, among industrialists, bankers, politicians of all groups, army officers and artists. His German was that of one speaking his mother tongue, his knowledge of music, painting and engraving was accurate and catholic. His impartiality, both personally and as representative of a great disinterested power, was acknowledged. His wisdom gave depth to his flat Boston voice and personality. His sincerity was tempered by irony. Once the Department of State was contemplating changing his commission from that of Commissioner to High Commissioner. The suggestion had apparently risen at the instance of our Commissioner in Budapest, Mr. Grant-Smith, who found himself outranked by some of his colleagues who carried the higher title.

The *Foreign Relations of the United States, 1920*, published Dresel's reply : "August 11 — So far as I am concerned, I see no sufficient reason for a change. In fact at present it might prove trying as I am very anxious not to make my position here the subject of further discussion. I have uniformly experienced considerate and courteous treatment in diplomatic circles and from government officials regardless of title. If Grant-Smith feels a more ornate halo would help him and strengthen his position, I should be heartily in accord. However, I do not aspire to such unaccustomed eminence."

I have recorded before, and I record again, that when an ambassador was appointed to Germany after the signature of a treaty of peace and under Mr. Harding's administration, the failure to utilize the services of this consummate diplomat either in Berlin or elsewhere, was a striking waste of valuable material, and a further commentary on our adolescent outlook on foreign affairs in regarding diplomatic offices as plums for reward and not as jobs to be done. Lord D'Abernon assumed office in Berlin a relatively short time only before Dresel's departure, but certainly up to that moment Dresel had enjoyed the authority and respect in Germany which D'Abernon subsequently achieved.

The mark kept slipping. Prices kept rising, but not rapidly enough to compensate for the fall of the mark. A gold reserve was non-existent, a Socialist Government was trying in agitation to take up unemployment by supplying Government jobs. Reparations of unspecified figures loomed in the background.

Foreigners continued to have faith in Germany's future and absorbed untold quantities of marks. We spent countless hours with American visitors to the Embassy trying to demonstrate to them that an investment in marks was like putting your faith in the Cheshire Cat. The marks would expire without even leaving a grin.

"If you must invest in Germany," we said, "buy real estate, something that will keep a permanent value."

Moritz Bonn, the German economist, used to analyze the situation with his acute and disillusioned penetration. He used to say, "You know, the only reason the mark has any value is because the British and yourself have faith in us. We haven't any in ourselves, and if you cease buying, the mark will hit bottom."

The reparations discussions at Brussels and Spa brought no relief, the sums specified were too big, the problem was too complex to be solved by the mere setting of a figure. Many people believed at the time, and some still believe, that the German Government was letting the mark slip deliberately. Certainly the act of Chancellor Cuno during the occupation of the Ruhr by the French, in 1923, was deliberate. He printed unlimited quantities of money and broke down all barriers with the calculated intention of bankruptcy. But in the time of which I speak, 1920–1921, I never felt a deliberate intent. There was bewilderment, socialistic ideas as to expenditure, inexperience, and, above all, lack of faith in the Government, all of which undermined credit.

However, whether deliberate or not, the effects of devaluation are appalling. If I were given the right to condemn to punishment the most iniquitous of peoples, I would never condemn them to devaluation, the results are too barbarous. It meant the destruction of the result of all thrift, the impoverishment of the most stable and bourgeois elements of society. It meant the ruin of the integrity of the civil servant and employee, it meant driving the girls of respectable families onto the streets. It meant debauch for those who had money, wild attempts to get "value" for cash before it lost its value. It meant starvation and misery for the laborer and his family whose increased wages never kept pace with the diminishing purchasing value of the pieces of paper he got for the sweat of his brow. It meant the rise to power of a group of profiteers, predatory adventurers, who reveled in a decadent and shameless night life in the great cities. War is a dreadful experience, but it brings out some virtue and, in

some cases, martyrdom and self-immolation. Devaluation
has no redeeming features, it brutalizes those whom it does
not turn into cringing cowards. It is the last crucifixion that
a people can suffer.

In these conditions anti-Semitism reared its ugly head.
Millions of returning soldiers out of a job and desperately
searching for one, found the stage, the press, medicine and
law crowded with Jews. They saw among the few with
money to splurge a high proportion of Jews. A number of
the leaders of the Demokratische Partei, that fraction of the
Reichstag most closely identified with the type of government in power, were Jews. The leaders of the Bolshevist
movement in Russia, a movement desperately feared in Germany, were Jews. One could sense the spreading resentment and hatred.

I remember writing home at the time that if there ever came
a reactionary movement, whether military or monarchist — I
didn't dream of a Nazi Party — that movement would be anti-
Semitic in character. It has been widely assumed that Hitler
and his followers invented anti-Semitism in Germany. The
facts of the case do not bear this out. When Hitler inserted
an anti-Semitic plank in his platform, he doubtless was acting
in accordance with his own hatred and prejudice. Nevertheless, adroit politician that he is, he was inserting a plank to
catch the votes.

Even in those early years the Weimar Republic was not
popular. It was a government of defeat, a government of
humiliation. It had incredible difficulties to confront, financial chaos, unemployment, a people underfed for years and
in despair. All the parties to the Right were frankly mon-

archist, the Center or Catholic Party was lukewarm. The Democratic Party were philosophically convinced republicans, but the party failed to produce leaders who appealed to popular imagination. The great Socialist Party preached the doctrine of republicanism but its members were bewildered and troubled. Unused to responsibility, they were frightened when it came, and timid in the application of power. Those in power failed to clean out the disaffected, the traitor within the gates remained within the gates and spoke his mind freely. The idea of a democratic government had been accepted by the German people because it was felt that a democracy would be pleasing to the victorious Allies. When it came into being, however, it encountered rebuff and humiliation from the other democracies. It was a muddled, slovenly and ineffective government. The German people, with their instinct for order and power, did not like it, it didn't work.

Poland was the most restless of the Central European States, its frontiers were dubious and its historical claims and dreams unbounded. In the spring of 1920 the Polish Government launched an attack on Kiev. The attack went through the Ukraine like a knife through butter. A counter-attack by the Russians suddenly turned the advance into a retreat, and the speed of the Polish advance was equaled only by the speed of their retreat. The Polish forces rallied before Warsaw, General Weygand arrived from Paris to assume direction, the Russians were beaten back and driven from Polish soil.

The French had desired to send troops to Poland over Germany and had demanded permission to do so. The Ger-

mans were terrified lest they become involved in the struggle
and find their country the battlefield for Russian and French
forces.   The trade unions threatened a general strike if French
troops attempted to cross their territory, and the German
Government refused the French demand.   I subsequently became acquainted with M. Patek, who was Minister for Foreign Affairs in Poland during this war.   While he was Ambassador to Tokyo he related to me with considerable satisfaction his part in having persuaded the Polish Government
to launch this "preventive attack."

The responsibility for having launched the attack does not
matter as much as the consequences thereof.   The rapid advance of the Russians against the Poles and their threat to
Warsaw created a situation in Europe which was the most
precarious that has existed between the two wars.   The whole
social structure of the continent was in such a fluid condition, Bolshevism and its doctrines were so wide-spread and
enthusiastically preached, that the fall of Warsaw and the
advance of the Russians up to the boundaries of a Germany
without defense and in a state of chaotic disturbance, might
well have spelled the ruin of western civilization, at least as
far as the Rhine.   The line held, and from that crucial moment the influence of Bolshevism became less menacing.

Considered from the point of view of its effect on history,
the Battle of Warsaw constitutes one of the great turning-
points.   Compare it, for instance, with the Battle of the
Marne, in 1914.   A victory over France at that time by an
Imperial Germany, not a Nazi Germany, would have been
unlikely to produce shattering effects upon western civilization.   The Battle of Warsaw, on the other hand, had it been

won by the Russians, would have brought about untold and incalculable consequences for our whole civilization. We have to go back to the defense of Vienna against the Turks and other crucial battles in the world's history to find one of equal significance.

Writing of Poland leads me to speak of General Hoffmann, intimately associated with Hindenburg and Ludendorff on the East front, eventually commander-in-chief of the Eastern Armies when the commanding generals moved to the West, negotiator and signer of the Brest-Litovsk Treaty. General Hoffmann was a frequent guest at the Embassy and I retain vividly the impression of the huge figure erect and military, mighty chest almost bursting from the unaccustomed civilian clothes that he wore at that time. He was a man of driving force, decided opinions, and unswerving loyalty to the House of Hohenzollern, indeed, he never spoke of the Kaiser save as *"Mein Kaiserlicher Herr."*

I was talking with him one day of the negotiations at Brest-Litovsk which he and von Kuhlmann carried out for the Germans.

General Hoffmann spoke somewhat as follows : "Nearly all men have something in their lives that they regret. It may be a love affair, it may be treatment of one's parents, it may be a missed opportunity. I have only one great regret in my life, in spite of the fact that I have lived the life of most men. That regret is that at the time of Brest-Litovsk I did not break off negotiations, march into Moscow — I could have done it easily at the moment — and hang about a score of these rascals. I could have put an end to Bolshevism with relative ease and I could have saved the world untold misery for the future." Perhaps this over-simplification of a complex situation gives a key to the General's character.

I once saw a striking example of his moral courage and his ability to handle men. From time to time we would attend Communist meetings in Berlin and other cities, listen to their speakers, and try to get an estimate of the effect that they were making. One night I was present at such a meeting in the workmen's section of Berlin. A foreigner was speaking, presumably a Russian, although I could not be sure from the accent. He inveighed against the German Army, held it up to ridicule and accused it of breaking down before the enemy and allowing Germany to be plunged into the present disastrous condition. From somewhere in the back of the hall rose the huge figure of General Hoffmann.

Clad in a military greatcoat and military cap, he strode to the platform, seized the speaker by the shoulder and dropped him down among the audience. He then turned on the Communist meeting in a fury, denounced the treachery and the falsehood of the previous speaker, called on the Germans present who had served in the war to back him up in his statement of the virtues of the German Army. He rebuked and scolded his listeners as if they were children, indeed, he called them "*Kinder.*" He ceased abruptly and strode from the room and to my complete amazement the assembly echoed with cheers for the General as he departed.

It was only a few months after the defeat of the Russians before Warsaw that I made a visit to that city and stayed with my friend Hugh Gibson, who had been appointed American Minister there in the early months of 1919. Hugh had taken the beautiful old "Blue Palace" belonging to the Zamoyski family and possessed of one of the most interesting libraries that I have ever seen. The library was in an annex separate from the house and the librarian was maintained by the family and remained at work there. I remember seeing the original treaty of incorporation between the Grand Duchy of Lithuania and the Kingdom of Poland and other documents of high historic interest.

Prince Sapieha had succeeded Patek as Minister for Foreign Affairs, and since I had come to know the Prince well in Switzerland he frequently came to meals at the Legation and we had many interesting conversations about the war just terminated in which he himself had served as a lancer.

From Warsaw I went to Cracow, I don't remember why, but I do remember the incomparable beauty of the tapestries in the cathedral and the incomparable ugliness of the ghetto of the city. Until that visit to Cracow I had always felt reasonably equipped from a language standpoint to travel any place in Europe. I had assumed that a knowledge of French, German and English was adequate to meet practically any situation. I was proved completely wrong at Cracow. I got out on the station platform and was unable to find anybody who appeared to understand even such international words as taxi and hotel.

I carried my own suitcase to the street, saw an ancient fiacre, climbed into it and merely waved my hand to the driver. He clattered out and delivered me at the hotel. There, of course, I found a concierge who like every concierge on the continent spoke every known language. I had to bribe him heavily to get into the fiacre with me and show me the city, as my short experience at the station had shown me that I was quite unable to get about by myself. My only experiences comparable to this helplessness have been subsequent visits to towns in the interior of China and Japan.

Among the numerous figures that crowd my memory of this period I like to think of Wilhelm Cuno. Cuno was president of the Hamburg-American Line and subsequently had the misfortune to be Chancellor of the Reich during the fateful days of the occupation of the Ruhr. Nobody could ever have mistaken Cuno's nationality. He was tall, extremely blond, short blond moustache, intensely blue eyes, as Germanic in appearance as Hans Sachs. He had married a woman from Hamburg. These Hamburg women, most of whom maintain close relationship with England, are among the most attractive that Germany produces.

Cuno once told me that he was about to proceed with his wife to Freudenstadt in the Black Forest. It appeared that President Fritz Ebert was on a vacation there and Cuno had some business to talk over with him. In as much as I was departing within the next few days on some business to Stuttgart, Cuno, his wife and I joined forces as far as Freudenstadt. After dinner, Cuno and I walked through the charming surroundings of that countryside to a modest hotel where we were shown into the presence of the President of the Reich.

Fritz Ebert was a saddler by profession, one of the leaders of the Majority Socialist Party. I suppose no man on earth has ever become president of a great country more to his own surprise. He was a simple man of unquestionable honesty, deep devotion to this country, a bewildered man in a situation which he had not coveted and which he did not understand. He sat at ease at a table, he and his companion smoking pipes behind their mugs of beer, his collar was unbuttoned, and he looked at that moment the picture of contentment. I talked to him for a brief space before Cuno got down to business. I found him friendly, kindly, benign, very much interested in the United States but completely ignorant of it and astounded at the war effort which we had made. Cuno and I took a walk in the woods in the moonlight when he had finished his business, and discussed the German President. I found that Cuno held him in deep affection but it was a tolerant affection, it was a liking in spite of his knowledge of Ebert's background and limitations. Cuno's attitude toward the President typified that of thinking Germans toward their Government. They were willing to give it a try, the Allies seemed to like this sort of thing, but they watched the Government's efforts with feelings that varied from friendly amusement to contempt.

One of the most vivid and dynamic personalities of those first two years in Germany was Matthias Erzberger, leader of the Center or Catholic Party. We never saw a great deal of Erzberger. A man of deep political instinct, he had a reluctance to be seen too much with foreigners lest it affect his position in his Party and lest he be suspected of being under foreign influence. Nevertheless, Dresel and I had an exceedingly interesting conversation with him which I subsequently drafted in a report to Washington. It may be of interest if I quote a paragraph of this report which shows how the personality of Erzberger impressed me.

While the Department is of course familiar with Erzberger's history and activities a word about his personality may not be misplaced. He makes the impression of a man of super-abundant and Rooseveltian vitality ; small, thick set, a round face, blond mustache ; speaking with a strong Bavarian accent, the words and ideas pour from him in a torrent. The ego plays a great part in his conversation. He speaks of "my program," "my offer to the Entente," "my desires," etc. In this country in which the great majority of men show the effects of the war in a certain listlessness and indifference, Erzberger's extraordinary energy and determination shine by contrast.

I have re-read the report in the archives of the State Department and find it voluminous and of genuine interest to me. There is only one phase of it, however, which is perhaps of general interest, that portion in which Erzberger related the plans which he was entertaining for setting up a system of obligatory work for all youths in Germany. This was the first time that I had ever heard of this idea and Erzberger was probably the first person to entertain such a scheme as a serious political possibility. The idea took root first in the form of voluntary labor camps for the sons of trade-union members, and finally developed into the mighty Arbeitsdienst of the Nazis. Assuming that Erzberger's idea is the origin of this movement it will, I think, be of interest if I cite that portion of his remarks which dealt with obligatory work :

(2) The Government must inaugurate a forced service for the benefit of the nation of about one year's duration of all healthy youths between the ages of 18 to 25. These youths will be housed, clothed, equipped, and fed but receive no pay. The Government will inaugurate a propaganda campaign to appeal for willing acquiescence to this law, relying on the patriotism of the youth of Germany and pointing out that their elder brothers have served six years in the war and they should serve one year

in labor for the Fatherland. 200,000 of these youths will be installed as miners. Barracks must be built, and other arrangements made for their schooling, feeding, amusements, etc.

It would be impossible to carry out this scheme of forced labor for the benefit of any man's pocketbook. It can only be done for the benefit of the State. Therefore socialization is essential. On the other hand, experience has shown that socialization does not increase production (witness the railroads), and therefore forced labor is an essential corollary to socialization. The two must be produced together.

Further numbers of these youths can be used in farming and allied industries on those great properties in the possession of the State. This will be pure gain in that no payment will be made for labor; they can produce their own foodstuffs, and the land is already owned by the Government. The present system is to let it out to operators who make a profit on it, and there is no reason why this profit should not go to the State. They can also be employed in forestry, cattle raising, etc.

The places that these four or five hundred thousand able-bodied young men leave vacant when they leave for forced service can be immediately refilled by those officials who are dismissed in the economy program. This will at one blow overcome the unemployment question of the released railroad and post employees and will greatly increase the productivity of the nation, causing an automatic reduction of the present number of unemployed.

The trades unions in the mines will probably be dissatisfied, but the reasonable elements will recognize that no competition will be made in their work by these untrained youths. It takes some years to produce miners for the skilled jobs, and the young men who undertake forced labor will not compete with them. The trained miners will have the same food, the same living conditions, the same privileges as at present; the others will be merely additional and untrained labor.

Erzberger stated that a system of a fixed amount of production would probably be used for forced labor. In this way a man who works well will be free sooner than those who loaf on the job. Also, less discipline will be necessary, as the men will discipline themselves in the endeavor to be free from the labor. This plan will be brought out in the next session of the Reichstag and will be debated there.

I have saved to the last the person that I like most to talk about, the one for whom I entertained genuine affection and admiration, Walther Rathenau. Rathenau, the son of a Jewish mother, succeeded his father as president of the great electrical plant, the A.E.G. During the war he had charge of provisioning for Germany. At the time when I knew him he was the German representative in the discussions on reparations. He had a face of singular beauty and sensitiveness. An accomplished linguist, the beauty of his voice lent color and warmth to any language he spoke. He was a man of vast erudition but he was never dogmatic. He knew literature, art and music and knew them as a master knows his subject, yet he was as simple and as unassuming in his expression of an opinion as if he were a mere dilettante. His views on sociology had remodeled the A.E.G. and had affected profoundly all great industry in Germany. He was wise, kind, selfless and intelligent. He became Chancellor and an assassin's bullet put an end to his existence. This man, one of the finest human beings that I ever knew, was killed by the hand of a brute.

On March 4, 1921, a Republican régime came into office in the United States. As long as President Wilson had been in power his disappointment at the rejection of the Treaty of Versailles had prevented him from taking any steps to regularize our position with Germany. Mr. Charles Evans Hughes had hardly taken over the office of Secretary of State before his mind began to turn to this question. After considerable discussion in Washington and after sounding the opinions of the German as well as the Allied Governments,

Mr. Hughes eventually sent to Berlin the text of a proposed treaty of peace.

Throughout the summer months of 1921 we negotiated this matter with the German Government. It was eventually signed on August 25. One can hardly believe one's eyes in reading that treaty today. We asked for and obtained from the Germans all the benefits accruing to anybody under the Treaty of Versailles. We disclaimed, and the Germans acquiesced therein, all of the responsibilities arising out of the Treaty of Versailles. It is an extraordinary document and one of the most tangible evidences of the breakdown of the German will to resist and their readiness to acquiesce in the wishes of the victorious powers.

It was at the height of these negotiations that a telegram reached me from Washington. It read somewhat as follows: "You are assigned to the Embassy at Tokyo as Counselor. Please arrange to proceed at your earliest convenience after the signature of the Peace Treaty."

CHAPTER X

Long, lazy days on southern seas, a brilliant sun on slow moving swell, deep blue water ruffled by a gentle breeze. Those are the memories of the trip from Marseilles to Tokyo. We boarded the French steamer *Anckor* ; it had been torpedoed and wrecked during the war, had just been recommissioned, so appeared new and spotlessly clean. We soon found that the chef was an artist. He had been carefully chosen by the captain, a citizen of Marseilles, so that he was unusually competent on fish food. His bouillabaisse was the only one I have ever eaten with genuine satisfaction.

We ran through the lovely Straits of Messina, steamed through the Suez Canal, and put in at Djibouti. It was my only glimpse of equatorial Africa, and I stared with admiration at the black women carrying baskets on their heads, bodies, carriage, and walk of a grace and beauty that one imagines for Diana. Some days later as we were approaching Colombo, a Belgian fellow passenger and I asked the captain how long we would stay in the port. The captain replied that he had no cargo for delivery there so that he could probably be under weigh again in a couple of hours. We expressed disappointment as we had anticipated a game of golf, whereupon the captain decided that he could just as well wait six hours ; that would give us time for a game and for dinner at the hotel on the shore. From then on we considered the ship as our private yacht.

We docked at Saigon on Thanksgiving Day. Kate and I gave a joyous party for the captain ; turkey was unobtainable, but we managed a small pig. From Haiphong through the Straits of Hainan to the incomparable beauty of Hong Kong, Shanghai for a couple of days and thence to Yokohama. On the trip for the first time I began to talk to my son in my own language, he had had first a French then a German governess. My wife and I decided it would be too much to bear if we had to talk to him in Japanese, so we had engaged an English governess. The boy had forgotten his other tongues by the time we reached Japan.

I have recounted this trip in some detail because of its effect upon me. I had lived the better part of five years in and around Germany, years in which I had seen a people in bitter struggle go down into the valley of despair. I had not been aware of the need of it during this experience, but in the peace of that voyage I found a calm pervading my spirit and a healing for the hopelessness which had entered me. I began to see that a world still existed with hope and a future. It needed but this glimpse of the East to feel the immutability of nature and to take comfort from it.

The ship moved slowly into the dock through the dusk of a December evening. Two tall figures were waving excitedly in greeting, and I recognized Alexander Kirk and Pierrepont Moffat from the Embassy. The former is now Chargé d'Affaires at Rome, and the latter has just been appointed Minister to Canada. It was delightful to be greeted by these two friends. While the Chancery messenger busied himself with our luggage we were taken to the station at Yokohama. I peered out interestedly at the passing lights and rickshas, renewing my acquaintance with the scene of Japan, so changed since my last visit in 1906. I had first visited Japan in 1892, a little boy with a negro mammy. I could remember little of the first visit save the curious crowds that always followed Emma and me when we set forth. My father had gone east on a silk buying expedition and had had the courage to take my mother and four children with him. We must have been a caravan as we moved about the country. The visit in 1906, however, was clear in my memory and I could note the change into Western costume and Western ways, especially among the men. The women, happily, continued to wear kimonos, a garb which flatters them much more than Western frocks.

The boys took us with pride, not unmixed with amusement, to our house in the compound. As Counselor, I rated "No. 2 house," "No. 1 house" being, of course, the residence of the Ambassador. Bright fires burned in the open grates, the boys had arranged the scanty furniture as advantageously as possible, it looked cheerful and comfortable that winter's night. "No. 2 house" was a rambling one-storied affair of frame construction ; it had grown into a tradition that each succeeding Counselor should add something to it. We added another bath. Construction was simple, you only had to build an additional shed and knock a door in the wall. We grew to love the little house and sincerely mourned its destruction in the great earthquake of 1923. Kate always spoke of it as "our greengrocer's cottage."

The Chancery of the Embassy presented something new to me, something peculiar to the Far East, a Japanese Secretariat. This office is run by a "Japanese Secretary," not, as

his name implies, a Japanese national, but an American Foreign Service officer who has studied the language as a student
interpreter, obtained a fluency in the tongue, and has spent
most of his career in Japan. He is assisted by other officers
of like qualifications and does the translation work of the
Embassy, oversees and examines the corps of student interpreters, and gives advice on matters involving the peculiari-
ties of the Japanese customs and people. Such a Secretary
and staff are indispensable in dealing with a language so in-
credibly difficult as Japanese.

There is perennial argument between those who have
studied Chinese and those who have tried Japanese, as to
which is the more difficult. I belong to the Japanese school
because I made serious efforts to learn it. I acquired a Japanese teacher and tackled the *First Reader*, produced in their
simplified phonetics called *Katakana*. The third lesson was
the story of George Washington and the cherry tree. It is
relatively easy to speak a Japanese jargon, this is acquired by
a lot of business residents who confidently assert that they
speak Japanese. A little study beyond that, however, shows
the unbelievable discourtesies and blunders of such a scanty
knowledge. The very forms of the verbs and phrase change
in accordance with the status of the person whom you are
addressing. I acquired enough knowledge to dispense with
couriers on travel, to get about the city on simple errands.
I did not stay in the country long enough, however, to dare
to carry on business or a social conversation.

As for the written language, it was so difficult that it had
a genuine fascination. If a sentence fell into place in your
mind, you had the same thrill of accomplishment that you get

when you put in the last piece in a jig-saw puzzle. The written characters are taken over bodily from the Chinese, but, whereas the Chinese is a monosyllabic tongue, Japanese is polysyllabic, thus a Chinese character may represent an entire polysyllabic word. It may, on the other hand, represent merely the monosyllable sound of the Chinese word which forms a part of the longer Japanese word. Erudite gentlemen know twenty thousand characters.

There is no way to learn them but to look at and memorize them, the strain on the eyes and on the endurance is terrific. The *Katakana* is added to the Chinese characters to indicate termination, it cannot be used adequately for the expression of thought. The number of words in Japanese is small and many have several meanings; the only way in which they can be distinguished one from another is through the Chinese character.

The American Ambassador in Tokyo was Mr. Charles Beecher Warren, a lawyer from Detroit, a member of the Republican National Committee, and later High Commissioner and Ambassador to Mexico. A man of exceptional intelligence, he became a successful diplomat in both posts. Short, clean shaven, thick set, he had the lawyer's habit of exploring any case to the last dot. He did not act by instinct, but by reasoned and calculated logic. We spent innumerable hours in his office, he with his inevitable cigar, I with my pipe, while we explored to the ultimate some problem before us. I learned much from this contact with a trained legal mind, with a spirit disciplined by such a mind. There was complete assurance in his own judgment, but, since the judgment was worked out with such care, the assurance was usually justified. Mrs. Warren, whose sister my wife had known years before, was gracious and charming and quickly made us members of the family. It became a ritual that on return from parties we would go to the Embassy to have a final drink, and to talk things over.

Social diversions in Tokyo as a rule were solemn affairs, elaborate dinners beautifully cooked but bearing a strong family resemblance one to another, which seemed to indicate either a rotating chef for Western food or a group of chefs all trained by the same master. Wealthy Japanese usually had one wing of their houses built Western fashion with salon and dining room. This wing would be used to entertain foreigners, closed again after their departure, when the Japanese family returned to its existence on straw mats.

To a Westerner, the Japanese leads the most unendurably uncomfortable existence that one can imagine. He sits on the floor in an agonizing position. Without central heating, he wraps himself in numerous kimonos and warms his fingers over charcoal brasiers. He eats food that our palates gag at. Shark fins and raw fish are delicacies, sometimes the fish is served with scales and fins, curled up with its tail in its mouth. A large vegetable called DAIKON looks like a turnip and has a most pervading odor. The Japanese use it more lavishly than the Italians use garlic. Kate used to eat at home before she set forth to a Japanese dinner, and frankly admitted it.

No other of the civilized races lives in the same measure of discomfort from our standpoint. The presence of women at social gatherings is largely a concession to Western habits, the Japanese women are seldom at ease socially and seem to feel themselves out of place.   There are frequent stag parties at tea-houses where geishas do the entertaining, and where humor is boisterous and somewhat sophomoric in tone.

Nowhere in the world, not even in these United States, is there such persistent speech-making as in Japan.   I probably made more speeches there during my two years of residence than in double the period in any other part of the world. In listening to speeches the Japanese are gluttons for punishment.   This obligation is a formidable burden, particularly if one does not speak readily.   My predecessor as Counselor, Ned Bell, had been a brilliant conversationalist, one of the most persistently entertaining and engaging talkers I remember, nevertheless when he rose to his feet every idea fled from his mind.   He knew his weakness and in general flatly refused to make a speech.

Once it was unavoidable.   Brother Thompson, a missionary, had died and, as Chargé d'Affaires, Ned had to offer testimony at a memorial service.   Ned took the precaution of building up a modicum of Dutch courage and rose to his feet with a charming tribute fully prepared.   He began to speak, and here is what he said: "Brother Thompson is dead." Here he paused, cleared his throat.   "Our dear Brother Thompson has died."   He halted again, looked wildly about. "Brother Thompson is dead — and that's that," said Ned and sat down.

Tokyo itself is a huge, sprawling, relatively uninteresting city, it does not compare in charm with the old capital, Kyoto. But the countryside is an unending joy.   The mountain areas of Miyanoshita and Hakone are charming, Nikko and Chūzenji conbine the loveliest works of man with the best efforts of the Creator. I made numerous trips, mostly on foot, whenever I could get free from the Chancery.

One especially has added to the riches of my memories. Pierrepont Moffat, my wife and I set out on foot around the base of Fujiyama. We wandered along the edge of Shoji Lake, surely one of the most beautiful settings of any mountain water, reflecting the peerless mountain on its calm surface. We slept in tiny inns on straw mattings and struggled to find something edible in Japanese food. Kate's feet became blistered, so we dressed her in a pair of my breeches, shod her in bedroom slippers and mounted her on a tiny mountain pack horse we were able to rent. We ran the rapids of the Fujikawa in a flat-bottomed sampan. To those who like their thrills without physical effort I commend this experience.

In one of the inns during the evening, I was conversing as usual with other guests in my halting Japanese when one of them demanded what I was doing in Japan. I replied that I was in the American Embassy. "Ah," said he, "you are a member of Mrs. Burnett's Embassy." Mrs. Charles Burnett, wife of the Military Attaché, had studied Japanese when her husband was a student officer. Of a sensitive and poetic nature, she had fallen under the spell of Japanese poetry and had concentrated on the archaic form which is the conventional medium for the expression of poetic thought. Several years before our arrival she had submitted a poem in the annual national poetry competition, and had won first mention from a board who judged the competitors without knowledge of their identity. In a nation with a genuine love of the beautiful, Mrs. Burnett's fame spread far and wide in the land, and inhabitants of tiny villages who were unaware of other foreign names had heard of Mrs. Burnett and esteemed her.

A famous diversion for the Diplomatic Corps, at least for the chiefs of mission, is an Imperial Duck Hunt. As I was in charge of the Embassy when the hunt drew near, Kate and I were invited. As usual in such perplexities, I consulted the Japanese Secretary as to costume for the event, and was told that since the invitation came in the name of the Emperor, and since he would be represented by one of his Imperial relatives, the proper costume for my wife would be an afternoon gown, and for me a cutaway coat. From this advice I began to have suspicion of the hunt.

The guests met in the morning on a private train which was to carry us to the country. We were received by an uncle of the Emperor, an extremely exalted gentleman in a land where the Emperor stands as something more than mortal. On the trip out, an Aide informed me that His Highness desired to talk with me. I had heard, of course, that the Imperial Family spoke French; the expedition to Europe in the seventies under Marquis Ito had drawn up an elaborate code of Imperial etiquette on its return, mostly based on Prussian practice.

Among other provisions, French was to be the foreign language of the members of the Family. So His Highness asked me a question in French about my previous posts, and I, pleased to have this common language and to dispense with an interpreter, answered at length. From time to time, His Highness would bow and smile, so I rambled on contentedly enough until he beckoned to our Japanese Secretary who was seated across the aisle from us and said something to him in Japanese. The Secretary's face went suddenly crimson with suppressed emotion, but he turned to me gravely and said, "His Imperial Highness says if you will talk French to him he can understand it." I began then to talk in words of one syllable and slowly, and he did in this case follow me.

The Japanese Secretary later explained that Japanese tradition would not tolerate the presence of foreign tutors in the Imperial Family so French had to be taught by a Japanese tutor, thus they never became accustomed to the sound of the tongue in foreign voices. Tradition must have become relaxed, since the brother of the present Emperor, Prince Chichihu, at that time the heir to the throne, was sent to Oxford, in 1926, for a year of study.

But I have strayed away from the duck hunt. Imagine a circular lake of perhaps a quarter mile diameter, entirely surrounded by a tall bamboo fence. The lake is a sanctuary, no gun has been fired for years, and, when you peer through a hole in the fence, is nearly covered by gaily feathered Japanese duck, looking like Chinese toys for a child's bathtub. All around the lake radiate a dozen trenches, perhaps a yard wide, with both banks elevated above the ground, and with a zigzag entrance screened from the lake by a fence which protects the trenches from the sight of the duck on the lake, as well as hiding the lake from the hunters. Decoys are tethered in the trenches, food is supplied abundantly, so the duck get the habit of swimming in whenever they want a meal. Large plaques with numbers mark the stations behind the elevated embankments, odd numbers on one side of the trench, even numbers on the other.

The Head Huntsman arranges his hunting party, ten in number, and pins numbered buttons on them to indicate their places behind the trench embankment, five odd, five even. Think of the men in their cutaways, the women in high-heeled shoes, lace gowns and picture hats. The Huntsman then presents to each the weapon of the chase, a butterfly-net on the end of a long pole. In two columns, the odds and evens, and in complete silence we followed the Huntsman who carried hooded falcons on his arm. We took our positions stealthily according to our numbers, the Huntsman waved his net over the trench, the duck rose with a squawk and we pulled them down in the air with our butterfly-nets. A duck escaped, the falcon was loosed, he rushed like gray lightning and brought the duck to earth. The Huntsman explained that no duck should escape from the trench and return to the lake, he might tell his fellow duck about it and the hunt would be spoiled.

They gave us a magnificent meal after these exertions in a shady pavilion by another lake, pressed duck such as one used to get at the Tour d'Argent in Paris when I was a boy, but with a special flavor of orange peel. Then we went hunting again. I was number three, number five was a gentleman unknown to me dressed in a black cutaway, gray derby, check trousers and white spats. I addressed him in every tongue I knew but got only mutters for reply. I decided he was a bad linguist or that he had done more than justice to the admirable Burgundy they had just served with the pressed duck. We had hunted one trench and had lined up for another when we discovered that number five was missing. The Huntsman and I conferred, then ran back to the last trench. There we discovered number five. He was kneeling on the embankment, fishing the decoys out of the water with his butterfly-net, and wringing their necks one by one. I learned subsequently that he represented one of our sister Republics in the Americas, and that he was, in fact, a competent linguist.

On the train going back we were each given a present of duck. It didn't matter how many you had netted, ambassadors got seven, ministers five, and chargés three. This type of hunting is a special appurtenance of the Imperial Family and, presumably, is a survival from the days of the Shogunate when the members of the Family were kept from any participation in the Government and were amused by elaborate and traditional forms of diversion to fill up their existence.

CHAPTER XI

I liked the people. I know that most Westerners don't. I know that the comparison between the Chinese and Japanese is always to the disadvantage of the latter. I like the Chinese, too, they laugh when we laugh, and no two people can have a stronger bond of sympathy. I like the Chinese civilization, sense of beauty and philosophy. But if we like one race must we necessarily hate another? The Japanese are as different from the Chinese as black from white. Let us isolate the Japanese and get him away from the inevitable comparison and see what he is like. We must enter again the realm of sweeping assertion, so let me hasten to admit the thousand exceptions to the statements I am about to make.

I like the two extremes of Japan, the millions of simple people and the members of the great families. The extremes have common characteristics; a deep sense of personal dignity, an expectation that they shall be treated accordingly, corresponds with their habit of punctilious courtesy toward others. Traditionalists to the backbone, they have built life into a series of ceremonies, and this applies to the peasant in his cottage as to the nobleman in his palace. Deficient in humor, but always smiling, they lack all traces of irony. Their conceptions of life are simple. I know of no Japanese outstanding in the field of philosophy, indeed, it is doubtful if the speculations of philosophers have ever interested the Japanese deeply. This does not mean that they have not a firmly fixed *weltanschauung* in the German sense, but they have no philosophy in the English meaning of the word.

Their faith in their race, in their throne, in their caste is unshakable. After nearly eighty years of official dissolution, the influence of the clans is still potent. The descendants of the Satsuma clan have first claim to high posts in the Navy, those of the Choshu clan to the Army.

The tradition of politeness goes to the extreme of depreciating all personal possessions, of understating all affections, of hiding all sorrow and disagreeable news, certainly from the casual outsider. The Japanese argue, and rightly, I think, that true politeness demands a cheerful exterior to one's fellows, and the suppression of news which might depress others. Not for the Japanese is the luxury of self-pity. It is a hard and somewhat lonely standard they have set, but it is a standard of consideration for others. Perhaps, as well, it forms an indispensable shell for the deeply emotional and excitable nature of the Japanese, of which the foreigner has occasional glimpses only, perhaps in the theater, perhaps in moments of disaster.

In no other race lies so deep-rooted a sense of the beautiful. There are certain famous cherry trees that are visited by thousands of travelers each year in the spring, there are famous scenes to which other thousands make their pilgrimages. The appreciation of beauty is not an acquired taste among the Japanese ; entire classes of school children join in the trips and stand in awed silence before some lovely scene. A delicate piece of procelain or ivory is not hung on the wall in a Japanese house, it is taken out of its silken wrappings from time to time and handled reverently by the members of the family, admired by the littlest children in their turn.

In most countries the lower middle class is regarded as the backbone of the nation, it husbands the staid and enduring virtues of thrift, respectability, devotion to duty. It is usually a conservative and dependable element. Not so in Japan; it has been explained that under the old régime the merchant ranked last in the grades of honor, far after the soldier and farmer. Hence, they argue, the class is new and without standards, they have neither the code of honor of the samurai nor the tradition of the soil. Whatever the explanation, and the foregoing may be valid, the lower middle-class Japanese is the least attractive to the Westerner. He seems to have broken the shell of politeness and can be bumptious and curious, and permits himself violations of good taste which other Japanese would be the first to condemn. Perhaps I may phrase it this way : the Japanese gentleman is one of the most admirable that I have met, the Japanese peasant has to an outstanding degree the virtues of the peasant the world over, the Japanese *petit bourgeois* is a *nouveau* who is hard to bear.

I was fortunate during my stay in Japan to have had my sojourn correspond with the period of increasing good will between the two countries. During the war against Germany the Japanese had seized the occasion of the preoccupation of Great Britain and the United States to issue their twenty-one demands to China, to occupy the province of Shantung, to bombard and seize Kiaochow, and to utilize the pretext of the rescue of the Czech brigades in Siberia to send a vast expeditionary force into that area and to occupy it as far as Lake Baikal.

The end of the war, coupled with the release of the American and British Navies from their duties in European waters, coincided with a swing of the pendulum in Japanese public opinion, which had become increasingly tired of the expense of these adventures abroad. The powerful merchant and banking classes with their desire for better international relations and freer trade possibilities gradually came into the ascendancy. This movement for conciliation with world opinion was typified by such men as Count Uchida, Baron Shidehara, Baron Makino, and others, so when the occasion of the Washington Conference arose the Japanese public was ready to grasp this opportunity to better its relations with the two Anglo-Saxon States.

The American Ambassador, Mr. Warren, had frequent occasion in Tokyo during the negotiations in Washington to assuage the anxiety of the Japanese, to explain the motives behind the insistence of the Americans and British for a better order in the Far East, and to use his influence with the American Government for the preservation to the Japanese of the battleship *Mutsu*. The original plan of Secretary of State Hughes had provided for the scrapping of this partly completed ship. However, the ship had become a symbol to the Japanese, due to the fact that most of its construction had been paid for by the contribution of small amounts from millions of simple people. The permission given to Japan to complete and retain the *Mutsu* did much to strengthen the hands of the conciliatory elements in Japan.

Another step which marked an improvement in relations

between the two countries was the abrogation of the Lansing-Ishii Agreement. As the name indicates, this agreement occurred during the war when Mr. Lansing was Secretary of State, and was formalized in an exchange of notes between the Secretary and the Japanese Ambassador, in which the Secretary recognized that Japan had "special interests" in neighboring Chinese territory. While the agreement in itself stated what was, after all, an acknowledged fact, since obviously the condition of these neighboring areas was more important to the Japanese than to anyone else, nevertheless the Japanese press had been distorting the agreement into an acknowledgment by the American Government that Japan had something more nearly approximating "special privileges" than "special interests."

The exchange of notes and the Japanese interpretation had aroused widespread criticism in the United States, criticism which imperiled relations between the two countries. It was therefore with a sigh of relief that we learned from Washington that the agreement had been abrogated peacefully; we had all worked persistently to stimulate a frame of mind among the Japanese which would admit the necessity for this abrogation.

At the close of the Washington negotiations, and before awaiting even the formal exchange of ratifications, the Japanese had begun to retire their troops from Siberia and during my stay complete evacuation was accomplished. In accordance with the terms of the treaty, shortly after the exchange of ratifications the Japanese entered into negotiation with the Chinese for the evacuation of Shantung. The negotiations, involving the sale of the railroad, were protracted and arduous but eventually were carried through to a successful conclusion.

Although the Washington treaty and subsequent Naval treaties are now as dead as the proverbial mutton, nevertheless there is one point covered by the Washington treaty which arises perennially and which still, I think, may flare up at any moment into political importance. In connection with self-denying ordinances contained in the Nine-Power Treaty and other documents of the Washington Conference, the United States undertook not to fortify the island of Guam.

One really needs an atlas to appreciate the strategic importance of Guam. One of the Ladrone group of islands, its lies in the heart of the Japanese mandates, the Marshall, Carolina, and Paloa groups. While it is some 1500 miles from Guam to Wake Island, perhaps half way to Honolulu, while it is some 1600 miles from Guam to the Philippines, from Guam to the Japanese Bonin Islands is only a bit over 700 miles, and to Yokohama itself some 1300. A strongly fortified Guam would mean one of the best positions from which to blockade Japan in case of war, curtail its supplies and cut communications with certain of its possessions.

I have never met an American Naval officer who did not feel that in renouncing the fortification of Guam, the United States had sold its birthright, but, if one tries to put oneself in the other man's shoes it is easy to see why the Japanese feel convinced that such fortification would be a serious menace to them. It is as if a power with a strong Navy with whom our relations were not of the best should fortify one of the islands of the West Indies. We can easily imagine with what apprehension we should regard such an effort.

Certainly through the peaceful era, approximately to the end of 1931, the non-fortification of Guam contributed strongly to the maintenance of good relations between the United States and Japan. It is to be remembered that President Wilson returned from the Peace Conference in Paris and made a public demand upon the people of the United States to construct a Navy second to none. The Japanese were convinced that this construction could have for its object only the design of forcing our will upon Japan. They argued that the war in Europe was over, that battle between the United States and Great Britain was inconceivable, and that, therefore, there could be no potential enemy except Japan against whom we were planning such colossal construction.

The fear of this construction was intensified by the talk of the fortification of Guam and the Philippines, thus giving us a chain — Hawaii, Guam and the Philippines — from which, with a Navy of such force as projected, we could close to Japan access to the rest of the world. Security is a double concept, there may be security for one party by domination, but security for both parties can only be achieved by some form of balance, by a mutual belief that the situation has been so arranged that the home areas are safe from attack. Our Navy has repeatedly brought forward the claim to fortify Guam ; so far the claim has been resisted by Congress. May it continue to be so, for I fear that those fortifications would never be completed, at least they would not be completed before battle had been engaged between the Japanese and American fleets, unless we have available in Pacific waters a fleet of much greater preponderance than the present one.

In the early summer of 1922 my wife and I took a trip to China on a short leave of absence. On a blazing hot day in Shanghai I sent a telegram to a classmate of mine, John Magee, a missionary in Nanking, telling him we were taking the boat for Hankow and urging him to get aboard and accompany us up the river, since this was the only good boat for a number of days and our stay was limited. I was not too optimistic as to the possibility of John falling in with our plans since he is the vaguest saint on earth, but I did receive a reply to the telegram saying that he would meet us at the boat in Nanking. Before sunrise the next morning the boat moved slowly into the port and I scanned the yelling mob of rikishamen, porters, coolies, in vain for a sight of John. He wasn't there, so I went to the captain who told me I had plenty of time to take a rikisha and visit John's house. He instructed the rikishaman where to take me and the coolie trotted me far beyond the walls of the city to a tiny house on the edge of a green pond where the women were washing their vessels.

A lovely tenor voice raised in song floated from the open window on the morning calm. I looked up and saw John, half shaved. To my blasphemous reproaches he turned an angelic smile and remarked, "Well, Hughie, I thought you weren't due until tomorrow." John explained that he had an important engagement that afternoon which he could not omit and that it was therefore necessary for us to get off the ship and stay with him. Accordingly we rushed back, woke up Kate, made her pack and dragged her to John's house for breakfast. During the day John showed us Nanking and at somewhere near four o'clock in the afternoon I warned him that he had better hurry back to keep that important engagement that he had mentioned.

John said, "What engagement?"

I replied, "The one that prevented you from accompanying us."

He said, "Oh, that? I can do that just as well tomorrow."

After a day or two in Hankow, which I remember chiefly as the hottest place that I ever had the misfortune to encounter, we took a train for Peking where we stayed with Albert Ruddock and his wife, Margaret, in the Counselor's house of the Legation compound. In spite of the fact that Kate and I succumbed to the sickness that is apt to attack foreigners in the summer in China, we spent a memorable few days before we were afflicted. Peking has something unique; one is conscious of the uninterrupted flow of history, one watches the caravans arrive, identical to the caravans that Marco Polo watched from the same gate, that Genghis Khan sent in, that thousands of emperors and kings, in an era of history so remote that it is not even recorded in writing, watched arriving by the same paths.

There are motor cars, there are gentlemen in white breeches mounted on polo ponies, there are plenty of other signs of the twentieth century, but they blend into antiquity in this city and the whole vast place seems changeless and eternal. Rome gives one somewhat the same feeling. Both are places where the most jaded traveler devotes himself to sight-seeing, both are places where the past lives in the present and where each human being must realize that not only he himself but his whole generation is but an incident in the vast book of history.

I wanted to see Manchuria and had hoped to go to Mukden and to visit Harbin. The Chinese were beginning to trek in, in vast numbers, and I was told that the scene resembled the opening for settlement of Kansas or Oklahoma. Unfortunately, one of the never-ending battles between the Tuchuns was going on near the Great Wall, and railroad traffic was interrupted.

There are a great many things that have deteriorated in recent years. Among them are battles in China. In those days people in the Legations at Peking packed up a picnic box and took the day off to ride out and see a battle. A lot of shots were fired, the army did a lot of shouting, but you could count the casualties on your fingers. Since the Japanese have taken a hand in the matter, however, things have become more serious.

Unable to go to Manchuria, we did what we thought was the next best thing, took a ship from Tientsin to Antung, on the mouth of the Yalu River. Next we proceeded to Seoul, in Korea, and returned by the Straits of Tsushima, where the Russian ships of Rozhestvenski went down before the guns of Togo, and thence home. China had been fascinating. The interest in China is almost breath-taking ; but it had been hot, it had been dusty, it had been yellow, it had been barren. To return to the greenness, the neatness, the order of Japan made one take a deep breath of satisfaction.

My wife had spent one summer in the heat of Tokyo, a heat which is only equalled in intensity and humidity by that of Washington at its worst. The second summer we decided that she and the boy would take an apartment at the hotel in Chuzenji and that I would come up for such week-ends as I could. September first, 1923, was a morning of torrential downpour. The children were playing games in the billiard room and we were engaged with two Japanese in a game of bridge in our salon. The hand had just been dealt, the dealer was about to declare, when the earth rose under us, gave itself a violent twisting shake and crashed back again. Mutters like thunder sounded underground. Shock succeeded shock. We rose to our feet, still clutching our cards ; one of the Japanese said, "This is serious ; we must get out."

We rushed into the corridor, an undulating path of linoleum, staggered down the stairs and thence into the drenching downpour. My wife and I rushed to the play room where we found that the nurses had deposited the children under the billiard table and they were playing ship. The children were delighted. All that afternoon the shocks continued. The clouds cleared away and a soft moon came out in the evening. I proposed to take a boat on the lake and avoid further shocks ; Kate, however, preferred the dry land, so we lay in bed waiting for the ceiling to descend.

The next morning I tried to telephone to Tokyo but all wires were down. Bear in mind that we in Chuzenji thought that we were in the center of the shock, and we could not understand why the capital had not already sent out workmen to repair the lines and re-establish communication. As I tried to puzzle this through I grew more apprehensive and wondered whether the silence might mean something more sinister than neglect. I talked it over with Hulings, one of the assistants to the Naval Attaché, who with his wife and family also lived at the hotel. We decided we had better get back to the capital and see what had happened.

The road from Chuzenji to Nikko, the nearest railroad station, is a steep winding descent that can be made in a rikisha but we usually went on foot, sending the luggage by coolie. The shocks were continuing; it gave one the strangest impression, one lost the feeling of certainty that a solid earth gives. How much of our life is predicated on the fact that the earth is solid. When you find that this is not the fact, all your certainty vanishes. As I felt the path heave, I would not have been surprised to see mountains disappear and gigantic pine trees swallowed up by the earth.

At Nikko the Military Attaché was living in a temple loaned by the Empress. We stopped to find whether he had any news. As we drank our tea and talked matters over, in came Mrs. Burnett, whom I have mentioned before. She explained that a messenger had just arrived from the Imperial Palace. The messenger stated that an airplane had flown over the palace and had dropped a message for His Majesty. The message contained but one phrase, but one pregnant with significance: "Yokohama obliterated, Tokyo in flames."

At least our path was clear, we must get back to Tokyo. Hulings and I hired a motor car and then went shopping. We piled the car with everything we could think of that was obtainable, first aid packages, sacks of rice, whiskey, packages of biscuits, anything and everything that we could conceive of as useful in a devastated area. Leaving our wives and families in Nikko, we pushed on. Miles outside of Tokyo we began to meet the refugees, whole families evacuating the city, exhausted, frightened, eyes staring. We had to stop the car again and again or they would have walked right into us.

Men carried their household furniture, their children, their mothers. Some carried the most bizarre packages, bird cages, and parrots.

Japan is a land almost without wheeled vehicles, so everything was carried on peoples' backs. We tried to get news from them ; all they would say was "The wall of fire, the wall of fire." Eventually, just before sunset, we reached a slight elevation whence the city should have stretched out at our feet. There was nothing but ruin, devastation, bordered by dense clouds of smoke pierced here and there by bright flames. There was hardly a landmark that we could recognize, there was nothing that could tell us even where the Embassy lay in this unknown aspect of the city.

Impossible to proceed by motor, the streets full of debris, telegraph poles, abandoned wagons, we had to leave the car and push on by foot. We eventually spotted a huge iron torii, one of those T-shaped gates which indicate the temples of Japan. We knew to what temple this belonged and we knew that a straight line drawn from this torii to the sea should take us past the Embassy ; in fact it did, and we found the smoking ruins of our houses. Nothing was left. The Embassy, the Chancery, and our little greengrocer's cottage, the garage and servants' quarters, had all been destroyed.

The servants were gathered in the garden, having salvaged a few belongings, even, I was happy to notice, some tapestries of mine as well as an enormous stock of wine. They were giving themselves a cheerful time in this scene of ruin. We indicated to them exactly where we had left the car and sent them back to carry in the supplies, then pushed on, footsore and hot, to see what had happened to Hulings' house — a short distance from the Embassy and in a cup-shaped valley, invisible from the Embassy.

As we tipped the rise of the hill we were astonished and overjoyed to see that Hulings' little house stood intact, it stood alone amidst the devastation. By some freak of the wind, that one little house had been spared the flames. Water mains had burst, of course, so there was no method of getting clean, but we ate some sardines and biscuits, brushed our teeth in Japanese whiskey, and wished more than ever that water was available to kill the taste. Up in the bedroom we found the mattresses covered with plaster from the ceiling, turned them over and fell asleep in exhaustion. Ten minutes later the earth quivered and muttered, plaster fell all over us, and, silently, as if by tacit agreement, we dragged the mattresses downstairs and into the open air. The only open space in the neighborhood was the cemetery, it was true that some of the monuments had been toppled about, still we could find a place where nothing was likely to fall, so we spread out the beds and slept like logs.

Next morning we went back to the Embassy ruins looking for transportation. My car had disappeared; I found later that during the fire the Dutch Minister had told my chauffeur that I had given instructions for him to drive the Minister to Nikko, and that the chauffeur, not overgifted with brains, had believed him. We must have passed each other en route.

The servants at the compound reported to us that the Ambassador was at the Imperial Hotel, an Aztec-looking structure which had withstood the shocks, and thus fortified the reputation of its American architect, Frank Lloyd Wright. Thither we repaired and reported for duty — dirty, smoke-begrimed and unshaven.

Americans in Tokyo quickly began to appear at the Embassy with the offer of services. Charles Burnett, the Military Attaché, entered at once upon the task of organizing expeditions of relief and information. All motors were requisitioned and visits were made to American houses about the city, to Yokohama, Kamakura, and Miyanoshita, to all the resorts in the earthquake area where Americans might be found or news of them obtained.

As these men reported their findings, we began to get a picture of the disaster which for sinister horror has rarely been equaled in history. Yokohama had been literally obliterated. Our American and British friends had been gathered at the bar of the club for the Saturday noon cocktail. The building collapsed, few were saved. Men and women had plunged into the bay to avoid the fire and had been obliged to swim for ships at anchor through water literally ablaze with burning oil. The miracle was that some arrived. The American Consul and his wife had been killed, their two little boys survived.

Bizarre things happened ; an American Vice Consul had been caught in the ruins of the Consulate, pinned down by a beam but unhurt. He saw the high wall of a neighboring building waver above him, he saw it lean over, and he saw it fall upon him. He was framed by a window frame and not even wounded. An American woman was bathing in the third floor of the Grand Hotel, the façade fell out to the street, her floor tipped outward and she coasted quietly down on the rubbish still in her tub. Lifted out by two young Americans, they all plunged into the harbor and clung to a rowboat while the fire devoured the city.

An event happened in Tokyo ; when I think of it now I still feel the sensation of gruesome horror which flooded me when I first heard it. The devastation caused by the earthquake itself in Tokyo was not so disastrous, it was the succeeding fire that caused the widespread destruction. Not only was there a furious wind, but September first followed a long drought, everything was dry as tinder. The water supply had broken down, pipes and conduits had burst, there was no controlling or checking the conflagration. The terrified people ran by thousands from the flames. They reached the river bank where the police had thrown a cordon to prevent the death of hundreds by drowning. The police urged the people into what they considered a safe place, a huge square used as a shipping yard by the Ministry of Munitions. The square became so packed with people that they could not move. The flames came, the surrounding warehouses were destroyed. Morning found those thousands still standing, held together by their own mass, and roasted to death.

A couple of days later, there was ushered into my office an astonishing figure for those days. He was clean, he was clothed in a spotless white uniform with gold braid, his youthful face was shaven ! Like the climax to the plot of an old-fashioned movie, the American Navy had arrived and our troubles were over. At the first news of the disaster the Admiral had rushed the China fleet over to Tokyo. This caused some apprehension to the Japanese Navy, lest we were seizing the occasion of their helplessness to destroy them. But this was quickly allayed, the Navy was tactful and unbelievably helpful with supplies and wireless facilities.   Communications had been interrupted for all practical purposes, and the Navy gave us first touch with the world.

A few days later, supply ships from Manila steamed in ; General Frank McCoy arrived from Shanghai to supervise distribution, and did it admirably.   The American people poured out aid in unstinted generosity through our Red Cross, millions of dollars were subscribed without urging.   This spontaneous and practical aid from America deeply touched the Japanese, ancient grudges were forgotten.   We regained the place in Japanese affection which we had held in the days of Townsend Harris, first American Consul to Japan.   It seemed safe to assume that our relationship would remain cordial and sympathetic for many years to come.

Alas, this was not to be, and the fact that the deterioration set in by our own frivolous act does not make it easier to forgive.   But that is a matter for a later chapter.   The era of good relations was a satisfaction while it lasted and I was proud to be working in the American Embassy through those days, and I remain proud as I think of it.   Our people reported for duty more promptly, our local relief organizations functioned earlier and more efficiently, our Navy arrived first, our country poured out relief in unbelievable generosity ; no other nation compared with it, and the Japanese recognized this fact and were grateful.

The rumor ran about Tokyo that Koreans had been responsible for setting fire to the city after the earthquake.   There had been examples of terrorism on the part of Koreans from time to time since Japan had annexed the country, and these rumors found ready credence among a portion of the population, terrified and excited by the scope of the calamity. Cases of mob violence occurred and some of the Koreans paid with their lives for the fact of their nationality alone. Aside from these incidents, the behavior of the people was beyond praise. In the breakdown of all organization, in nights of complete darkness, there was no looting, there was no disorder. The people went about dazed, it is true, and it was some days before they began to take up their work, but I saw no examples of disorder, nor heard of any beyond those lamentable attacks on Koreans. In going about all sections of the city for the relief of Americans, we found the people helpful and ready to do what we asked them, rather eager than otherwise to be given an occupation.

I had visited San Francisco, in 1906, a few months after the earthquake and fire. I had heard stories of the immediate organization and energy of the people, an energy that turned in a few hours to reconstruction. The Japanese did not show this same talent and energy ; at the same time there was no need for soldiers and firing squads to quell the looters in Tokyo.

It was in the third week of September that a telegram from Washington asked news of my plans and referred to a previous message sent on September first. Of course I had never received it, so requested its repetition. The telegram was dated noon, September first, the day and hour of the first great shock, and transferred me to Mexico City as Counselor. It came as a great relief. Except for a trunkful of summer clothes at Chuzenji, and odds and ends of things that the servants had rescued from our house, my wife and I had practically nothing, so it was good to feel we could return to America and replenish our necessities.

Accordingly I was pleased when I sent word to Kate to come to Tokyo, that we were going home.   She arrived with several little wooden boxes under her arm, the unfailing indication of fresh purchases in Japan.   I inquired about them and was shown some little jade cups.   Thinking of the ruin of all our belongings and that toothbrushes would come in more handy, I exclaimed in astonishment, but Kate remarked, as if it were the most normal behavior, "I am beginning my collection again."

We were made welcome by Lee Kaufman, an American in Tokyo whom we had known and liked, and were given bedrooms on the second floor to which one climbed by a little wooden staircase from the garden.   The Kaufmans were fortunate in having a house which had withstood the shock and had suffered nothing more serious than leakages in the roof. The earthquakes were still continuing, nothing like the violence of the original day, but enough to cause continued anxiety. Incidentally, the seismograph registered 1066 shocks in the fourteen days following the first one.   The figure has always stayed in my mind as that of the last invasion of Great Britain. The first night the shocks drove us downstairs helter-skelter, clad in pajamas and nightgowns, into the garden where we met Lee Kaufman, discussed the situation, and went to bed again. But we soon found it more convenient to lay mattresses along the edge of the garden under the projecting roof and to sleep there, where one jump would take us into safety.

Our steamer was scheduled to leave early in the morning from Yokohama.   The port and the normal facilities for landing had been destroyed so we had to board a lighter and wait for hours in the harbor for the arrival of the ship.   Accordingly, we came down from Tokyo the evening before to spend the night in the ruined port.   Nelson Johnson, now Ambassador to China, had hurriedly arrived to act as Consul General after the earthquake.   He had set up a series of tents on the consular compound and this was the only station of hospitality in the whole of the city.   I remember that he had salvaged a phonograph from the ruins and had one cracked disk which played *Yes, We Have No Bananas.* My little boy, then five, was fascinated with the surroundings and with the disk.   We must have played it over forty times during that night.   It was a strange sensation to be the only living things in this huge city and to have the lanterns in our tent shed the only artificial glow in the scene of devastation.

The ship moved out of the harbor, land disappeared from sight.   In the late afternoon the skies cleared, the clouds parted and the perfect form of Fujiyama lifted itself above the horizon.   The lines of its symmetrical base disappeared in purple mist.   The Japanese say that the departing traveler who is vouchsafed this view of the mountain is sure to return to Japan. I have never returned, perhaps I never shall, but I am grateful to the country and its people.   The months there had brought me to a more normal existence.   I had lived in a land which did not seem to be aware that there had been a war in Europe, where people followed their normal avocations, where there was time again in one's life to read and to study.   I felt a peace again such as I had not experienced since August 1914.

CHAPTER XII

The State Department, to which I returned in the early part of 1923, under Mr. Charles Evans Hughes, Secretary of State, was full of friends. William Phillips and two other Assistant Secretaries, Leland Harrison and Butler Wright, were Foreign Service Officers whom I had known for many years. I called on William Phillips to discuss my situation. I explained that if the Department felt it essential, I would proceed at once to Mexico, as ordered, but that my wife and I had both been badly shaken about by our recent experience in Japan and would appreciate a stay in Washington if it could be arranged. I further explained that I had grown deeply interested in Central Europe and only less so in the Far East, that I had not been in Latin America for a number of years, that it seemed remote from the problems which I had been studying and to which I had given so much time.

Bill was most sympathetic and told me that the position of Chief of the Division of Current Information, the State Department's press section, was open through the departure of Ned Bell to Peking, and that if this interested me I could take it on. Further, he suggested that I take leave for a couple of months in anticipation of starting work in the Department. I readily acquiesced, and left with Kate for Aiken, South Carolina, where my brother had a house. We motored down in November. It is odd to compare that trip with subsequent trips that I have taken south over beautiful highways, the contrast between now and sixteen years ago is striking.   At that time we ran through mile after mile of yellow mud where enterprising farmers waited with teams of mules to haul out the motorist in difficulty.

I knew little about the Division of Current Information when I took it over, but was greatly helped by the presence of the Assistant Chief, Michael McDermott.   McDermott has subsequently become Chief of the Division and has remained so for many years.   A man of quiet competency who knows the problems of the newspapermen as well as they do themselves, his long record with them has been one of helpfulness and sympathetic co-operation.

When I entered the Division the only knowledge I had of it was a story Ned Bell had told me when he had stopped over in Tokyo on his way to Peking.   He said that on one hot summer day he had brought the Secretary of State to meet the assembled newspapermen in one of the daily press conferences. In the heat of the day all the windows of the reception room were open and a hot breeze blew through.   One of the correspondents had put a question to Mr. Hughes involving some phase of constitutional law.   The Secretary, thoroughly at home on this subject, gave a lecture, pouring out his thoughts in a torrent of words lucid and comprehensive.   It was the habit in those days to take notes in longhand of the press conferences, to write them up subsequently and to post them in the press room for the benefit of those correspondents who came in later.

Dripping from every pore, Ned leaned over the table, writing rapidly ; one by one he tore off the sheets from his pad. When the Secretary finally paused, asked if there were no further questions, and left the room, Ned turned to gather up his notes and to his dismay found that the breeze had scattered them far and wide. He had not taken the precaution to number them, but he returned to his office and endeavored to dictate his summary. Alas, the continuity was lacking ; he could not find out how the notes ran, or in what order. He returned to the Secretary's office, explained his predicament, and begged the Secretary to give him a brief repetition of the statement. The Secretary looked at him in surprise and remarked, "Why, Mr. Bell, I had thought my explanation would be plain to the meanest intelligence."

It was extremely hard work, this assignment in Current Information. There was no such thing as office hours. When I left the Department and was out of my house I invariably left a telephone number where I could be reached. I was summoned from dinner, I was waked up in the night. Whenever a cable arrived in the press associations dealing with foreign affairs the first effort of the correspondents assigned to the State Department was to obtain a "reaction" from the State Department at Washington. This "reaction" had to be given regardless of the time of day. It is no easy thing to be wakened by the jangle of a bell in the middle of the night and to give a "reaction" to a story involving a threat to American oil properties in Rumania. But the task had great compensations.

Nothing happened in the State Department in which the Chief of the Section was not actively concerned. I sat in on the most intimate conferences in order not to be surprised by developments when they were released for publicity. Such a position gave one the opportunity of participating in events which ordinarily the Chief of a Section would not even have known were taking place. It involved continuous study not only of the telegrams and despatches of all types of activity in the State Department but of the history or what the press knows as "background" of events. Whenever a story broke I had to be in a position to give the correspondents the full history and events leading up to the situation of which they were writing. I had to know it thoroughly myself in order to make it clear to them.

These men assigned to the State Department, whether by the press agencies or by the individual newspapers, were men of experience and competence, many of them knew foreign affairs intimately. Even though they were a selected group of their profession, nevertheless I am happy to state that in an experience with them lasting over three years and dealing with some who represented the opposition to the party in power, I never suffered from a breach of confidence, and always found them ready to treat me in the most open and loyal manner.

In view of the story that Ned had told me I began working with the Secretary of State with some trepidation. I soon found, however, that the inspiration and joy of working with him far outweighed any apprehension that might have come from his occasional caustic manner. It quickly became apparent to me that there was one thing Mr. Hughes would not tolerate ; he would not talk with anybody who came to him who had not mastered the last word of his subject. Even on most pressing matters it was essential to be in possession of the full facts before you presented yourself to the Secretary. Not that we usually had to recite these facts to him, he was to such an extent master of his material that he rarely had to ask questions, nevertheless when he did ask them he expected a thorough and immediate answer.

It was admirable training, it was more than that, it was inspiring. I felt that I never visited the Secretary without leaving his office a wiser man. I don't want to give the impression that the Secretary was always abrupt. Far from it. At times his booming laugh would burst forth, at times he would enter into reminiscence, and on those occasions no character could have been more interesting and more fascinating. Even after months of experience with him one was startled at the breadth of his knowledge, at the penetration of his intellect, at his ability to thrust unerringly and swiftly to the heart of any matter. More than most men, I suppose, in my travels around the world I have come in contact with the outstanding men of our generation. I have found none to compare in wisdom and intelligence with Secretary Hughes.

Shortly after our arrival in Washington an episode occurred which I am inclined to relate. I relate it not so much for its intrinsic interest as because it typifies that sort of incident which makes the life of a diplomat so precarious, and because it serves to show that the dangers which lie in the path of a diplomat are often those not associated with the work in his office but rather those which arise when he is off his guard in his ordinary life. Kate had always been on happy terms with the various Ministers and Ambassadors who had been our Chiefs, but there had been one exception which proved the rule, an Ambassador for whom she had less than no use. Neither had I. The Ambassador had resigned and at the time of which I write had just been nominated for a lucrative Government position at the insistence of Senator A.

One evening we were dining with friends. As I looked about the table I saw Kate nearly opposite me, seated between Senator A and Senator B, the latter a good friend of the former but a gentleman of somewhat Puckish humor, taking a sort of twinkling enjoyment from a friend's discomfort. In one of those pauses that occur in dinner conversation I heard Kate's voice ring out, "But he is a dreadful person." Due to the pause, the attention of everybody was caught and held while my wife continued her exposition in vigorous terms of the demerits of the Ambassador. Kate, of course, was blandly ignorant of the fact that Senator A had sponsored the Ambassador for the new post. I knew it, and did my utmost to create a diversion. In vain, alas. Senator B was thoroughly enjoying himself and everytime Kate paused for breath he urged her on. Senator A looked more and more discomfited. Kate subsequently explained that Senator A had opened the subject by asking her what she thought of the Ambassador. Kate is nothing if not forthright, and told him honestly what she thought. The dinner seemed interminable.

In the smoking room Senator A came to me, and said, "Look here, Hugh, this is a very serious matter. You realize that I sponsored the Ambassador's nomination. I didn't dream of some of the things your wife has told me. Do you support what she has said or was she talking with undue exuberance? In the former event I am afraid I shall have to ask you to come before a Senate Committee and testify as we could not go through with the nomination if the things that your wife has stated are sustained."

I gulped, took a deep breath and said, "Needless to tell you

I would not have brought this all up, but my wife has done so and I support her in every particular."

Kate and I lay awake most of the night, going over the evidence we would submit and making plans for what we would do when I left the Service.

Early in the morning the telephone rang, Senator A on the wire. "Hugh, I have been thinking this thing over."

"My Lord, Senator, so have I," said I.

He continued, "I have come to the conclusion that no useful purpose could be served by having your wife and you testify and we are not going to summon you before the Committee. I will talk to you about it later."

He never spoke to me about it but within a few days I read in the paper that the Ambassador's nomination to the post had been withdrawn. My days in the Foreign Service had not come to an end.

In the spring of 1924 William Phillips went to the mission in Brussels and Joseph Grew, at that time Minister in Switzerland, became Under Secretary of State. This was a cause of rejoicing to me as I had worked with Joe both in Berlin and Vienna and we were close friends, united, I think, in both esteem and affection. Those occasions of my life when I have been surrounded in my work by friends have been those of deepest satisfaction and this period in Washington stands out in that respect.

The pressure for living accommodations that had prevailed in Washington during and immediately after the war had diminished. Most of the dollar-a-year men had gone back to their vocations and had left the capital. Nevertheless the nation was prosperous, it was the beginning of the era which culminated in 1929, and life ran at a high pace. The customary points in bridge were two cents, and poker, of which a vast amount was played, was so high as to exclude all but a very few. The effects of prohibition were vivid and obvious, people were drinking extravagantly and recklessly, many of them people who had had little or no interest in liquor before the passage of this unfortunate law had turned their attention to it.

Kate and I took a house some distance out Massachusetts Avenue, Villa Rosa it was called. It still stands. It was a beautiful place in which to entertain, spacious drawing rooms and a charming terrace for the warm weather. In the summer when our wives left us to escape the Washington heat, Joe Grew, Leland Harrison and I used to rent a little farm house some miles out on the Rockville Pike. It made a pleasant and peaceful retreat for the evenings. A little stream ran through it, perhaps two feet deep, a cheerful place to bathe before going to work in the mornings. At that time the country around Washington was, of course, much less cut into subdivisions. The area beyond Nebraska Avenue was delightful to ride in. We used to have the horses brought to the corner of Massachusetts and Nebraska Avenues; from there we rode on paths in rolling wooded country through what is now the Foxhall Road area.

During the first months of my work in Washington we were all deeply interested in the legislation which had been introduced by John Rogers of Massachusetts for the re-organization of the diplomatic and consular services. Up to this time the two services had been separately administered under a very different scale of pay ; the maximum salary, for instance, for a counselor of embassy was three thousand dollars while that of the senior consular officer more nearly approximated the present level, with its maximum of 9000–10,000 dollars. At the same time advancement was quicker in the diplomatic branch, the turn-over by resignation was higher, there were fewer candidates for the reason that a relatively small number of men felt that they could get along on the salaries offered without independent incomes.

The Rogers Act was finally passed and became law on July 1, 1924. It amalgamated the two services, put them on a scale which compares favorably with that of the foreign services of other nations in so far as it applies to officers below the rank of chiefs of mission. The Constitution of the United States reserves for the President the right to appoint ministers and ambassadors. There can therefore be no legislative restriction upon this constitutional right of the President ; the legislation applies only to Foreign Service officers up to and including the grade of counselor of embassy or consul general.

In accordance with the act all members of both branches were to be commissioned "Foreign Service Officers," class one to nine, as the case might be, class one being the senior men. I have no hesitation in saying that the Foreign Service of the United States is a vastly better organization because of the Rogers Act. It gave renewed ambition and additional incentive to work to a number of men interested in political problems, who had been unable previously to accept positions in the diplomatic service because of the salaries. It eliminated political preference in the appointments and promotions. It offered assurance of a life career on good behavior and thus improved the quality of the young men who presented themselves for examination.

Nevertheless, at that time, and since then, I have been apprehensive about one phase of the Service. Because of its stratification into numerous classes and its promotion by seniority only in the lower classes, it is highly unlikely that intelligent and ambitious young men will find themselves content with the slow promotion and the uninspiring drudgery of junior office. This factor has not yet proved to be important since for approximately eleven years the nation has not enjoyed genuine prosperity. No period during those years has brought forth demand from American businesses for young men to fill lucrative positions. If such a period does come, however, the experienced, well-educated, well-trained young men in the Foreign Service will be strongly tempted to leave the slow career for the more brilliant opportunities of business life.

Our loss was heavy from this cause during the period from 1923 to 1929. If such a period comes back, or conditions approximating it, we may see the very best young men that we have, lost to Government Service because they have become discouraged by the slow promotion and bored by the routine work which they are obliged to carry out through their early years of experience.

I know numbers of young men who would have been admirable Foreign Service officers, interested in the life, but who declined to take their examinations because of this phase of Service administration. I know a number of us senior men who would have hesitated to enter the Service as boys had

present conditions existed then.   I recognize the demerits of
the old system of administration in the diplomatic service but
at least it offered the probability of work of immediate interest,
of considerable responsibility.   It offered young men of ability
the inspiration to enter a field of adventure rather than one of
security.

The present system is too successful to scrap.   The remedy,
it seems to me, lies in administration.   The seniority promotion in the junior grades should, I think, be less rigidly administered, and every opportunity should be seized to give
interesting work to those who show promise in early years,
and rapid promotion should follow good performance.

I had other doubts about the Rogers Act.   When the bill
was in malleable form during the committee hearings in the
House of Representatives I went to the Secretary of State and
declared to him that it seemed to me that the proposal to establish a board of personnel was faulty, I felt that the members
of a board could never have that intimate contact with the
men which would enable them to know the problems of each
one, the possibilities of each officer.

I was afraid that the board would act on rule and precedent
and without that consideration for human factors so indispensable to the proper handling of personnel.   I pointed out
that big industries, big department stores, all had their chief of
personnel who was himself ultimately responsible for decisions in this field.   It seemed to me a good precedent and that
we should establish a similar chief of personnel, a permanent
official in the State Department who would learn to know the
men by years of dealing with them and, hence, would avoid the
defects of a board.

Mr. Hughes replied that he knew that a board was defined as "something wooden and narrow," nevertheless he had served for years in active political life and had found that the organization or man dealing with personnel was invariably the spot most subject to attack by political influences. Given that fact, he felt that the board could resist pressure better than any one man. He felt further that an opposition Government coming in would at once replace a chief of personnel with an appointment of its own selection, that the whole organization would thus fall under political domination. The defects of the board were many but in the long run Mr. Hughes felt it was a superior method of operation to a single chief.

The past years have proved him right, I think. The board has made its mistakes, as any human organization makes them, but it has resisted pressure and as time goes on that pressure becomes less and less and the decisions of the board are now freely accepted in all quarters.

Entertaining the doubts that I did about the act and its effect on the future of the Service, I rebelled when the Secretary of State and Joe Grew informed me that they wanted to name me Chief of the newly established Section of Personnel and as such an ex-officio member of the Personnel Board. I struggled my hardest to keep out of it ; I pointed out that my work in Current Information was such as to occupy me day and night to the exclusion of anything else, that I didn't want to be in a position where I would have to determine the fate of my friends. Something in me told me that the job was thankless and would be repugnant to me. Nevertheless I was overruled and forced to combine the duties of chief of the two divisions at once.

This would have been harassing enough under any circumstances but was made doubly so by the fact that the offices were physically separated, Current Information being on the second floor and Personnel on the first. I ran up and down that stone staircase scores of times a day when the telephone in one bureau brought the information that something urgent was occurring in the other. It would have simplified the matter to put in a fireman's pole.

The Personnel Board was made up as follows: Joe Grew, the Under Secretary, was chairman; Butler Wright and Wilbur Carr, Assistant Secretaries, were members. Mr. Carr had been for years director of the consular service, knew its problems intimately and had a just pride in the group that he himself had done so much to build up. I was a member of the board as was my assistant, Edward Norton, a consular officer. There was no basis of comparison at that time between members of the former consular service and of the former diplomatic service. In awaiting the time when inspectors' reports and other material would give us a basis on which to compare the relative merits of the men, we continued to make our promotions as within the two original services. This resulted in more rapid promotion for those of the former diplomatic branch than those of the former consular branch.

When I left the board, honesty compels me to admit that it was the subject of bitter attack because of this disparity in promotion, nevertheless it is difficult to say how we could have avoided it in those early years and, in any case, I do not remember a single incident in which the decision of the board was taken other than by unanimity. The presence on the board of Wilbur Carr and of Edward Norton, both of them deeply interested in the consular service, would seem to be a sufficient guaranty that they were adequately protected. Critics of the board's administration labeled us a "Harvard clique," this in spite of the fact that although Joe Grew came from Harvard, Butler Wright came from Princeton, Wilbur Carr and Edward Norton from no university, and I from Yale.

The work on the board justified all the apprehension that I had entertained in regard to it. I hated dealing with my friends ; I found that after a man is given a post he wants or a promotion, he treats it as a matter of course. This is a human failing to regard all good things as nothing less than one's just deserts. At the same time there are many others who can't get the post or promotion that they want, and they become enemies.

Human beings are constructed on different patterns. Howland Shaw, one of the most competent men in our Service, is now Chief of the Personnel Section. He sought this post, he finds it deeply interesting and wants to continue in it. I can only say that I never laid down any work with greater enthusiasm when the time came to do it. In my entire life in the diplomatic service it is the only work which I have undertaken which was repugnant to me in anticipation and in practice.

Mr. Coolidge was to enter on his second term as President of the United States on March 4, 1925. A few days before, a rumor went around the Department that Mr. Hughes intended to resign as Secretary of State and return to private life on that date. I was deeply distressed, so deeply that I determined to urge the Secretary to alter his decision, futile though I was persuaded it would be to attempt to change his mind. I urged upon him that the Foreign Service had just been initiated, that he had taken a deep interest in it and that I was very much afraid that the entry of a new Secretary of State would weaken the influence of the new Personnel Board and that decisions would be taken by the Secretary on a political basis.

Mr. Hughes was charming ; he explained that he had just passed his sixtieth birthday, that he had given a great number of years of his life to public service, that he had a family to provide for and that he must go into private life to make this provision. Obviously there was nothing further for me to say in the face of such reasoning.

On the eve of his departure, Mr. Hughes made a speech at a luncheon of Foreign Service officers. Amid the thousands of speeches to which I have been subjected, this is one of the few that stands out vividly. The Secretary spoke of his faith in the Service and his deep interest in it. He was convinced that we were building something that would endure and would prove of genuine and lasting benefit to the nation. He gave us two points of advice ; the first related to health. He said that men who could keep their health after fifty years of age were the men who made the great records. Thousands of promising men had ruined their health by that time, and it was the survivors among this promising group that earned the great names. His second piece of advice related to the type of work that one undertook. He warned us against the search for titles, the desire to assume a title as sort of a feather in the cap.

"The satisfaction of getting a job," he said, "lasts only for two or three days, then you begin to be occupied by its worries and by its responsibilities. Unless the nature of the work is such that you can be profoundly interested in it, the title of the job itself will be of less than no satisfaction. The only enduring thing is the nature of the work itself."

CHAPTER XIII

The successor to Mr. Hughes was the most striking contrast to him that one could imagine. Mr. Frank Kellogg left the Embassy at London to become Secretary of State; he had served a term in the Senate before becoming Ambassador. Mr. Kellogg had been a partner in one of the most powerful law firms of the Middle West, in St. Paul. He had made his first reputation in the time of Mr. Theodore Roosevelt as a "trust-buster." He was raised on a farm, and had worked extremely hard physically in his youth. To this he attributed his health and his ability to continue active work at an advanced age. His rugged gnarled hands were the result of farm labor. His character endeared him to us quickly. A short figure he was, with snow-white hair, a nervous trembling of the hands, a powerful thick-set body and a clean-shaven vigorous face. He had a hasty and explosive temper but he bore no grudges.

His temper would blaze without regard to the type of person he was talking to, or to that person's position. He used to get to his office about a quarter to nine in the morning. On his desk was a sort of keyboard with buttons which summoned the various officers of the Department. If Mr. Kellogg had read something irritating in the paper before he reached his office he would strike the keyboard like a piano concert-master, all fingers at once, and summon everybody he could think of. As we entered his room one after the other we were greeted with a storm of rage. An immediate council was held, Mr. Kellogg still sputtering, and out of that conference would come a calm and reasoned decision on the part of the Secretary of State. I never understood how it worked, but it seemed to.

In my first interview with him I told him the type of work I was doing and what it involved. I said that I was of no particular use to the correspondents if I always played safe and held off for advice. The element of time in news is so important that in many cases I had to give snap judgment and verify it subsequently. I told him that he had to expect that I would make some dreadful mistake about once a month but that I thought the advantages of this system would outweigh the occasional mistakes.

Mr. Kellogg seemed to agree, and said something like this : "All right, we will follow that procedure. When you make a mistake I will probably blow your head off but I will back you up."

He followed this literally ; he certainly did explode when things went wrong but, as he promised, he would back me to the hilt with anyone, including the President of the United States. I remember in this connection one time when he rang me about midnight. He had just learned of an article that was coming out in the morning paper and demanded, blasphemously, whether I had been the source. I said I had. He called me every name in his very considerable vocabulary and then stated, "Now don't worry, I will see the President the first thing in the morning," and he did.

Mr. Kellogg was an ardent golf player and those of us in the Department who knew the game found ourselves subject to call at any moment when the Secretary could get free. At the end of the game he loved his one whiskey and soda and the conversation which followed. Once on this sort of an occasion he told us all that the happiest time of his life had been when he was Ambassador to Great Britain ; he had loved his work and had had a staff all of whom were golf players. He thought when he gave up being Secretary of State he would ask the President to send him back to England.

Mrs. Kellogg was present. She was a woman of extraordinary charm and graciousness ; we were all fond of her. When she heard her husband make this remark she raised her eyebrows and said, "All right, Frank, if that is what you want to do, but you will have to divorce me first and marry some young strong woman because I will not go through it again."

President Coolidge's personality is so well known to the American public through countless stories and anecdotes that it seems superfluous to add to the chronicle. I had numerous interviews with him, however, and one of them fits in so well with the conception usually held of the President, that I shall describe it. The Secretary of State had sent me to see the President about a statement that he was anxious to make to the press. He felt that the statement would do away with a good deal of resentment which the French entertained because of our attitude in respect to the war debt, if I remember rightly. When I entered the Oval Room at the White House, Mr. Coolidge was smoking a cigar and looking out the window. I stood there. When he continued to smoke his cigar and look out the window, I sat down. I waited for him to speak. He didn't. Whereupon I stated my case and read the statement.

Without removing the cigar or looking elsewhere than out the window, the President said, "No, I don't want to please the French."

I got up, bowed, said, "Very well, Mr. President, good day, sir."

I got my hand on the door when the President's dry voice said, "What's the hurry ?   Come back here."

I did, and sat down.

His voice went on, "State the case again."

I did so to the best of my ability, putting in such additional arguments as I could think of.   There was silence from the President, he still smoked his cigar and looked out the window. I became uneasy and started for the door again.

The President remarked, "I don't see why you are in such a hurry.   Sit down."

This time I kept silent and after a considerable interval, probably longer to me than it really was, he remarked, "All right, have it your own way."   This time I got out the door successfully.

Mr. Coolidge could be loquacious on occasion but those occasions were seldom social ; I think his taciturnity may have been due to shyness and boredom rather than to an underlying habit of mind.   I have heard him genuinely eloquent when really stirred.   Some years later I had my last glimpse of Mr. Coolidge in a public act.   A newsreel in Geneva was showing his departure from Washington when Mr. Hoover was entering the presidency.   The reel showed the back platform of the train banked in flowers, Mr. and Mrs. Coolidge standing there.

The crowd was yelling and cheering and you could hear the cries, "Speech, Mr. President ; say something, Mr. President."

Mr. Coolidge leaned over into the crowd, took a megaphone from the hands of one of the audience, put it to his lips and his nasal New England voice came out, "Good-by."

I have tried to sketch a general picture of the type of work that the Chief of Current Information finds among his duties. Perhaps it would be of interest if I related one or two of the episodes in more detail.

In the first year of my work the American arbitration of the Tacna-Arica dispute took place. The dispute was one which arose out of the war between Chile and Peru, 1879–1883. It was complicated by the claim of Bolivia for a corridor to the sea and direct access to ships for its exports. Numerous attempts had been made to settle the sovereignty of this arid strip of land but all of them had been unsuccessful. The dispute had been referred to our Secretary of State for a decision. He sent General Pershing with a numerous staff to the area, held plebiscites to determine the wishes of the inhabitants and on the basis of this material issued his award. Obviously, while the studies were being made the result of the award was guarded in the deepest secrecy.

The correspondents made repeated efforts for weeks preceding the issue of the award to get some kind of an indication as to its nature. Especially for the press services, that is, the Associated Press, United Press, and International News Syndicate, all of whom had clients in Latin America, the story was of supreme importance and rivalry was heated. Each hoped to beat the other by several minutes in getting out the news on the streets of South American cities.

I had arranged that I would read a summary of the award at four o'clock in my office and I laid down the rule that no correspondent should leave my room until I had finished reading. After that they could break their necks getting to the telephone. At four o'clock I duly read the summary to a packed room and

watched the stampede which followed my last words.   What
was my surprise to learn an hour later that the Associated Press
had beaten the others by five minutes and that their papers in
South America had appeared on the streets in extras, before the
others.   I was full of curiosity to ascertain how this had been
done and McDermott, on inquiry, was able to satisfy it.

At that time the Associated Press maintained two correspondents attached to the State Department, Kirk Simpson and
Stephen Early, the latter now Private Secretary to President
Roosevelt.   These two men had arranged a finger code between them.   Kirk Simpson stood at the open door with his
hands behind his back.   Releasing one finger meant Peru had
won, two fingers meant Chile had won, three fingers meant
that the award had not been decisive for one or the other, et
cetera.   Steve Early sat at a telephone in the next room, having
already opened the connection with his office ; as soon as the
signal was given from Kirk he began to talk and dictated his
message as I read the summary.

Of course it is highly important to those in charge at the
State Department that news be presented in a way to win
sympathy among the American people for acts which might be
contemplated or already performed.   It is often important also
to create a type of atmosphere in public thinking which may be
favorable to contemplated action.

Sometimes, however, attempts to influence public opinion
come home to roost in the most startling manner.   Robert
Olds was Under Secretary during Mr. Kellogg's incumbency.
Olds called me into his office one day, being somewhat new
at his task, and asked me whether he could talk with the pressmen in such a way as would not reveal the source of the infor-

mation but would furnish them with material to create the atmosphere desired. Specifically, he was troubled about the situation in Mexico ; the Administration felt that it had to take a firm stand for the protection of certain American interests. Olds wanted the American people somehow to be brought to the realization that the firmness of the contemplated action was justified, that there was no other means of dealing with the highly radical, perhaps communistic, elements in the Mexican Government.

I told Mr. Olds that whether he could get stories printed or not depended on the news value, that he would have to give facts on which a story could be built up, since the correspondents were not encouraged to write editorials. Furthermore, I added that there was always some risk involved that the source might ultimately be revealed and that this risk was increased geometrically by the number of men you took into your confidence. I suggested that if he wanted to give such a talk he confine it to the representatives of the four big press associations. Accordingly I invited the four of them in and Mr. Olds talked, vigorously and startlingly. He revealed a number of episodes which had taken place in Mexico tending to show great danger of a Communist seizure of power.

I was uneasy while this was going on. The episodes were so startling that I could not imagine what the results would be of such disclosure. Barely had I reached my house when Kirk Simpson called me on the telephone.

He said, "I suppose you realize that this is a startling story, and to let you realize it I am going to read you my first paragraph." The story started as follows : "The specter of Communism stalks abroad in Mexico." It went on to say that apprehension of this condition was wide-spread in Washington in most authoritative circles and then cited the episodes. Kirk said, "I want you to think carefully and tell me if that is a fair picture of what he said."

I replied that it was, that the statement given by Mr. Olds clearly justified this story. I then rang Mr. Olds and told him that the story of the Associated Press was dangerous but accurate from what he had said. He replied to let it stand.

The next two days were a storm. All over the United States violent criticism of the Administration broke out ; the Administration was building up hatred of Mexico for a war with that country, we were about to launch an invasion, we were about to send our soldiers to rescue oil investments. The storm was of such dimensions that it shook the Administration. Secretary Kellogg telephoned Mr. Frank Noyes, president of the Associated Press, and stated that the story was unjustified and outrageous. Mr. Noyes demanded an interview, there were present at the interview Secretary Kellogg, Mr. Noyes, Mr. Olds, Mr. Simpson and myself. Mr. Noyes said that Simpson had reported to him just what had been said by Mr. Olds and that he felt the story was well written under the circumstances and completely justified.

The Secretary denied that it was justified from the story which Olds had given, then he turned to me and said, "Hugh, you heard this. What do you say ?"

I was forced to reply that Kirk had read the message to me over the telephone and that I felt it completely justified, from the story that Mr. Olds had given. This was one of the times when the Secretary did as he promised, blew my head off and then justified me to the President.

We fell under another evil time with the press, although this time there was no one episode that brought it about. One of the perennial difficulties in Nicaragua was taking place — a revolution was on. The question arose of which government we should recognize, considerable looting took place, we landed marines both in Managua and on the north coast. This time, however, the people and the press of the United States were in a very different frame of mind from that which prevailed when Mr. Knox was Secretary of State. In the old days of "dollar diplomacy" such episodes were taken lightly ; in 1926 we had a radically different point of view as to armed interference with our neighbors. The press was in a fury, complaints poured in from all sides. It took weeks of the most careful work before the clamor aroused by these episodes had died away.

The correspondents are incalculable in some respects ; I could never be sure of what was "hot news" and what fell into the category of news that could be handled at leisure. General Dawes had gone abroad as American representative to work out with the French, British and Belgians the plan of German reparations which became known as the "Dawes Plan." General Dawes had cabled from Paris that the plan was to be initialed and would be put on the cable immediately thereafter. He warned us that it was long, some thousands of words, and it would begin to arrive about two A. M. I marshaled my entire force to get this off the wire, to have it mimeographed, and distributed with the utmost possible speed. The first sheets began to come in about two-fifteen.

In order to save the time of the correspondents, while mimeographing was going on I posted the first sheet in the outer office.

From time to time I rushed out with additional sheets. About four o'clock I paused to notice that a number of the pressmen were sitting with their hands in their laps.

I said, "Good Lord, do I work here all night to give you this stuff in a hurry when you haven't any interest in it ?"

One of them replied, "Oh, we are waiting until you are free to tell us about it."

Whereupon I had to assemble the sheets myself, read them with care, master their meaning, and then go out and lecture to the correspondents. They immediately departed to write their stories.

In the summer of 1926 my wife and I decided that since we were in the United States we would undertake an American experience of which we had often read but which we had thus far been unable, through our absence, to share — we would visit Newport. We found rents of course staggeringly expensive, but we finally took a small house behind the enormous structure of Mr. Perry Belmont ; the house was so small that I imagine it had been built for the coachman. In any case it had charm, was near the beach, and we had a most delightful summer. I could only get there for week-ends, but I found that I was sharing this experience with the great majority of the male population of Newport, the men all flocked in on Saturday mornings and left on Sunday nights.

Newport was totally unlike any foreign resort, there was a formality about entertaining, an organization of amusements which would be unknown in Europe. I got a little bored with continuous conversation about the stock market of which I unfortunately knew less than nothing but, on the whole, was content to have gone through this experience as characteristic of one phase of America as an oil field in Oklahoma, or a professional baseball game is of other phases.

As we drove through the streets of Washington Kate always used to ask me to turn up a street called Woodland Drive.   On one side of it, nearly opposite Senator Wadsworth's house, was a white structure of French appearance with a terrace and ancient oaks.   If the family were away we used to stop while Kate admired it and, I must confess, even peer in the windows when it was locked up.   It was during that summer in Newport that I suddenly read that the house was to be sold.   I telephoned to Kate, who immediately boarded a train for Washington and we purchased the place within twenty-four hours.   I took out a mortgage on the land and paid it off in the next three or four years, taking advantage of the enormous extra dividends that came from all holdings during that fabulous period. When I look at the house now it gives me genuine comfort. It is so much more satisfactory still to hold something tangible and visible from that fantastic financial experience, something which is not represented only by pieces of paper of considerably shrunken value.

In writing of Japan I have described the happy state of our relations at the end of 1923.   A relatively few months later those relations were strained, suddenly and violently, through a diplomatic episode which remains still in some degree inexplicable.   All of us who had lived from time to time in Washington knew and esteemed Mr. Hanihara, the Japanese Ambassador at that period.   "Hani," as we all called him, had been Secretary of Embassy in Washington at various stages of his career and had mingled freely with all circles in Washington.

He was animated by a genuine affection for the United States, he loved the capital, he loved his friends, he loved our way of life.   A new immigration act was in the process of debate before Congress and at the instigation of the representatives from California an amendment was offered to close immigration completely to the nationals of races that were not eligible for citizenship.

Because of the existing laws respecting naturalization and immigration from China, this amendment, while not so stated, was aimed exclusively at Japanese immigration.   Japanese immigration at that period was limited by unilateral act of the Japanese under an agreement embodied in a series of letters exchanged between Washington and Tokyo in 1907–1908. The understanding attained at the time was known as the "Gentlemen's Agreement."   Japan undertook on its own initiative to restrict the immigration of its nationals into the United States, hence the procedure contained nothing derogatory to the self-respect and pride of the Japanese nation.

The Japanese public and Government were much upset about the possibility of legislation which in their eyes was not only discriminatory in that it was aimed at Japan alone, but was of a nature to offend their susceptibilities.   The issue was the more clear-cut in that only a handful of Japanese were arriving each year under the "Gentlemen's Agreement" and for practical purposes that agreement had solved the difficulty.   After numerous conversations with the Secretary of State and Mr. John MacMurray, at that time Chief of the Far Eastern Division, Hanihara wrote to Mr. Hughes a considered argument of the Japanese point of view setting forth the earnest desire of the Japanese Government that the exclusion be not incorporated in the act of Congress. Mr. Hughes forwarded the document to the Senate Foreign Relations Committee which was sitting in hearings on the act. The communication of Hanihara dated April 10, 1924, terminated in a paragraph worded as follows:

Relying upon the confidence you have been good enough to show me at all times, I have stated or rather repeated all this to you very candidly and in a most friendly spirit, for I realize, as I believe you do, the grave consequences which the enactment of the measure retaining that particular provision would inevitably bring upon the otherwise happy and mutually advantageous relations between our two countries.

The press seized upon the words "grave consequences," tore them from their context, charged that Japan was threatening the United States and endeavoring by this threat to interfere in the course of domestic legislation. By a most unhappy coincidence the publicity broke on the very day of the consideration of the bill in the Senate, and such administration supporters as Moses, Lodge, Reed, Pepper and Willis stated that they were constrained to sustain the exclusion act because of this "threat." The act went into effect and Hanihara was recalled. The Japanese press, the Japanese public, the Japanese Government were exceedingly bitter about the whole matter, and the genuine regret which was expressed by the President of the United States and the Secretary of State could do little to mitigate the hostility that was inflamed.

The whole episode was one of the most unnecessary and lamentable that I have encountered in diplomacy. It suffices alone to read the paragraph which I have quoted to see that no threat was intended. If anyone were not convinced by this one paragraph and cared to read the entire note (*Foreign Rela-*

tions of the United States, 1924, Volume II, Page 369) he could not but be persuaded that the tone of the note was manly and friendly and that it did nothing further than deplore what the Japanese Government considered an unnecessary lessening of those friendly sentiments which had existed traditionally between the two nations.

I have never been able to understand why such competent lawyers as the senators whom I have cited above were able to regard this note as a "veiled threat." Had they not been lawyers one would assume that they had not read the note but had taken their position on the press reports; I am told, however, that no member of the legal profession would take position without thorough study of the documents.

The relations between Japan and the United States went from bad to worse. The press of each country resented the attacks of the press in the other and in that resentment went a little further toward provocation each time. The whole thing appeared unnecessary and the time had come for positive effort to be made to undo what had been done by Hanihara perhaps carelessly, and by the Senate of the United States perhaps frivolously.

A new Japanese Ambassador, Matsudaira, was about to land in San Francisco. I went to Secretary Hughes and told him I felt that the arrival of Matsudaira offered a heaven-sent opportunity to get rid of the recrimination between the press of the two countries. I pointed out that Matsudaira came of one of the most distinguished families of Japan, that his wife was of the Nabeshima family, that her father had been a Daimio, that Japan was sending us her most exalted subjects and that their arrival might give an opportunity for the Secretary to tell the press that there was nothing between Japan and ourselves but a state of mind, that all we needed was calm on both sides of the Pacific and that there was nothing to imperil our friendship. I realized that the correspondents could not be expected to write editorials and, therefore, urged the Secretary to issue a warm statement of welcome to Mr. and Mrs. Matsudaira and at the same time to preach the gospel to the correspondents.

I found Mr. Hughes in one of the rare periods in which he was discouraged. He said that it did not matter what one said to the press, they preferred to be critical and antagonistic to foreign nations, that he doubted whether such a move would prevail ; nevertheless he was willing to try it, and bade me prepare a statement about the arrival of the new Ambassador. He told me to select a group of correspondents and that he would talk to them. I followed his instructions and when the correspondents came into the Secretary's office every trace of Mr. Hughes' discouragement had gone. He spoke to them like a prophet and so deeply did he persuade them that every man in the room went out not only to give an enthusiastic reception to Matsudaira but to point out to the American people "that there was nothing between Japan and ourselves but a state of mind."

This episode caused one of the most extraordinary reversals of public opinion that I have ever seen. All over the country editors recognized the reasonableness of the Secretary's position, all over the country editorials appeared calling on the press to make a thorough examination of the subject and pointing out that there was nothing tangible and difficult which stood in the way of better relations with Japan. Such a thing cannot be done often and it can be done only when there is no basis for the existing hostility ; if the hostility is based on something more tangible than irritation such an attempt would be futile. It is safe to say that until the autumn of 1931 — the date of the Manchukuo incident — relations between Japan and the United States were not only correct after this episode but were even cordial.

One further incident occurred during this period which was related to my stay in Japan. His Imperial Highness Prince Chichihu returned to Tokyo by way of the United States after a period of study at Oxford. Since I had served as Counselor at Tokyo the Secretary of State designated me to meet Prince Chichihu at New York, bring him to Washington on an official visit, and then escort him to San Francisco for his departure. The visit and trip were of genuine interest. Prince Chichihu had a voracious appetite for knowledge and I was forced to do a considerable amount of study and investigation in order to keep one lap ahead.

For example, we visited the Lincoln Memorial in Washington and in the course of looking at that lovely piece of architecture I read to the Prince certain words of Lincoln's which are engraved on the frieze. That night we took a special train to Chicago. As the train was pulling out of the station the Prince took a suitcase from the table, turned it upside down on the floor and emptied out more than a score of books on Lincoln which he had had purchased that afternoon.

He then said to me in his precise English, "Those two quotations on the monument, what were they ?"

I took a sudden guess and replied, "*The Gettysburg Address and The Second Inaugural Address.*"

"Find them," said the Prince. I looked into the books and,

sure enough, my guess was verified ; I found them where I had told him.

We had, of course, taken every precaution to have His Highness securely guarded during his expedition through the United States.   A number of secret service men from the State Department and the White House accompanied the Prince on the special train, elaborate precautions were taken in each city where we stopped to have the local police collaborate in this protection.   When the train was approaching Chicago I spoke to the detective in charge and asked him what the plans were, since we were intending to spend three or four hours in that city.   The detective replied that the Chicago police had arranged to clear the platform.   Nobody was to be there when we got out but ourselves, the mayor of the city, the Japanese Consul, and two or three Chicago detectives.   We were then to proceed from the gate through a cordon of police to the motor cars waiting at the door of the station.

The train pulled in, the Prince descended, and I introduced him and his staff to the mayor.   We turned and strolled up the platform.   At the gate we were asked to pose for photographs and the bulbs flashed in front of us.   We then continued our walk through the cordon of police and boarded the motor cars. Nothing could have been more thoroughly and apparently safe.

However, when I returned to Washington and the Prince was safely aboard his ship for Tokyo, I opened an envelope one day which appeared in my mail ; the envelope contained nothing but a photograph — a photograph of the group taken at the station in Chicago.   In the front row were the Prince, his gentleman in attendance, the mayor and myself.   In the back row were perhaps a dozen secret-service men.   A cross in ink indicated a large man in the back row whose face was unknown and on the bottom of the card was printed the following : "Tell the man who is marked by the X that we see he had an opportunity to do his duty and that he failed. We will not forget him."

I hurried to the secret-service man in the State Department ; the face was unknown to him. We went to the White House ; it was unknown there. We sent the picture to the police of Chicago ; they had never seen the face before. I don't know to this day what happened, but certainly in spite of all our precautions an unauthorized man had been within a yard of the Prince.

Hugh Gibson had been serving for several years as Minister to Switzerland. He came back to Washington frequently in connection with his work on what was known as the "Preparatory Commission on Disarmament" then sitting from time to time in the League of Nations at Geneva. Toward the end of 1926 or the beginning of 1927, he came into my office one day and confided to me that he was to go to Brussels as Ambassador, that he had been asked by Secretary Kellogg his advice as to who should go as Minister to Switzerland and that he intended to recommend me for the post if I was in accord. I don't suppose that I need to assert that I was immediately and enthusiastically in accord. Not only had I known and loved Switzerland but the work in the League of Nations for an American representative was becoming more and more interesting.

The appointment did not go through without considerable difficulty ; as the news got about that Gibson was leaving there were many applicants for the task. Happily for me, however, the united efforts of Hugh and Joe Grew, added to what I hope was the Secretary's own disposition, led the latter to urge the President to appoint me. Mr. Coolidge did so.

The announcement was made in the press on the same day that the nominations of Leland Harrison to Sweden and of Butler Wright to Budapest were also made. This was the first time that three Service men had been given posts at the same time and few Service men had ever been given posts of such desirability. It was a big story in the press and telegrams of congratulation and messages of all kinds poured in. I felt feverish that afternoon and went home ; by evening I had a high temperature and by midnight the doctor had diagnosed a case of scarlet fever.

I had never before been delirious and the impression of delirium even now is deeply implanted in my memory. I can remember taking part in the pageantry of a crusade, I can remember being an officer on Sir Henry Morgan's ship when he looted a gold-laden Spanish galleon, I can remember floating gently out of the window to call on the Secretary of State to thank him for my appointment. The disease is beastly, there is something obscene about it, but the memories of delirium are rich in color. Hence I was delayed in my departure and was able to sail only in the month of May, 1927.

PART II

CHAPTER I

Ten years in Switzerland. The years were so full of events, so packed with incident, that it is going to be difficult to select my material. The events in which I participated, watched or recorded, were the epitome of history for those years — if not of the world, certainly of Europe. The scope of events was so vast that I have had to approach my task with a definite plan of limitation. I cannot undertake the history of Europe for ten years, much less the history of the world, hence I am driven to report only some of the things I saw myself, some of the meetings at Geneva where the delegates took their positions, and took them for reasons which I could not hope to evaluate in their entirety.

I have another conclusion to state. I have read so many diaries and memoirs written after the fact, which show the writer's foresight and perspicacity, that I shall attempt to give an honest picture of the bewilderment, perplexities and uncertainties that face a man in the midst of great events, I shall try to state how I felt at the time. At the risk of criticism for lack of penetration, I shall state my contemporary convictions, regardless of whether subsequent developments have shown them unfounded. Such comment as I may make in the light of later developments I shall characterize clearly as more matured judgment.

Sir Nevile Henderson, the last British Ambassador in Berlin, has published a book *The Failure of a Mission* which is a model in this respect ; it is one of the few patently honest reports. It pictures a mind of unusual acuteness, but nevertheless finite, faced by overwhelming events. It shows the hesitation and doubt, the grinding uncertainty that besets the human judgment in the face of gigantic decisions influenced by a multitude of factors impossible to assess with mathematical exactitude. Few indeed are those who penetrate the future with certainty, who see their objectives clearly illuminated by a beam of light piercing the obscurity of doubt. I say that such men are few indeed, so few that I have never met them outside the pages of their own account of history. I don't want to labor this point unduly, but it does seem pertinent in this connection to cite the case of Lincoln.

Recent studies, particularly Carl Sandburg's *Abraham Lincoln : The War Years*, seem to bring out vividly the fact that Lincoln was great beyond his contemporaries because he clung with tenacity to a simple thesis, "The Union must be preserved." He did not know how, he was beset by perplexity and doubt as to method, he saw no blazing revelation of the path to be followed, he merely applied every decision to the touchstone of his article of faith : Would the decision help to preserve the Union or not ? If not, it was discarded, if so, it was adopted. He made no claim to superior penetration and foresight.

One other observation about this chronicle of mine. I have determined that it shall be a tale of personal experience, hence I make no apology for the introduction of personalities and of my own episodes and reflections. This is to be an account of one period of one man's life ; that period included a share in some great events, but it included as well a number of events of no importance to others but perhaps of a measure of interest, and often of much greater satisfaction than the more important matters.

Every man, if he is fortunate, has lived through one stage of his life when everything is good, when there is nothing in life which he would wish otherwise.   A recognition that I was passing through such a phase of my life swept over me as I sailed for Europe.   I had been selected as Minister to a post of singular interest, charm, and importance.   At the age of forty-two I was Chief of Mission and would work in the future under my own name and responsibility.   I had won the position on service record ; I had never sought to utilize political influence for preferment, indeed, I had none that might have been used.   I was going back to a land that Kate and I held in deep affection, a land full of old friends and old memories. The United States was prosperous as never before, but each year of its prosperity made me the more ready to go abroad again, to live again in a simpler life, in a less exacting social measurement, and above all to consort with people less interested in the stock market and prohibition.   It was in a happy mood of anticipation that I watched the gray old city of Cherbourg reveal itself in the morning mist.

My wife went on by train, our small son and I by motor. The boy had been upset by the thought of leaving his school and friends in Washington, he was not much impressed by my title of Minister, he feared I would have to do too much preaching.   We pulled up the first night at the Hotel Normandie in Trouville, and I, gladdened at the prospect of French cooking again, ordered dinner with particular care.   Among other dishes I remember we had *haricots verts*, served as they do in France, heated over a spirit lamp with butter and ground pepper added. My son was already a bit of a gourmet, and when he tasted the beans he remarked, "You know, Dad, I think there is something to this Europe that you like so much, I think I am going to like it."   It was the first word of approval from him since we had left the United States.

. We drove in leisurely fashion over southeastern France, stayed a night in Dijon where I heard *Martha* given in the open air in the public square, on through the foothills of the Jura and into Switzerland.   It was the month of May, the countryside at its loveliest, fruit blossoms and the delicate new green of springtime.   Switzerland itself was a delight, the compact and neat little houses, boxes of flowers gleaming at every window, cows in fields patterned in flowers.   It was all as I had remembered it, but with a difference.   In the six years of my absence peace had come back to these lands.   The signs of war had disappeared and the world looked again as it had when I was a boy.   Cresting a rise above Neuchâtel, the range of the Bernese Oberland broke into view, pink in the setting sun, the Jungfrau, Mönch, Eiger cut the horizon with their lofty snowy peaks.   Another hour and we had entered Berne.

Returning to that city was doubly like returning home because of the friendly faces around me.   Fred Dolbeare was Secretary of the Legation.   One of my closest friends, he had arranged for my reception by the President and Federal Councillor in charge of Foreign Affairs the very day after my arrival.   These two gentlemen, Schulthess and Motta, had been the men I was most intimately associated with in the last two years of war, the former in the Department of Public Economy, the latter in the Foreign Office.   Barely had we terminated the formal exchange of speeches when the conversation became that of old friends, full of reminiscence and affectionate family inquiry.

Schulthess is from Zürich, his French is fluent, his wife is a Frenchwoman, but the intonation has that harshness of the Germanic Swiss. A tremendous worker, fierce in the defense of what he believes, he is staunch and dependable, but a formidable opponent. Motta was from the Ticino, Italian Switzerland. Supple and friendly, an impassioned patriot, and dominated by the thought of Swiss neutrality in all his public acts. One of the most accomplished linguists I have met, he not only spoke Italian, French, German and Swiss German, but could speak publicly and eloquently in any one of the tongues.

He spoke for Switzerland as Chief of the Foreign Office for more than a score of years and attained a weight and authority in European councils out of all proportion to the influence of his country. Shrewd and cautious in spite of his warmth of manner, he held the delicate position of Switzerland in unassailable integrity through the last dangerous years of his life. When he died a few months ago, Switzerland and Europe lost one of the few figures in public life who were actuated by principle and deep religious conviction.

The Chief of the Political Department, who holds the position of our Under Secretary of State, was Paul Dinichert; when I left the country in 1919 he was already in office. We had been good friends in the past, and continued so. When I came to Berlin years later as Ambassador, Dinichert was Swiss Minister there, so we were able again to take up our association. The thought comes to me, as I write this, that amid all the difficulties and drawbacks of life in the Foreign Service, there is one consolation on which you can count with certainty. After a few years of service, wherever you may be sent you find old friends and acquaintances among the representatives of other nations, so that it is rare that you enter a new post without friends already at hand.

When I mention Switzerland to most of my American friends, certain images arise in their minds. They suddenly remember the sight of the Dent du Midi from the hotel at Vevey, they remember the stupendous outline of the Jungfrau at Interlaken ; or their thoughts turn to the times when they climbed the Matterhorn or tore down the slopes of the Männlichen on skis. The people they think of in Switzerland are hotel keepers or sturdy guides. In other words, the conception of my friends is the travel-bureau poster of Switzerland, the scene for a happy vacation, a land given over to the tourist and his whims, a land in which the Swiss people do not count except as they contribute to the comfort or amusement of the traveler. I don't condemn this conception. This is what my friends were looking for when they went to Switzerland and this is what they found, abundantly and pleasantly. It remains the fact, however, that this is but a small portion of Switzerland and a portion which is perhaps the least interesting to a man who comes to know that land.

The Swiss people are far from homogeneous in race and language ; there is singularly little outward resemblance between the Italian-speaking inhabitant of Ticino, the French-speaking inhabitant of Geneva, and the German-speaking inhabitant of St. Gallen. I use the word "German-speaking" somewhat loosely. The Swiss do not speak German in the sense of speaking a tongue which is comprehensible to the inhabitants of Germany. They speak a variation of the Germanic tongue, slight differences exist in the pronunciation as between the people of Basle and Zürich, for example, but in general the Swiss German is understood throughout the Germanic cantons. But this language is a spoken tongue only. The child studies German and learns to read and write it ; in the majority of cases, however, he speaks "Hoch Deutsch" as a foreign tongue. In the last couple of years the Confederation has admitted the language known as Romansch as a fourth official language of the nation. This tongue is spoken by the inhabitants of the mountain districts of the Engadine and is derived from a Latin source.

There are other points of disparity within this nation. The Swiss peasant is a sturdy conservative, he can be counted on to vote "no" to practically any petition or referendum submitted to him. A knowledge of this fact is of no small importance to the politician who is framing the question to be submitted to the people. The industrial worker in the big cities tends, of course, to a more socialistic, international outlook on life. The Swiss Government has always extended a high degree of assistance and protection to the agricultural element. This policy was determined not alone by recognition of the difficulty and toil involved in reaping a livelihood from high mountain slopes and rocky land, but also because of the political conception that the peasant class must be maintained as a conservative balance against what would become an overwhelmingly socialist nation were the peasants to migrate to the cities.

With all these disparities and with such apparently disruptive factors, the Swiss people have achieved a national unity of purpose and culture far beyond that of many peoples thoroughly homogeneous in race and language. Common ideals are taught in the schools, common ideals are pursued in the relation between parents and children, common ideals animate each citizen in his obligation to his state and in his faith in a democratic system.

Democracy in Switzerland goes back into the dim Middle Ages. When feudalism prevailed over the whole of Europe the peasant woodsmen of Uri, Unterwalden and Schwyz as well as sections of Lucerne were engaged in forming a coalition to rid themselves of alien overlords. The first formal agreement was made between the three forest cantons in 1291 and this agreement became the nucleus around which the Swiss Confederation coalesced. Obviously the Government has become more complex in modern life, but in some of these forest cantons the citizenry makes its decisions and governs its lands in exactly the same form that the citizens of the first three cantons used when they took their oath of brotherhood. The institution is the most perfect survival of pure democracy and is known as the Landesgemeinde.

I have attended several Landesgemeinde in different remote villages. The citizens, in their Sunday clothes, assemble at the local capital. A holiday spirit prevails, bands playing, local orchestras showing their prowess. The voting male population of the canton forms in ceremonial procession in the capital's square and marches to the pavilion, an open space usually just on the outskirts of town. Here the cantonal authorities make their report. Each voter has the right to speak, criticize, or suggest, and he makes use of the right.

I found the Landesgemeinde exceedingly businesslike proceedings, there was very little clap-trap, there was next to no emotional appeal in speeches, there was hard-headed and stubborn argument on expenditure and the cantonal treasurer was often hard put to it to justify his act. Voting is done by a show of hands. I understand that when and if a vote is exceptionally close a separation of the voters is made for counting purposes, but I never happened to see it. Proceedings close by the singing of the cantonal hymn and the *Federal Anthem*. A Landesgemeinde is not only picturesque, it is a moving sight to a man with faith in democracy, it is the final proof — if proof were needed — that a democratic institution can exist for centuries and remain orderly, effective, businesslike and honest.

The Swiss Government is modeled in many respects upon the Constitution of the United States. The separate cantons retain those attributes of sovereignty which are not specifically alienated to the Federation. There is an Upper House and a Lower House, there are Federal courts for intercantonal matters. Resemblance ceases, however, when we come to the attributes and functioning of the Executive. Executive power lies in a Federal Council of nine members. Members of the Council are elected by the Federal Assembly for a period of seven years, but in fact are nearly always re-elected on good behavior. Each member of the Council assumes charge of one specific branch of government ; there is a Councillor in charge of public economy, of finance, railroads, foreign affairs, and so forth. The President of the Confederation is merely the presiding officer of the Council ; each one assumes the Presidency in rotation for a one year period, he has no power beyond that of his colleagues. The permanency of office gives to the members of the Federal Council unusual competence in the administration of their bureaus ; it also gives them high prestige in parliamentary debate.

The members of the Council, while not voting members of Parliament, nevertheless have access to both Houses and spend a large amount of their time while Parliament is in session in attending and participating in debate. The mastery that they have of their subjects gives them formidable power in persuading Parliament as to legislative necessities. Parliament so far recognizes the competence of the Federal Council that a member of Parliament frequently introduces a resolution demanding the accomplishment of a certain objective and instructing the Federal Council to present a bill for this purpose.

There is little or no glamour about public office in Switzerland ; public duty is merely another form of business. Every peasant in the nation, if he so desires, has access to the Councillors. On market days in Berne a number of farm wagons were lined up outside the Federal Palace after market was over ; their owners had entered the Palace to issue complaint in person about their troubles to the Federal Councillors. They work exceedingly hard, their salary is something like twenty-seven thousand francs a year, and they live in the same simplicity as the ordinary citizens of Berne.

In the many years that I spent in that land I have never seen financial scandal touch the high officers of the country and, indeed, it was something very rare even among the lesser politicians. The Swiss have achieved an applied democracy which remains, as the word indicates, simple, direct, and of universal participation. The initiative and the referendum are part of the legislative system and frequently applied. Voting occurs on Sundays, the booth is usually the local café, where the men come on Sundays in any case after their shooting practice, which represents their Sunday sport. The percentage of voters participating in even small affairs like referenda is exceptionally high. The percentage of votes cast in Switzerland is far above the percentage of either England, France, or ourselves.

When I have talked in other lands of the virtue of this democracy I am frequently met by the assertion that it is all very well to think of this direct democracy working in a land of only four million people, it is a very different matter, they assert, to attempt to use such methods for fifty or a hundred million. I always reply that we have some cities of about the same size as Switzerland and a number of them slightly smaller, where the problem should not be very different from that which confronts the Swiss, yet the management of the Swiss Republic is infinitely better than that of any one of our cities, at least of any one that I know. I don't think it is a matter of size ; I don't think the area of the country or the number of its population determines its character ; I think this is rather determined by the interest of the individual in his government and by the probity and integrity with which he fulfills the duties of a citizen.

For generations the Swiss have had universal obligation to military service. It is a militia system ; the length of service does not bear too hard on the individual, but its effects upon the manhood of Switzerland are apparent to anyone who has studied that country. Recruits of all classes of society are thrown together and learn to appreciate and esteem each other. In the competition of the soldier, the son of a cab driver may prove himself superior to the son of a banker ; this is the lesson that the son of the banker needs to learn in every land. During the course of our debate in America on the question of universal training I often read protests from so-called liberal elements who claim that conscription is an undemocratic form of legislation.

I assert on the contrary that conscription contributes to the highest development of democracy and that true democracy can be achieved only by something of this character. We can make conscious and responsible citizens, only, it seems to me, when every man has done some service to his country, has been inspired by the ideals of his country, and has met his countrymen on a basis of friendly competition without the accident of birth or fortune.

Democracy in Switzerland is a vital and living thing, government in Switzerland is an honestly administered business, justice in Switzerland is carried out as wisely as human brains can conceive. In respect of government and freedom of opportunity it is my belief that the youth born in Switzerland has a better chance of a self-respecting, honorable life than the youth of any other nation. May this oasis in the desert of controlled thinking which is now Europe long endure, and may it continue to flourish in the difficulties which are certain to confront it in the next few years.

Berne is essentially a Swiss city. Its architecture shows influences of the warmer climate of northern Italy in shady arcades along its flagstone streets, nevertheless the general aspect of the town is essentially Swiss. Street junctions form large squares where gaily colored statues are surrounded by flowerbeds ; the steep tiled roofs form a homogeneous and irregular pattern from the distant hills. The original city was built on a high promontory in a sharp curve of the Aar River. Massive fortifications and topography made the city almost impregnable to weapons of former days.

Throughout the Middle Ages and even until the middle of the eighteenth century, the great families of Berne, the "patricians," as they were known, enjoyed considerable wealth and prominence in European affairs. This was primarily due to a factor in the evolution of military strategy. The Bernese were among the first to discover that rows of pikemen were able to resist the attack of armored knights on horseback. The decline of feudalism and the emergence of the common man into a position of importance, were certainly coincident with that discovery and may in some measure be due to it. These regiments of Bernese pikemen were rented as mercenaries to the great armies of Europe and for a long period it was a bold captain who set out on expeditions without such a staunch body of troops to hold his center. Members of the patrician families accompanied their troops as captains or generals. European history is full of such names as von Reding, von Gerlach, von Wattwyl, and de Salis.

One reads of Swiss as marshals of the armies of France and of the Holy Roman Empire. One finds Swiss counselors to the kings of Europe, one finds especially highly trusted bodyguards of Swiss troops under Swiss officers. The growth of the use of artillery and the spreading knowledge of the methods of its employment put an end to the predominant role of pikemen and re-established the cavalry, but a lighter and more mobile cavalry, in European wars. This brought about the gradual decline of the fortunes of the Bernese.

The city has never developed much industry. The descendants of the marshals and captains of Europe still live in Berne and constitute Bernese society; they are the doctors, the lawyers, and often the leading businessmen of the capital. From this background society has retained a certain conservatism, a tendency to live in the past, a separation in thought, at least, from that assertive democracy which is the predominant characteristic of Switzerland.

We found a house in the old section of Berne standing high above ancient battlements, bordered by a wide sweep of brick terrace, with linden trees giving shade from the summer sun. The slope fell away steeply in a series of terraces and gardens until it reached the battlements above the river. The view from the terrace was theatrical in its beauty. From the rapidly flowing river, steep wooded hills dotted with villas rose on the opposite bank. Far away the background of the Bernese Oberland gave an ever-changing scene of grandeur.

Our life in Berne was simple. Few of the patrician families had sufficient fortune to entertain on an elaborate scale ; they did entertain, but simply and infrequently. There came to Berne, however, innumerable friends from America, England, France, and elsewhere, and it was a Swiss doctor who was responsible for their presence. Dr. Kocher, the son of a perhaps more famous father, also a physician, had established a practice among the women of other countries of such a scope that scores of them returned year by year to get the benefit of his treatment. So much did I find myself in the company of the patients of Dr. Kocher that it became my boast that I was the only foreigner after years of residence in Berne who had never consulted him.

The sports of Berne were to me, at least, exotic. Although there was a charming tennis club, the season for tennis was so short that I had to search for other diversion. I took up fencing and not only fenced in competition at the local club and in the club at Geneva, but used to bring the fencing master to my house early in the morning where we would practice for an hour on the terrace before breakfast. It has always seemed to me that of the competitive sports the best are those in which you face your opponent. There is a satisfaction in this sport which means not only well-trained and supple muscles but the necessity of thinking a fraction of a second quicker than your opponent or of guessing that fraction of a second ahead of him as to what he is going to do.

In my case, at least, skiing was a noncompetitive sport. I took it up too late to risk the danger of racing and jumping. In my first years in Switzerland mechanical means for climbing the mountains were rare, if not nonexistent ; one carried one's lunch and spent from three to four hours gaining altitude ; sealskins on the bottom of the skis prevented slipping backward. One climbed through forests covered with snow where the sun made a prismatic aura about the dazzling branches. There was a silence, a majesty about these snowy altitudes which I never could find in the summer. The snow gives a friendly aspect to rock and gorge ; the cruelty of the mountain is not visible, although a sudden blizzard can make you realize its presence. Skiing has an added fascination in that there is a tinge of apprehension in the excitement of the rush of descent. One comes to a sudden steep descent, one's heart leaps up : Can I do it ? Yes, I am going to. Then the rush of a turn, and the immense satisfaction of having outdone oneself. In the years that have passed since Switzerland I have missed this amusement deeply.

The physical life was engrossing and satisfactory, let me turn suddenly to an experience of the mind or Spirit. In the life of every man and woman certain incidents have occurred which are beyond the explanation of life in the dimensions that we know of. Certain episodes seem to prove that a purely mechanical explanation of existence does not suffice. Such an incident, and the most striking of my experience, happened at this period. Among the yearly visitors to Berne to consult Swiss doctors was King Feisal of Iraq. He was a pleasant enough acquaintance, but no more. My wife and I usually gave him a bridge party during his visit as he was inordinately fond of the game, and the British Minister had asked us to help in making his stay agreeable. His appearance was distinctive, a slender figure, a narrow dark face, with a pointed beard.

When our son attained the age to be sent home to school, Kate and I used to take him to London for a week or ten days in September and then put him on the boat for the United States. On one of these occasions, and on the eve of his departure, we told the boy that he could choose his amusement for the evening. He selected a play followed by supper at the Berkeley where a famous prestidigitator was giving a floor-show. We were seated at the table watching a remarkable exhibition of dexterity, when at eleven-thirty my wife suddenly straightened in her chair and said, "Hugh, King Feisal has just come in, looked around the room, and is coming over to speak to us." I rose, but could see no one resembling the King. I turned to my wife, her face was a study of puzzled incredulity. She said, "That's strange, he's gone ; I don't see how he could have disappeared so suddenly."

At breakfast my wife complained in irritation that she had

been troubled during the night by a repeated dream of Feisal ; time after time she met him in the corridor of the Hotel Bellevue at Berne, each time he would greet her and state that he was going away. The three of us took a taxi to the station. Our boy leaned out the window and announced excitedly, "Mummy, the placards of the newsmen are saying something about your King Feisal." We stopped the taxi, bought a paper. King Feisal had died in Berne at eleven-thirty the evening before.

CHAPTER II

At the moment of my arrival in Switzerland the relations of the United States and its representative to the League of Nations in Geneva were still in a state of doubt. It will be remembered that Mr. Harding's election, in 1920, had been hailed by the Republican Party at least, as a repudiation by the United States of the League of Nations. Accordingly when Joe Grew came to Switzerland as Minister shortly thereafter, he felt constrained to considerable circumspection in his dealings with the League and its personnel. If he had a message to deliver to Sir Eric Drummond, the Secretary General of the League, it was usually delivered at Drummond's house. Toward the close of his stay, Grew took part in one discussion group on armaments questions. The heavens didn't fall, the United States did not regard it as a "commitment," indeed, public opinion seemed to feel that on the whole it was the common-sense thing to do.

When Hugh Gibson succeeded Grew as Minister to Switzerland he was thrown more and more into the work at Geneva. The press had become more accustomed to the presence of Americans in the old National Hotel where the League Secretariat functioned; nevertheless it was still a matter of doubt as to how far the United States might go in its co-operation and how public our participation in the work of the League might be.

Sir Eric Drummond, now Earl of Perth, had been Secretary

General of the League since the inauguration of that body ; indeed, he was named to his post in the original Covenant of the League. A Scot of considerable acumen, Drummond had been in the British Foreign Service, and his appointment provided that a man singularly equipped for his task should be the dominant personality of the Secretariat in the formative years of the League. He had an unusual gift for conciliating divergent points of view. I have seen him repeatedly sitting in committees where the discussion became heated. He would intervene, and in a modest and deprecating manner make a suggestion which would save face on both sides and enable the work to be resumed.

Many delegates to the League felt that Drummond played too active a role and that his presence gave a disproportionate weight to the British thesis. In my experience, however, I felt that Drummond regarded himself as nonpolitical, that his whole energy was bent on making the machine function and that his intervention in a debate seldom maintained a thesis of his country but was rather a contribution to a general agreement.

However this may be, the machine that he set up functioned admirably. I never ceased to be astonished at the smoothness with which the Secretariat handled the vast volume of papers, information, research and translation. In all meetings of the League English and French were the languages permitted. If a delegate spoke in another language he was obliged to bring his own interpreter. In very small committees, and in order to facilitate work when all members spoke either French or English, interpreters were occasionally dispensed with, but such action was rare. The interpreters were astounding men. Not a few times I found that a speech extremely dull in its original presentation became alive and sparkling in the mouth of the interpreter. I have never seen them halt for an expression ; I have never seen them make a serious omission, and this in spite of the fact that they did not make shorthand transcriptions but relied on brief notes and on their memory.

Sir John Simon, during his frequent visits to Geneva as British Minister for Foreign Affairs, used to lay traps consciously for the interpreters. I remember on one occasion he concluded a speech somewhat as follows : "I am now going to offer a piece of advice to the delegates present. I am going to offer this advice in an English expression which I defy the interpreter to reproduce. Here it is : 'Don't look a gift horse in the mouth.'" Naturally we all listened intently to see how the interpreter could take this hurdle, but he took it in his stride, without blinking, in an almost literal interpretation : "*A cheval donné, regarde pas la bouche.*"

That evening we were dining with Sir John and we endeavored to find whether this expression existed in other tongues, and made the curious discovery that in other languages as well the same homely expression is commonly current. A Spaniard present contributed this : "*A caballo regalado, no se le mira el diente.*" A German contributed : "*Geschenktes Gaul, guck nicht ins Maul.*" I would be interested to learn whether human experience has reduced this piece of homely philosophy to a colloquialism in languages of the Orient. I can't leave the subject of interpreters without recounting an episode wherein a gentleman began speaking at one-fifteen in laborious South American French, continued exhaustively until about one-forty-five, when he remarked that he thought he had better bring his speech to a close as some of the delegates might find that he was encroaching on their lunch hour. Russell, a British interpreter, leapt to his feet, omitted the usual translation completely, and declared amid cheers, "The Honorable Delegate suggests that in view of the late hour it is time to adjourn for lunch."

I have mentioned above the concern that was felt at home in Washington as to how far we could share publicly the work of the League. This concern was largely dissipated by the decision of President Coolidge to summon the Naval Conference of 1927 in Geneva and to request the League of Nations to loan its secretarial services for the purposes of this conference. The conference itself arose from the conflict of opinion in the so-called "Preparatory Commission for Disarmament" between the British and ourselves as to the question of cruiser tonnage. My first task in Geneva was to serve at the same time as a member of the American delegation and as Secretary General to this conference. Great Britain, Japan and the United States were participating members of the conference and representatives of France and Italy were present as observers.

I must go back to the Washington Conference in 1921–1922 to remind readers that whereas that conference established a ratio of 5:5:3 for capital ships and aircraft carriers for the United States, Great Britain and Japan, respectively, no such ratio had been established for auxiliary craft and submarines. The Washington Treaty had defined battleships as surface craft of greater than ten thousand tons or mounting larger than eight-inch guns. Auxiliary craft, then, were all surface craft which did not come within this definition with the exception of aircraft carriers.

The record of the Washington Conference is not entirely clear as to whether the equality established for capital ships and aircraft carriers was to prevail as well for other types of craft as between Great Britain and ourselves. However the record may stand, the fact remains that throughout the United States the principle of equality with Great Britain, or "parity" as we phrased it at the time, had been acclaimed and it was the general understanding that such parity would apply throughout the entire Navy. Although conservative circles in Great Britain had declined to admit such parity for the rest of the fleet, nevertheless Mr. Bridgeman, First Lord of the Admiralty, expressly stated in Geneva that Great Britain admitted the principle. The question before the conference then was how to apply this principle.

I have no wish to become too technical ; I shall therefore explain quite simply that Great Britain with its vast empire felt the need for a large number of cruisers and it was not important to Great Britain that these cruisers should be of the largest possible type. The American thesis, as stated repeatedly by Admiral Hilary Jones, who assisted Hugh Gibson as delegate to this conference, was that we desired the smallest possible figure in total tonnage of cruisers but that we reserved the right to utilize that tonnage in any way we saw fit. Our Navy felt at the time that the only useful cruisers for our purposes were ten-thousand-ton ships mounting eight-inch guns which could have a wide cruising range to compensate us for the lack of fueling stations dotted all over the world. The British feared that this large number of heavy cruisers would give the United States fleet a predominant combat value : therefore, they could not acquiesce in such an arrangement. The Japanese were in the happy position of being able to agree with either thesis, although they did urge a slight modification of the 5:3 ratio.

It was a distressing conference.   We, that is the civilian element involved in the American delegation, felt that war between the United States and Great Britain was unthinkable and that, therefore, it was folly to wreck a conference between our two nations over a point that involved combat superiority. We felt that there was no such thing as absolute needs in a Navy, that these needs were relative and dependent upon the force and type of potential enemies.   The British and American Navies were, however, stubborn, and we had to come to the conclusion, reluctantly, that there was no means at the time of harmonizing the views.

During the conference I used to have repeated talks with the British Admirals.   They pointed out to me their honest conviction that our Navy was wrong in wanting its entire cruiser tonnage in eight-inch-gun ships.   They claimed that the fact that the six-inch gun was man-handled instead of machine-handled gave it a rapidity of fire that in some types of combat would be enormously useful ; also that the smaller ship had a maneuverability which since the days of Francis Drake had been one of the prevailing factors in sea battle.   Impressed with these arguments I would go to Admiral Jones and tell him that after all the British Navy had had a creditable record for some hundreds of years and that if they firmly believed such doctrine at least we should take it into consideration.   The Admiral was adamant.   No settlement could be accepted by the American Navy which did not give us the full right to put our entire cruiser tonnage in the type of craft we desired.

I should here say a few words about Admiral Jones.   He was

a man of simplicity and of an honesty so limpid that a glance at his clear eyes convinced you of his character. He was one of the most lovable men that I have encountered and every member of the delegation felt deep affection for him. His idea of debate, however, might be said to lack variety. He made an affirmation, he listened politely to the other man, he restated his affirmation. This could and did become exasperating occasionally to his adversary, and in one meeting Hugh Gibson was forced to come decisively and effectively to his rescue. The Admiral had stated his thesis, Lord Cecil for the British Government had contested this in a series of arguments, the Admiral had quietly restated his thesis.

This episode had been repeated several times when Cecil burst out, "But, Admiral, try to see the other fellow's point of view for once in a way!"

Our chief delegate, Hugh Gibson, closed his briefcase with a snap, rose to his feet, and said, "Lord Cecil, if this debate cannot be conducted in parliamentary language I shall have to declare the session closed."

I am led to say more of the remarkable personality of Lord Robert Cecil. His tall black-coated figure, rounded shoulders and outthrust head, was one of the most familiar sights in the halls of the League of Nations. He looked like a benevolent vulture. He was a man of unquestioned honesty of purpose, of unquestioned loyalty to the cause he was advocating, but he was trained as an attorney, and from his arguments, Lord Cecil's high purpose was advocated with much of the deviousness of the courtroom. In the early years of the League of Nations he had been delegate from South Africa and as such had enjoyed a freedom in expressing his personal conviction which had won him a wide following and esteem among the more ardent of the League enthusiasts.

He was not at his best when he became representative of Great Britain; he lacked that freedom to act on his own conception of what was right and what was desirable; he became more the attorney for his government. He belongs to that family of Cecils which has given so many statesmen to Great Britain, which perhaps more than any other family has seen its descendants in successive generations endowed with high ability, deep patriotism combined with a sense of duty to the state.

Admiral Viscount Saito was the chief Japanese delegate. He rapidly earned our esteem and affection. A former naval officer, he had become Governor of Korea, and spoke with genuine authority for Japan since he had the backing not only of the Navy but of the highest political circles in the nation. He was a man of honesty and sincerity of purpose and he has joined that long and honorable list of public-spirited citizens the world over who have been assassinated for their convictions by their own compatriots.

As I think back over that unhappy conference it comes to my mind that a few years later the American Navy had a Chief of Staff who had come firmly to the conviction that we needed a considerable proportion of six-inch-gun cruisers. There has been an evolution in Navy thought in this connection and we are by no means so fixed in our determination that only the heaviest type of cruiser serves our needs. In this connection it is interesting to note that in the battle with the German "pocket battleship" *Graf Spee* off Montevideo a few months ago, that ship, mounting eleven-inch guns, was assaulted by three British cruisers; one British cruiser mounting eight-inch guns was put out of action in the first few minutes of engagement, the two smaller British cruisers carrying six-inch guns closed with the enemy and drove the heavier German ship into refuge in Montevideo harbor.   It would seem therefore that the tactics of Francis Drake still have some value in modern naval battle.

The approaching breakdown of the conference gave rise to much bitterness in both the British and American press ; recrimination was prevalent.   In order to mitigate as far as possible an unhappy effect upon the relations of the two countries, Hugh Gibson invited Mr. Bridgeman and Lord Cecil, as well as the Japanese delegates and certain members of the American delegation to my house on the evening preceding the final session.

Hugh spoke in the most careful selection of language and outlined, in full candor, his apprehension that a public debate on the conference would have unfortunate effects.   He explained to Mr. Bridgeman that he and his colleagues were as convinced of the rightness of their position as Mr. Bridgeman was of his own, that nothing could be gained by further discussion and that it was better to have a formal ceremony of closure than an argument.   Gibson pointed out that it was easy for him to make himself a popular hero in America by conducting a spirited debate, since this was the type of thing that the press would hail with joy.   He had no doubt that Mr. Bridgeman was in the same position.

A lengthy silence following his remarks was broken by Cecil, who said : "Then you really believe, Mr. Gibson, that such procedure is better adapted to accomplish limitation eventually and to achieve what we all have at heart than a public debate ?"   Hugh replied : "In all sincerity, I do."

A further silence was broken by Bridgeman, who stated that he had categorical instructions to make a speech and that he must do so. Viscount Ishii, for Japan, declared that he would have been glad to see the procedure adopted which had been recommended by Mr. Gibson but that in view of the apparently insuperable objections by Mr. Bridgeman, it seemed that they would all have to make their speeches.

The closing session of the conference was held ; the chief delegates of all three delegations made their speeches : Admiral Jellicoe made a further one for the British Navy. The net result was as Hugh had foretold, the press of Great Britain and the United States and, to some extent, of Japan, had a field day, and recrimination and resentment broke out.

Before I leave the subject of the Naval Conference of 1927 I am going to relate an episode which shows a characteristic aspect of that versatile man who spoke for the United States at this meeting. Hugh Gibson, as chief delegate, had received a note from Admiral Saito in which the Japanese delegation sent to the American delegation a formal challenge to a baseball game for the coming Saturday, the members of the teams to be selected from among the delegations and the correspondents of both countries. A press conference was scheduled a half-hour after the reception of this letter. As a rule only he and I attended the conferences ; this time, however, he summoned the entire delegation, and under his instructions we marched into the room in solemn order, two by two, and lined up behind the chief delegate. The press, sensing something unusual, became suddenly alert.

Hugh spoke with solemnity : "I have today a serious announcement to make. It is the more serious in that it comes to me in a formal communication from the chief delegate of Japan."

At this point every pressman was nervously writing on the backs of envelopes, pads of paper, or any material obtainable. Hugh continued : "A note from Admiral Saito came to my hand only a few minutes before this conference. I can do no better than to read it to you." He read the note. I heard a gasp of anger from the press, but within ten seconds it was succeeded by such a roar of joy and applause as I have never heard from pressmen.

Robert Dell, an Englishman, correspondent of *The Manchester Guardian* at Geneva and the most venerable correspondent there, roared from the front row : "Man and boy, I have followed the press for forty years and I have never heard the correspondents so properly had !"

It was during this conference at Geneva that I made the acquaintance of Alix Barton, a truly remarkable character. The granddaughter of Sir Robert Peel, who had been Prime Minister of Great Britain, she had married in her youth the British Consul to Geneva. He had been long dead but Mrs. Barton had remained in the city and had built monuments and buildings so that the whole city knew of her benefactions. She was either related to, or on friendly terms with every leading man in the British Conservative Party. She rapidly established the same relation with the principal leaders of Labor, MacDonald and Henderson. During my entire stay in Switzerland, I counted on her friendly assistance and relied upon her affectionate understanding. Her hope for the world lay in the League of Nations, and she entertained a conviction that the League itself would fail without intimate co-operation between the

United States and Great Britain. She died suddenly, in 1936, early enough not to see the complete disintegration of the League to which she had given her devotion through its entire existence. I wrote a description of her at the time which was published in a memorial to her :

I wish I were able to describe the elusive quality about Mrs. Barton that enabled her to maintain a "salon" in a period when that word has become an anachronism. It is easy to describe her appearance ; tall, slender, small head, lovely throat, with a back and carriage that every woman envied, uncompromisingly clothed in the models of her youth. The word Victorian came instinctively to the lips upon being presented to her. Her setting was equally Victorian. The Villa Lammermuir, in which she lived, lies in beautiful grounds formally laid out with a flavor of the past. The entrance hall of the house is flanked by small brass cannon with bunches of forget-me-nots in the muzzle, and has a stuffed walrus head on the wall. The latter we came to know affectionately as Monsieur Leygues ; it bore striking resemblance to the late French Minister of Marine with his drooping white mustaches. The house was packed with furniture of a type that one knew intimately as a child in the 90's.

But to seize those qualities that made Mrs. Barton what she was, that made us all hold her in such deep affection, is much more difficult.

Perhaps the catholicism of her interest was one of her most striking traits. I have sat at her table with experts and specialists on import and export restrictions, counterfeiting, protection of the whale, and disarmament. She not only permitted her visitors to talk shop, but shop was the type of talk in which she delighted. She always knew sufficient about the subject and about the problems which were confronting the negotiators to put adroit questions and draw them into earnest conversation. She could converse fluently in French, German and Italian.

Mrs. Barton's predominant characteristic, to my mind, was the degree of trust that she inspired in those who came in contact with her. There are few statesmen who came to Geneva during her residence who did not give her a large share of their confidence. Even the busiest and most harassed Ministers of Foreign

Affairs would find time to have tea with Mrs. Barton and discuss with her their difficulties, hopes and even their irritations. She was profoundly discreet. I never heard of a case in which one of the thousand confidences reposed in her was revealed. She had deep knowledge of the world, wide tolerance, and very great kindness.

With all that, she was a woman of deep conviction and senti-ment. I have seen her weeping over the defection of those she had regarded as her friends. I have seen her in a blaze of indigna-tion at what she regarded as a disloyal act. On one unforgettable occasion I saw her rend an eminent statesman for a piece of double-dealing.

Alix Barton was known as the "Queen of Geneva" and that title of affectionate exaggeration carried an element of truth. Her rule among those associated with the League of Nations was unchallenged but her rule was through the affections. A very great lady of a past generation, we who knew her are proud of her friendship and will never cease to miss her.

Scarcely had I returned to my office in Berne after the Naval Conference when a telegram arrived from Washington naming me American delegate to a meeting in Geneva that carried the resounding title of "Conference for the Abolition of Prohibi-tions and Restrictions on Import and Export." The World Economic Conference which met in Geneva in the spring of 1927 had recommended the calling of the new conference, and the Secretariat of the League had been busy preparing a sort of draft text as a guide to the work.

The State Department ordered me to go to Geneva at once, stating that detailed instructions would be telegraphed before the opening of the conference. It lived up to its promise ; I got my instructions, nine pages of them, the night before the de-bates opened, and was called upon in the general meeting the next morning to state the attitude of the United States toward the draft agreement. As far as I had been able to puzzle it out in the middle of the night, my instructions paid lip-service to the draft and then proceeded to tear it to pieces seriatim. I paid lip-service to the draft and stopped there.

The next days and nights were packed with activity. I seized upon the few delegates from other lands who had worked with the Secretariat in the preparation of the draft, made them expound this subject so unknown to me, convinced myself that while our criticism was justified in places, in others the draft was common-sense procedure. Then followed a battle with Washington, a somewhat heated discussion in which I had to carry conviction for the idea that the delegates of some forty other countries might conceivably be right, and our doctrinaire gentlemen doing the drafting might be at fault. We finally worked out a compromise platform on which I could stand.

This early conference experience impressed me deeply. From then on I bent every effort to have an American included in all initial discussions. I did my utmost to bring it about that our influence was exerted from the beginning of the discussion of every problem, to avoid a repetition of my unhappy experience of facing a general and previously discussed agreement by unilateral and doctrinaire arguments. It seemed so simple at home to let the others work it out and then see if we could agree ; unfortunately, our agreement or dissent often meant success or failure, and it was infinitely preferable to state our position early and before opinion had crystallized.

In the course of our debates the State Department became anxious for me to give publicity to a dispute with the French Government on the matter of the introduction of American films into France. The French had set up a sort of cultural censorship, ostensibly to check a much-feared "Americanization" of French youth, but also, at least so we maintained, as a measure of protection to the French film industry which felt itself badly outdistanced by Hollywood production. I prepared a most careful brief on the iniquity of stultifying the right of import by so-called "cultural" restrictions on the right of distribution. If I do say it myself, it was a document with a sting, and most entertaining to prepare.

The French delegate to the conference, M. Serruys, was a brilliant speaker, a scholar of erudition, a most entertaining man when in a good humor but somewhat irascible when matters did not go to his liking. I made my speech to an amused and attentive conference, they were not accustomed at Geneva to quite such directness of statement. M. Serruys demanded the floor before the translation was completed, answered me in biting sarcasm, pouring upon my bowed head many of the resentments which the continental entertains for America, but which he usually covers in the presence of Americans. Before I could speak again the chairman closed the meeting ; wisely, I think.

That skirmish with Serruys was widely publicized, with joy by the American press, with irony on the continent. Representatives of the American film industry were deeply interested, so I was not surprised one day in Paris to receive a telephone message from Mr. Will Hays, czar of the American movies, to lunch with him at the Hotel Crillon. I had had nothing to do with the film industry previously so was a bit startled at my first entry into this atmosphere.

Mr. Hays was most cordial when I entered his salon, was enthusiastic about my speech, and suggested lunch. At the door he paused and remarked that the boys would probably like to take some pictures while we were there. He pressed a bell, a dozen photographers poured in and exploded their flashlights. During an admirable luncheon, Mr. Hays called the head-waiter and asked him to get Mrs. Hays on the telephone, giving her address in the United States. At that time the transoceanic telephone was quite new, and its cost was considered prohibitive for all but most essential and urgent messages. However, when the telephone was plugged in the wall and brought to our table, Mr. Hays assured himself of the welfare of his wife and son and calmly resumed his lunch. Thus my own experience confirmed the accuracy of the stories of the superb disregard for money in the film industry.

In its second session the conference achieved agreement on a treaty. It was not a perfect text, many exceptions had been admitted. But it was the high-water mark of international endeavor to deal with economic ills, and had it become generally applicable would have done much to forestall, or at least retard, the rapid development, after 1930, of autarchic and controlled economy. Unfortunately, Poland alone among the signatories failed to ratify the treaty, but its failure was sufficient to destroy the effort, and it never came into general force.

The various types of conferences that I attended as American representative entailed continuous study and preparation on my part. The subjects considered were of the widest variety. The distance of the United States from Geneva made it difficult and expensive to send experts in every case so that I was usually designated and had to make myself as much of an expert as possible in the ten days preceding each conference.

Two conferences of this highly specialized type might be mentioned. One was a Conference on Communications and Transit where practically all the delegates except myself were officials of large cities dealing with traffic problems. As representative of the United States I became Chairman of the General Commission, and my leading preoccupation in controlling the debate was to reveal as little as possible of my vast ignorance of the subject. The second example was of much deeper interest to me. It was a conference called to tighten up international practice and law in order to prevent counterfeiters from profiting by the immunity given them by foreign lands against crimes committed on the soil of another land.

The debate was, of course, highly technical and even legalistic. I remember one exhausting afternoon in which the British delegate, Sir John Fisher Williams, and I searched for a satisfactory phrase in French for the Anglo-Saxon term "common law." The French were sure that they could translate it; we were sure they couldn't. If I remember rightly, we were finally obliged to insert in the French text of the treaty the English phrase as a footnote. The counterfeiting conference was attended primarily by representatives of the police organizations of the various continental countries. I noticed a startling phenomenon in regard to these people. A high proportion were deformed; they were men with club-feet, hunchbacks, twisted spines. I have no explanation for the phenomenon but have often wondered what Dr. Freud and his followers would make of this curiously high proportion of deformed characters engaged in manhunting.

In the summer of 1929 I attended one of the few conferences which were happy episodes from start to finish. This was a conference called by the Swiss Government, not by the League of Nations. It was summoned in Geneva for the purpose of drafting new treaties governing the Red Cross in war and the treatment of prisoners of war. The weather was lovely, Geneva sparkled with flags and flowers around the blue lake. None of us had very explicit instructions so we could enter into genuine negotiation rather than act as mouthpieces of our governments.

Drafts of the two conventions had been prepared by that extraordinary body known as the International Red Cross of Geneva, a group of devoted citizens whose appointment to that organization is the crowning achievement of a life of success and service. In as much as this conference was not under the auspices of the League of Nations, the entire proceedings were in French. I was chosen as chairman of one of the two committees preparing the prisoners of war convention. Eliot Wadsworth, my fellow delegate, headed our representation for the Red Cross convention.

At the time of drafting it seemed highly academic work to be preparing a convention for prisoners of war to be applicable in the next war, which seemed at that moment extraordinarily remote. Only ten years after its signature, however, that treaty came into application. France, Great Britain, Germany, Italy, had all ratified it and are all using the treaty as their criterion for the treatment of prisoners. This treaty incorporates one of the most advanced humanitarian theses yet accepted in the practice of war, namely, there shall be no retaliation on prisoners of war. This doctrine was proclaimed by Abraham Lincoln during our Civil War and was practised by our armies in that conflict. It was a simple doctrine, based upon the recognition of the inhumanity of punishing helpless individuals for the commission of acts over which they had no control.

For some months in the State Department in 1939 I had the melancholy satisfaction of directing the work of the American representatives in charge of enemy interests in belligerent countries, in execution of the terms of this treaty which I myself had participated in drafting.

CHAPTER III

Shortly after the conclusion and signature of these treaties I departed for the United States on the *Ile de France* in the autumn of 1929. In a corner of the smoking room, to accommodate an indispensable demand on the part of the American passengers, was a broker's office. The second day out it seemed as if the whole ship's company were suddenly packed into this small office watching the blackboard. The Great September Crash had begun, and the entire journey was spent calculating losses and discussing the reasons for this unprecedented collapse.

At home in America the crash had the effect of a cold shower. We were suddenly shocked back into a sense of realities and a recognition that an uninterrupted boom based on enormously expanded credit had come to an end. Within one week a school of philosophy had been destroyed. A few days sufficed to demonstrate the complete untenability of that school of thought so prevalent through the boom years and so wide-spread in the United States, which pretended that modern finance had achieved the means of eliminating forever the pendulum swing of prosperity.

Of course I was concerned personally, of course I was apprehensive, but even during this visit to the United States, so soon after the crash, I began to find compensation for the destruction of prosperity. I have had this impression confirmed year after year since that time. I felt through 1926 up to 1929 that we as a people could not stand corn. We were arrogant, we were materialistic, we laid down the law at home and abroad, we assumed an intelligence far superior to that of other nations and demonstrated that intelligence in no uncertain terms.

The Continent of Europe was full of American travellers, all colossally rich and all telling the unfortunate foreigner how to become so. I do not think that another swing of prosperity will reproduce this type of arrogance. We are a chastened folk, we have learned much of the virtue of thrift, at least in our private lives ; perhaps so much could not be said for our public affairs. People are living within their incomes and laying aside money for expenditure rather than expending on their expectations. But, most important of all, we are happier and a kindlier people ; adversity has made us more tolerant.

Travel through the United States during the past ten years as opposed to the four years which preceded the crash has shown an unbelievable change in courtesy, kindliness, helpfulness, on the part of our people. We had to pay a tremendous price for the attainment of these qualities. I am inclined to believe, however, that the attainment was worth the price. I wonder whether Americans who were not living abroad have any conception of these differences in the American people ; it is probable that the change occurred so gradually and normally as to be unobserved by those who shared in it.

I have learned subsequently from my friends that I was unbearable during my trips home while the country was in the boom. They say that my attitude toward my land, and even toward my friends, was insufferable. I did not realize this at the time, but it may well have been true. Coming from a land of simpler ways and more moderate appreciation of good business, I was profoundly shocked by my own people, even by some of those I loved. It seemed that the essential kindliness and friendship of America were threatened by the hard materialism of incredible success. It even appeared that our decencies were threatened by the abnormalities of a prohibition era. I know that I felt these things deeply, I didn't realize I had given voice to my thoughts so blatantly. I must have done so, no wonder I made myself a nuisance.

It was during this visit home that I began conversations which nearly led me into resigning from the Foreign Service. I think I was more tempted at this moment by the thought of private life than at any other time during my work with the Government. McCormick Blair, "Bill" Blair, as we always called him in Chicago, was a member of the firm of Lee Higginson and Company. He suggested to me the possibility of my working with the firm in their new office in Paris which they were about to inaugurate. As I say, the idea tempted me and I made several visits on my return to Europe to consult partners in Paris and elsewhere. I eventually abandoned the idea since I could not bring myself to forego a share in events of such interest as Geneva promised me in the near future.

This decision was a case where instinct served me better than reason. Reason told me to leave the precarious Foreign Service while still young enough to enter active life as a private individual; instinct told me to continue the work that interested me. Shortly thereafter, Ivar Kreuger, the Swedish financial wizard, suddenly committed suicide. His death revealed widespread falsification of accounts and stirred up an international financial scandal of magnitude. Heavily involved in the Kreuger enterprise, but above all personally involved through a fine conception of honor, the members of the firm put Lee Higginson and Company into liquidation. My adventure into private life, had I made it, might well have been short and disastrous.

Another incident of this visit home gives me satisfaction now when I remember it. We were discussing plans for the 1930 Naval Conference in London. I was under the impression of advices from Tokyo to the effect that growing dissatisfaction with the bases of the Washington Conference of 1921–1922 had brought the Japanese to a feeling of resentment against the 5:3 ratio as applied to those portions of the fleet not covered by the Washington Conference. Furthermore, the American Ambassador to Tokyo had died some months before and the post had remained vacant.

I had maintained in the State Department that it seemed obvious common sense that we should have in Tokyo during the London Conference not only an American Ambassador but someone so well connected with President Hoover that he could speak with authority in Tokyo and thus supplement the work of the negotiators in London. Finding that the principal men in the State Department shared my views on this matter, I called on President Hoover and pointed out to him the necessity for naming an ambassador immediately.

The President replied that he had offered the post to two gentlemen whom he considered competent but that neither of them, for family reasons, had been able to undertake it. I said to the President, "Why don't you send Bill Castle?"

William R. Castle, Jr. was at that time Assistant Secretary of State. The President thought well of the suggestion and asked me to speak to Castle about the matter. I did so, and found that he was willing to leave Washington for a few months on a sort of temporary assignment covering the period of the London Conference. The President issued the nomination and Bill Castle proceeded to Tokyo. He was there only a short period, but the success of his efforts with the Japanese was outstanding and was unmatched by that of any ambassador until the arrival of the present incumbent.

In discussing the Naval Conference of 1927 I sketched the divergent views between the United States and Great Britain in the matter of cruisers. Even before Mr. Ramsay MacDonald assumed the position of Prime Minister, but while in the expectation of doing so, he sent word to President Hoover that as soon as he took office he wanted to come to Washington and discuss this matter. Mr. MacDonald took the civilian's point of view in respect to the dissension, namely, that if we both meant what we said in our assertion that war was unthinkable between us, and if we both accepted the principle of "parity" between us, then it was ridiculous that we could not come together and conventionalize our belief in written form. Mr. MacDonald visited the President at Rapidan, Mr. Hoover's fishing camp, and the two men, animated by the same conceptions, came quickly to a meeting of minds on a broad basis. However, their informal accord left a number of gaps to be filled in by technicians. Further, the fleet of Japan had to be incorporated in the accord and due regard paid to the position of France and Italy. Accordingly the London Naval Conference of 1930 was summoned.

This conference in London was the last of the great conferences done in the tradition of the Congress of Vienna. This fact is partly explained by the spending habits of the boom years which still lingered in the spring of 1930, partly by the fact that Mr. Henry Stimson, then Secretary of State, is essentially a grand seigneur and proceeds about his high duties with the pageantry and suite that such high duties conventionally call for. The Secretary himself leased a country estate at Stanmore with a nine-hole golf course, the principal delegates were housed and had their offices in the Ritz, the rest of the delegation at the Mayfair, a block away from Piccadilly.

A detachment of marines accompanied the delegation and guarded the improvised chancery and code room in the Ritz. A fleet of enormous Daimlers was at the disposition of the delegates and Foreign Service officers acted as majordomos to allocate cars for duties, expeditions, and social obligations. The chief of the code room, chief of the press section, unnumbered stenographers, file clerks, et cetera, were in attendance.

The delegation itself was headed by Mr. Stimson. Mr. Charles Dawes, American Ambassador to London and former Vice President, was a delegate, as well as the Secretary of the Navy, Charles Francis Adams, Senators David Reed and Joe Robinson, Ambassador Hugh Gibson, and Mr. Dwight Morrow, formerly Ambassador to Mexico. Advisers included Chief of Staff of the Navy, Admiral Pratt, and various other high functionaries of the Navy. A competent legal section was also set up.

Hugh Gibson and I used to look at the organization and

weep. We thought of the struggle that we had had to get adequate money and personnel for the conferences that we had carried on by ourselves, with one stenographer, and how we had had to raid his office in Brussels and mine in Berne for temporary code clerks, and to plead for help, when under heavy pressure, from the Embassies at Paris, Berlin and Rome. I am convinced that the expenditure during one month of this conference at London would have paid the complete expenses of all the conferences in which American delegations participated during the time of Gibson and myself in Geneva.

I had never before visited London officially. I knew it, of course, as a traveler knows it. I had friends with whom I dined when I visited there, but that side of London which only the official visitor sees, its pageantry and formality, is something unique in the world. The conference was to be opened formally by an address by King George to the members of the conference sitting in the House of Lords. Elaborate preparations had been made for access and time of arrival of official delegates. Unfortunately, we awoke that morning to one of London's world-famous fogs, and I have vivid recollections of the trip from the Ritz via St. James Palace, over the Mall to Westminster, through an impenetrable gray-green wall broken every hundred yards by a blazing flambeau, where an immense policeman in glistening raincoat directed us to the next patrol. It is extraordinary that we all congregated without mishap. Mr. Dawes alone was forty minutes late, but his chauffeur had had the additional distance from the Embassy to negotiate.

The most interesting man in the delegation to me was Dwight Morrow. Harold Nicolson, who wrote his biography, informed me one time in London that he was not entirely satisfied with it.   Nicolson had realized the difficulty of seizing and portraying that indefinable charm which won for Dwight Morrow affectionate friendship from men with whom he came in contact.   It is indeed difficult to find words for the quality of the man which made him stand out so preeminently against the background of his fellows.

His intellectual equipment was outstanding and recognized. As an undergraduate he was a phenomenon at mathematics, as lawyer and banker he was among the most competent in New York, as Ambassador he was pre-eminently successful in his work with the Mexicans and is still remembered there with affection.   But these are not the qualities that endure in the thoughts of the men who knew him.   It was his eagerness, his persistent and insatiable intellectual curiosity, his readiness to seize upon an idea and to pursue it until he had satisfied himself of the ultimate answer.

In the pursuit of this idea he showed a complete detachment from the normal things of life, a detachment which led him at times into ludicrous situations.   He was talking in his room one day to Hugh Gibson and myself.   At that time he was pursuing the theory of French "security."   Since Hugh and I had listened to speeches on security for numerous years, we were able to indicate to him some of the early milestones along the road and to suggest to him experts on the question, like Louis Aubert of the French delegation.   In the midst of the conversation the telephone rang.   Mr. Morrow said that the Secretary wanted him, hung up the receiver, told us to remain where we were until he came down, and started out of the door still talking about security.   There were three doors on the exit side of the room; the first led to the corridor, the second led to the bath, and the third led to a coat closet.   Mr. Morrow entered the coat closet, slammed the door behind him, whereupon we heard shouts, yells, and the sound of rended clothing.   We hastened to let him out and opened the door into the hall, through which he departed still discoursing on security.

Another scene of Mr. Morrow remains in my mind.   The delegation had been invited in a body by the Lord Mayor of the City to a banquet at the Guildhall.   Now a banquet at the Guildhall is something to see.   It is served on gold plate.   Halberdiers meet you at the entrance, a herald with a long trumpet winds a blast to announce the speakers and in ringing tones prays silence for the gentlemen.   We had been requested to bring our cards of identification.

I walked down a long corridor and heard sounds of applause rolling out as I reached the corner.   There a herald took my card, raised a brass trumpet to his lips, of a shape and proportion of those used in the first act of *Aïda*, wound a blast and announced my name.   I looked down a long passageway, on both sides were seats arranged like bleachers where the British guests of the Lord Mayor were seated in tiers to look over the unfortunate Americans who had to run this ordeal. About the middle of the passageway another herald wound a blast and again announced my name.   I eventually came to a dais where the Lord Mayor in his robes was seated on a throne, flanked on the right and on the left by officials of his office, also on thrones.   A tall gentleman clothed in a black silk robe, a sword, and a powdered curly wig, presented me to His Worship and I then took my place with other guests behind the throne.

I watched with sympathy several friends who succeeded me, but it was a sympathy tempered by the satisfaction that I had already gone through it. Suddenly the timid-looking figure of Dwight Morrow presented itself at the end of the passage. He was a short man, with rumpled gray hair, glasses always slightly askew, and a certain surprised look on his countenance. His clothes must have been the despair of his tailors and his wife. He had quantities of them but they all looked as if they had been slept in. In this case his dress coat was slipping off his shoulder so that even at that distance I could see his shirt sleeve. The trumpeter wound his blast, Dwight Morrow started down the passageway peering uncertainly to right and left. He came to a startled halt when the second herald blew his blast, and suddenly disappeared into the tiers of guests. The large gentleman in the black robe and white wig hastily went under the ropes and retrieved him, pushed him up to the dais, held him firmly by the arm while he presented him to his worship.

Dwight Morrow in pursuit of "security." He learned on his arrival in London that the French had the peculiar idea that something had to be done of a political nature before they could talk tonnages, numbers, and guns. This was a philosophical conception of high interest to Dwight Morrow. He purchased a little red notebook, and at every gathering he could be seen, notebook in hand, tapping some Frenchman on the chest while he discussed the theory with him. I may seem to treat this subject of security lightly, nevertheless I knew its gravity and the importance of Dwight Morrow's investigations.

It is the first time to my knowledge that any Anglo-Saxon of position became aware of the immense importance of this conception to France and to the continent in general. The Anglo-Saxon was tempted to brush it aside as an inconvenience, to confine his observations to what he called "realities." The result was that of all American and British statesmen, Dwight Morrow, I think, came closer to understanding what the French were driving at and why, and as a result came closer than others to reaching tangible results with the difficult and temperamental French negotiators.

I became impressed with the high ability of David Reed as a negotiator. The antithesis of Dwight Morrow, Reed is prosaic in appearance, but he has an intellect of high order, great kindliness of heart, a deep and well-experienced knowledge of law, patience and determination. One of the most difficult questions of the conference was that of accommodating Japan to the general accord attained by Mr. Hoover and Mr. MacDonald. David Reed found after days and even weeks of experimentation, that Mr. Matsudaira, at that time Ambassador to London, was the Japanese with whom he could talk most freely and most fruitfully. The American delegation turned over these negotiations to him, and day by day, weeks on end, he and Matsudaira met in the quiet of their sitting rooms and patiently elaborated their points of agreement. They eventually presented a solution to this problem, the most difficult and puzzling of the points at issue. It was a personal achievement of high order by David Reed.

I have stated that the Secretary brought departmental press

representatives with him. It quickly became evident, however, that in discussions dealing with comparative tonnages, caliber of guns, maneuverability, speed, habitability, and other factors of comparative naval force, there was need for someone to maintain contact with the press who was competent to explain these matters. Both because a number of the correspondents had known me when I was in charge of press relations in Washington and because of my experience in the previous three years in Geneva discussions, the correspondents requested Secretary Stimson to assign me to them. He accordingly did so, and my work during those months was largely with the press.

The greatest difficulty which I found throughout this assignment arose from the fact that practically all the delegates were gentlemen of exalted position accustomed to doing their own speaking to the press and that, therefore, we would often find the morning papers giving divergent accounts of American points of view and purpose. It was difficult for men of this type to accustom themselves to a common front, one of the cardinal necessities in international negotiation. I remember at one stage of the proceedings Secretary Stimson had informed me definitely and vigorously that there must be no premature publication of a certain discussion he had held with Briand, chief of the French delegation. Accordingly I had declined to confirm, deny, or comment on such speculation as the correspondents had raised regarding this conversation.

The next morning the press service brought in a report that one of the New York papers had carried a full account of the discussion. I ascertained from the correspondent that he had obtained his information from Senator Joe Robinson. I decided to talk with the Senator, and came away with a deep impression of his reasonableness and southern courtesy. I explained in detail the difficulties into which we fell in international negotiation if we were unable to have one neck of the bottle for the issue of all publicity; six or eight men all giving their views of events inevitably gave rise to stories of discord and conflict within the delegation. This must be avoided at all costs if our thesis was to have a chance to prevail with the foreigner. I added that another factor was involved; that I had refused all the other correspondents on this story, that to give it to one man not only offended all the rest of the press but put me in a most embarrassing position in dealing with them in the future. I remember the Senator replied: "Mr. Wilson, I assure you I did not understand. I will not offend in the future, and I am exceedingly contrite."

There was an immense amount of entertainment for all the delegations and perhaps more for the Americans than for the others since we all had many invitations from friends, as well as the official receptions and dinners that we had to attend. Some of these affairs were picturesque and interesting, some as always were boring, but I gained the impression that official affairs in England were less boring than in any other land since nearly all were accompanied by the pageantry of the past or conventionalized by the procedure of history.

I have since found it amusing to tell my English friends of an adventure which happened to three Americans at one of their banquets. Admiral Pratt, Chief of Staff of the Navy, had the office next to mine, so when I received one morning a beautifully engraved invitation asking me to be a guest for dinner of the Knights of the Round Table, I wandered into the Admiral's office. I found him sitting with Arthur Page son of the former Ambassador, and asked them whether they intended to attend. We had been going out so much that all of us were reluctant, and had just decided to refuse when the door opened with a crash and Mr. Dawes burst in, smoking his inevitable pipe. He insisted that we must all accept the invitation since he himself was to be made on that occasion a Knight of the Round Table.

Presenting ourselves together at the Hall, Pratt, Page and I found ourselves, somewhat to our surprise, seated at a considerable distance from the head table and seated together. As the meal progressed the Knight Troubadour sang some ballads, the Knight Chronicler recited some poetry, and we got thirstier and thirstier, there seemed to be nothing to drink within our reach. Admiral Pratt finally summoned a waiter and said we would like some champagne ; the waiter produced a bottle and placed it before us.

The dinner went on and was consummated by the admission to Knighthood of the Round Table of the American Ambassador and others. While the loving cup was being passed from one to another of the guests at the principal table, a waiter approached and announced we each owed one guinea for dinner and that the bottle of wine was a guinea extra. This would not have been perhaps so overwhelming if we had not all discovered to our confusion that we had no money in our dress clothes beyond a couple of shillings. We took counsel together and decided that General Dawes had been responsible for our coming, attached the bills to a note to the General, and sent it to the head table for collection.

The conference at London was the last agreement between

the Great Naval Powers. It was designed to last for six years, and did cover those years in spite of the catastrophic events which occurred in that period. Before turning to other subjects, this may be the time to offer some observations on naval limitation. Limitation of fleets can take place, I submit, only under certain limited conditions. We must remember that the state which is limited by a number inferior to that of another state finds itself in a position where its pride suffers, particularly if the state in question lays claim to being a first rate power. Hence, such a state will only submit to an inferior figure of limitation if it is forced to do so either through being the loser in war or through apprehension lest the other party to the agreement will use superior wealth and potential of construction to make the discrepancy even greater. Germany had been limited by the Treaty of Versailles. This is an example of the first alternative. The limitation of Japan from 1922 to 1936 is an example of the second alternative.

Great Britain and the United States had emerged from the Great War so overwhelmingly powerful and with such industrial resource that it was obvious to the Japanese statesmen that unless they accepted the approximate existing ratios, these ratios would be widely changed to their disadvantage within the next few years. It was the part of common sense, therefore, for the Japanese to accept the inferior figure during a period in which that land could not hope to build an equality with us or even to maintain its existing position without treaty arrangement. In the Treaty of Washington, dealing, as I have said, with capital ships and aircraft carriers, the United States had not only the strongest existing fleet but had the wealth and the will to construct at a rapid rate following the

Great War. Hence, it was to England's advantage to acquiesce in equality.

The picture was different when it came to cruisers. Great Britain was vastly superior in cruisers ; we neither had them projected nor in construction. It was only the understanding by Great Britain of American psychology and a knowledge of American wealth that led them to acquiesce in equality for this type of craft. They recognized that if we became sufficiently irritated at an obstructive policy on their part we would, and could, project and construct a fleet of cruisers which would render Great Britain's superiority extremely expensive to maintain. To the outsider, it has always seemed a relatively simple thing to form an agreement to measure and limit fleets. I say what I do above merely to show some of the complexities and the elements other than ships and tonnage which must enter into such calculations.

Another factor was of interest in these years of discussion of fleets. Great Britain is an empire which has fueling and refitting stations in every corner in the world. The British Admiralty, through past experience and the knowledge of these accessible stations, invariably was able to know exactly what type of fleet they desired to hold in being and construct for the future. The Japanese Admiralty had an even simpler problem ; they had to construct and hold ready a fleet which would guarantee them against attack and maintain predominance in the seas around China. This was a relatively small scope of activity, hence the Japanese Admiralty, as well, knew exactly what it wanted, where action might take place, and had more decisive knowledge of its necessities even than the British Navy.

Our problem, that is, the problem of the United States Navy, was the most difficult of the three. Our Navy felt that it had to be ready to retake the Philippine Islands in the event of their seizure by a hostile power, and to retake them within an appreciable period of time, since they believed that they would be forced to such an attempt by popular clamor in the United States. The Navy had to contemplate also the possibility of another battle area in European waters. Both of these possible combat areas were an enormous distance from any American bases. This meant that our ships had to be so constructed as to carry supplies of fuel for long cruises and that some of the advantages of speed, armor protection, and even size of guns, had to be sacrificed to this need for fuel capacity. It was such reasoning as this that explains to a large extent our insistence upon the heavy type of cruiser in the 1927 Conference.

There was no political body in the United States that could give directions to the Navy as to the objectives for which the Navy might be used, hence the Navy was obliged to think in terms of all possible objectives for which its services might be called. There was no national board of strategy in the United States which could define those objectives, although several other nations have such a board and are able to lay down in broad lines the purposes of naval construction.

It was with such thoughts in mind that Hugh Gibson and I made repeated attempts to obtain from the President of the United States, either through his own ruling or through the findings of a board for national defense, decisive policies on which naval construction might be projected. Obviously, knowledge of such policies would have facilitated our discussions with other powers as to numbers and types of fleet. We made an attempt with President Coolidge and, later, one with President Hoover, but found both of these gentlemen unwilling to give precision to American policy.

Perhaps it is impossible in a democracy such as the United States to forecast long-range policy, nevertheless the desirability of doing so is patent and obvious. Such definition of policy should not be left to the Navy alone, although the Navy should give its best advice as to possibilities and strategy. At the present moment we are confronted with grave decisions of policy in respect to the American hemisphere, and I submit that the present, as no other period, calls for the creation of such a board of national defense as I have suggested.

The London Conference, then, was the last great success in the field of limitation of armament. The high point of economic collaboration in Europe was reached in 1928 with the abortive Treaty for the Abolition of Restrictions on Imports and Exports. In political collaboration, as well, the most ambitious attempt in Europe was made, and failed, in this year of 1930. For years, writers and thinkers had pointed out the obvious advantages of a European union, both economic and for the purposes of peace.

However, no genuine political attempt had been made, to my knowledge, to bring this about. It came, therefore, as a profound surprise when Briand introduced a resolution at Geneva calling for the setting up of a committee of the League of Nations to examine the possibility of such union. However skeptical the delegates may have been, the position of France at that time was sufficient to guarantee a study of any proposal made by that country — the possessor of an army of unequalled force and an unparalleled prestige among the other countries. It quickly became apparent, however, that even the prestige of France could produce nothing tangible in a meeting for such a purpose.

The theoretical advantages of a United States of Europe are so apparent that one is inclined to overlook the varied and profound obstacles in the path of its realization. It is not even clearly demonstrated that in practical application it would be economically advantageous to the entire continent to form such a United States, if we are to assume complete freedom of exchange within its borders. In thinking of this conception one recalls the words of Von Moltke regarding the abolition of war and the establishment of a lasting peace : "It is a dream, and it is not even a beautiful dream." I am confronted with the depth of racial and historical animosity, with the divergence of language and culture, with the enormous difference between standards of living in various parts of Europe, and confess that I can see only two possible ways in which these profound differences might be submerged for the purpose of European union.

It might be done if one state became so powerful that it could conquer and dominate the whole of Europe for a sufficiently long period to sweep out the barriers, maintain order during the economic convulsion which would follow, build the necessary communications, establish the necessary financial unity, and eventually bring out of the chaos something approaching widespread prosperity. The union might also come about through such a series of wars, devastation and suffering that the peoples themselves would overthrow existing governments and clamor for unity. Either of these two means of bringing about unity is so dreadful that it doesn't bear thinking about. If a United States of Europe is a state of health for that body, one fears deeply that the remedy to bring about that state of health is worse than the disease itself.

CHAPTER IV

I find that in this story I cannot adhere always to chronological order. Certain negotiations endured over a period of so many years that they cannot be made to fit a chronological pattern. Among these was the attempt under the League of Nations to write a treaty on the limitation and reduction of armament. When I arrived in Switzerland the League of Nations had already set up what was known as the Preparatory Commission for Disarmament. This body had functioned already for several years, and I participated in its meetings and debates until its final session. Normally, Hugh Gibson was chief delegate for the United States; in his absence I carried out this role. The task of the commission was to prepare a draft treaty, leaving the numbers in blank, on the basis of which a general conference on disarmament might be called. It was hoped that we could write such a draft that the task of the general conference would be fulfilled with a minimum of further discussion.

Thinking back over those years, it is difficult to see how the representatives of some twenty-five states, the principal military states of the world, could debate so long and so acrimoniously over the theory only of the method of disarmament. Yet such we did. I have no intention of giving a detailed account of the labor of the Preparatory Commission on Disarmament, both because it would be academic and dull to the casual reader, and because the task, at least from the

British point of view, has already been done adequately by General Temperley in his book, *The Whispering Gallery of Europe.*

The Commission was under the Presidency of M. Loudon, Minister of the Netherlands to Paris.   He had my sympathy then and he has it now, when I remember the acrimonious nature of some of the debate.   Italy was represented by General de Marinis.   A squat figure with an enormous head, short neck, half-closed eyes, he presented the appearance of a good-natured bullfrog.   Count von Bernstorff, Ambassador to the United States during the war, spoke for Germany, but he spoke, alas, in Germanic French, when he could have used impeccable English.   I always felt that some of the acrimony that crept into the debate between Bernstorff and the French delegation was due in part to the resentment of the latter at hearing their language so pronounced.   Our good friend Sato headed the Japanese group.   An honest and upright gentleman, we knew that we could count on Sato's word and we were proud of his friendship.

The French chief delegate changed with vertiginous rapidity in accordance with the equally rapid changes of the French cabinet.   M. Paul-Boncour, however, seemed to survive longer than most, and certainly played a more dramatic role than the others in the debates of the commission.   Like nearly all Frenchmen, Paul-Boncour spoke readily, but this is an understatement.   His voice was musical, his delivery magnificent. I once told him that I thought the rules of the League were grossly unfair.   Every Frenchman was a natural speaker ; practically no Anglo-Saxons were ; as for the other nations, they all had to speak in foreign tongues.   I said the only way to make things equal would be to oblige the French to speak English and us to speak French. We would then all be on an equal footing. I daresay that part of the influence which the French delegations always wielded at Geneva came from the fact that they were speaking their own tongue and speaking it beautifully.

Paul-Boncour was a short figure, powerful and stocky, a beautiful head which a sculptor would love to mould, abundant wavy white hair; one could picture him so easily in various circumstances of French history, mounted on a platform, haranguing a maddened mass of fellow citizens and pushing them into violent action. My fencing master at Berne had told me that Paul-Boncour was one of the ablest swordsmen that he had ever encountered. I repeated this to Paul-Boncour in one meeting at Geneva. He seemed to find the compliment natural, he said, "Yes, and do you know that the knowledge of my ability as a fencer has brought it about that I am perhaps the only Frenchman in public life of my generation that has never had to fight a duel?"

René Massigli was the right-hand man of the French delegation. An exact mentality, a retentive memory, an inexhaustible capacity for hard work, coupled with participation in nearly every French delegation to international gatherings since the Treaty of Versailles, gave Massigli a competence and authority in League discussions out of all proportion to his official position in France.

There was another member of the French delegation on whom we all depended for highly specialized advice. Jean Paul-Boncour, nephew of the Minister, was a competent man in many respects but in one he was outstanding. Jean Paul, as we called him, could always be counted on for knowledge of the best restaurants and the best wine within a radius of one hundred kilometers from Geneva. In as much as this part of France is admirable, even in France, for its cooking and wines, Jean Paul was always summoned to lead any group who desired to spend Sunday with the objective of lunch. Under his genial guidance I have gone as far afield as Lyons and Prier, Grenoble and Annecy. It was not always in towns, sometimes he would lead us to a tiny farmhouse where we would lunch off a roasted pig and cider. How he ever did his work and kept up his inexhaustible repertoire of good food, passed the comprehension of all of us.

I have spoken of the acrimony of our debates. The first years, however, in retrospect seem like a path of roses when one compares them with the years after the arrival of Litvinoff from Moscow. Many of the League members felt great satisfaction that Russia had accepted an invitation to take part in the Preparatory Commission. They had felt that this might be an indication that Russia was becoming "civilized" and that it would drop its former policy of antagonism and disruption toward the bourgeois governments. In his first appearances before the League, however, Litvinoff did little to give ground to these hopes. He took a mischievous pleasure in putting the others in the most embarrassing possible situation. His little eyes would twinkle as he drove home his shafts. Tempers grew frayed and outbursts were frequent. One of the most memorable of them occurred when the vast figure of Lord Cushendon, the British Delegate, rose slowly to his feet and shouted back a denunciation of the whole Bolshevist system, which was a credit to even a Conservative member of Parliament.

I believe that Litvinoff acquired his English in England, but wherever he got it, it was to a high degree incomprehensible; the accent was such that I used to listen for the translation rather than for the original to get an accurate knowledge of what he was saying. Many of the delegates fell into this habit, and there was a general exodus from the room when Litvinoff began, especially as he usually spoke at considerable length. The delegates would stream back to hear the translation, thus reversing the usual procedure.

Once during some lengthy remarks by Litvinoff, a delegate came into the room, leaned over Hugh Gibson and myself and said, "What is Litvinoff saying?"

Hugh Gibson replied, "He hasn't said yet."

Sir Alexander Cadogan occupied approximately the same position with the British delegation that Massigli held with the French. Cadogan was of an equitable disposition, profound common sense, and a dependable friend. He is now Under Secretary in the British Foreign Office.

I have gone at length into the personalities which made up this commission because our years of struggle, friendship and hostility engrave them deeply on my mind. I can't turn from this subject without mentioning one more man. Madariaga, delegate of Spain, was an outstanding intellect. He can speak or write in French, Spanish, or English with equal fluency. He is a widely known author and a gifted speaker. His talk would often throw a glint of humor into an otherwise dull debate — a theoretician, but with a basis of logic to his theory.

I do not need to describe him beyond saying that in the American delegation he was known as "Mickey Mouse." I once took my young son into the gallery to listen to a debate ; he emerged delighted, and informed us that he had at once spotted Mickey Mouse.

I have spoken already of our debate on the theory of disarmament. While we debated the theory alone, naturally the various theses maintained had a concrete application. The debates were not for pure dialectic sport, but for the purpose of making certain practical applications prevail, to the advantage of one state or the other.

No one question was so thorny as that of whether or not to include trained reserves in counting the numbers of men under colors. It must be remembered that under the Treaty of Versailles, Germany had been forbidden a conscript army and was held to an army of one hundred thousand men, all volunteers, with long terms of enlistment. Thus the numbers of men in Germany trained and capable of bearing arms was relatively small. France, on the other hand, and most of the other continental countries, had obligatory manhood service of from one to two years. This meant that every year there were turned out into the civilian population several hundred thousand well-trained and competent troops capable of being called back to the colors, and under the obligation to respond to such a call in a crisis. The French, therefore, and their allies on the continent, were determined that under no conditions should trained reserves be counted as part of the armed force.

The Germans — in the first instance — the British, and ourselves, all nations possessing small professional armies, were equally insistent that trained reserves should be included. Under the same impulse, if not under the famous French logic, the French were equally determined that all party-trained servants of a government should be counted ; for instance, the German "Schupo," or green police, carried rifles and occasionally had company drill, hence, according to the French, should be included at least as partial soldiers. I use the word "partial" advisedly, since the French eventually produced a scheme whereby different grades and categories of men in the national service but not a part of the army proper, should be assessed on a fractional evaluation for each man. This one controversy on trained reserves seemed so insuperable that we in the American delegation eventually came to the conclusion that a conference would never be held if we maintained our position. Our retirement from our position broke the log jam on a number of questions and precipitated the final elaboration of the preparatory draft.

The position of Germany in respect to disarmament was, of course, the dominating factor. The French and their friends, notably The Little Entente, seemed to believe that it would be possible to write a limitation of armaments treaty leaving Germany bound by the Treaty of Versailles. From the early years of our discussions, I was convinced that Germany would never tolerate such an arrangement nor could such an arrangement, I felt, be compatible with the obligations of the Covenant upon the states bound thereby.

During the course of the Preparatory Conference, Gibson and I made repeated attempts to persuade the French to make an offer to write into the treaty, presumably a relatively short-term treaty, a duplication of the obligations of the Treaty of Versailles. This would have given France a period of years in which Germany was bound and at the end of that period would have left Germany free to negotiate on an equal legal footing. We could make no headway with this thesis, and this controversy, like others, had to be passed in silence to the General Disarmament Conference. Legally, of course, the French were right; Germany was bound by an indeterminate obligation. Nevertheless, it was inconceivable to an observer from America that the German race would stay so bound in perpetuity, particularly as there was no thought of the others accepting like or even analogous obligations.

Painstaking labor of years had gone into the preparation of the draft convention. The best thought of naval, military, and political experts of the countries represented had been offered in its elaboration, and yet when we came to the General Disarmament Conference in 1932 I failed to hear a single suggestion that work should be continued to fill out the blanks for numbers in the draft convention. The result of these years of effort was buried in silence. I do not know of any other project elaborated internationally that met with such complete oblivion.

When we terminated the work of the Preparatory Commission we terminated such work of an international nature as was carried on in a world in which there was genuine hope of realization. In spite of the panic in the United States, it seemed as if the world was on the upgrade and that a spirit of international good will and collaboration might remove many of the ills of the economic body and might bring about a political appeasement (the word had then not acquired its special meaning). But in the spring of 1931 came the crash of the Kreditanstalt in Vienna. Widespread unemployment and suffering began in Germany, the British Government went off the gold standard, and it was under the impression of these events that the Assembly met in 1931.

British prestige was at the lowest ebb. The British Government was far more concerned by its internal situation than by any of the events of the Assembly, nevertheless those events were of formidable importance.

In the first days of the Assembly, Dino Grandi, Foreign Minister of Italy, proposed on behalf of the Italian Government that there should be a truce on all increase of armament, this in order to establish the proper sort of atmosphere for the General Disarmament Conference which had been called for February of 1932. The American Government expressed enthusiastic adherence to the proposal, and Grandi's suggestion was referred to what was called the "Third Committee," the committee of the Assembly dealing with disarmament. As I sat in the balcony at the first meeting of the Third Committee, I had the curious sensation of hearing discussed the advisability of my being invited to sit with the committee in its debates. Needless to say, I left the balcony in order to leave the discussion free. An invitation was extended to the American Government, and I was appointed to sit with the Third Committee.

Now it sounds like a simple thing to declare a truce in armament, but when you try to write such a truce a number of thorny questions immediately arise : What should be done about goods on order, tanks, airplanes, naval vessels ? What should be done about ships partially constructed ? What should be done about material for which appropriation has been made but for which orders have not been placed ? It was plain to most of us in Geneva that if there was to be a truce which would accomplish any psychological benefit it must be thorough-going and without exception. Under the impression of my government's enthusiastic adherence, I had preached the doctrine of a thorough-going truce.

My dismay can be imagined, then, when I received instructions that I had to reserve from the operation of the truce, work on certain destroyers, "which was part of our recovery program." I had to make the speech, I was under orders, but to do so was bitter. I had not been sure that a truce was possible ; I knew that a truce became impossible if we admitted reservations. I could see the satisfaction on the faces of some of the delegates present who had been reluctant to adhere to the truce but had been unwilling to assume the burden of breaking it down. The United States assumed that burden, and the truce was written with so many reservations that it meant nothing whatever.

In the midst of this debate came the stunning news of Japan's military adventure in Manchuria. The Council was summoned at once to discuss the situation. I was not a member of the Council, of course, but I might as well have been one since I usually met with Eric Drummond and members of the Council in the room of the Secretary General either before or after the Council's sessions, and sometimes both. The position that the United States might adopt was of overwhelming importance to these members of the League, an importance which makes somewhat ironic our inherent fear of commitment and involvement ; we were certainly involved, and, equally certainly, we were not committed.

There was a section of our public opinion which felt that

we were committed, either under the Pact of Paris, the Kellogg-Briand Pact, or the Nine-Power Treaty, one of the Washington Conference treaties. The first treaty, however, is a mere self-denying ordinance without any statement as to its implementation. The Nine-Power Treaty, as well, has no implementation for its enforcement. Our only obligation in the Far East for implementation was the Four-Power consultative arrangement and this, as far as I know, was never invoked during these discussions. We were "involved" through our interest in the Far East, through the outcry raised by our own people against Japan's act, and by the mere fact that we were possessors of an enormous fleet, so that any attempt at coercion by the states bound by the Covenant could be done only with our acquiescence, if not with our assistance.

To most of the members of the Council events in Manchuria had the geographical remoteness of events to us in the Antarctic. There was no one member of the Council who was aware of the special rights of Japan in Manchuria, no member had studied the history and the long series of treaties and conventions dealing with that region, no member had a conception of the long train of annoyances, irritations and incidents that had marked the relationship between the Chinese and Japanese in the Province. I sat listening to one meeting of the Council and heard Lord Cecil advocate that the Council summon Japan to retire all its troops forthwith from Manchuria. While the translation of Lord Cecil's remarks was being made, I wrote a note to Eric Drummond on the back of an envelope and suggested to him the wisdom of adjourning the Council for an hour in order to look up the treaties giving special police rights to Japan along the zone of the South Manchurian railroad. Drummond read it, looked down at me, grinned, and persuaded the presiding officer to adjourn the Council.

Perhaps here is the place to remark that when events occurred in remote parts of the world, the European delegates to the Assembly and Council always listened to an account of them with a certain air of pained surprise. The same thing happened in the dispute about the Chaco, while the dispute involving Letitia on the upper reaches of the Putomayo was more remote not only than the Antarctic, but it might have been in Mars. In the minds of the French delegates and others, particularly The Little Entente, the Covenant of the League was pre-eminently a measure for the maintenance of Germany in the position prescribed for it by the Treaty of Versailles ; anything that diverted attention from this, to their minds, dominating factor, had a tinge of bad taste.

I may say that this Alice-in-Wonderland type of debate in the Council rapidly changed. The delegates quickly recognized the overwhelming challenge which the Manchurian incident had brought to the Covenant of the League and to their whole international structure. Members began to study deeply, and, above all, hurriedly to summon their Far Eastern experts from the foreign offices.

These were eventful days not only in history but to me personally. I was dragged out of the Assembly to answer the telephone from Washington, I had constant conferences with members of the Council, the press was clamorous. Without appearing at the Council table, it was obvious that I represented the decisive factor in decisions which might be taken. Telegrams had to be sent and deciphered to all hours of the night. As usual, our staff was entirely inadequate, but they worked at a feverish pace. By the end of the Assembly I was thoroughly exhausted, and read with pleasure a telegram from Washington ordering me to come home for consultation regarding the coming General Disarmament Conference. My departure was facilitated by an apparently conciliatory attitude on the part of the Japanese which gave hope for the moment that the incident of Manchuria might be liquidated.

On the steamer, before I had even reached America, the wireless bulletins announced that fighting had broken out between the Japanese and Chinese at Shanghai, that renewed meetings of the Council had taken place, that the situation was even more tense, and that the American Consul at Geneva was sitting with the Council to collaborate. The Council met later in Paris and the Secretary of State sent General Dawes, Ambassador to Great Britain, to attend as American representative. When I arrived in Washington, I called on Secretary Stimson. He said, "It is a pity we ordered you home. I should have preferred to send you rather than General Dawes to the Council meeting in Paris, it would have appeared more normal and would have caused less sensation."

The World Conference for the Reduction and Limitation of Armament opened in February, 1932. It was probably the greatest conference numerically that the world has ever seen. It was probably, furthermore, as pregnant with disaster, as deplorable in its failure, as any assembly that mankind has witnessed. It was a colossal effort, an effort made by a number of men of limited wisdom, perhaps, but of a sincerity of purpose which made the failure still sadder and more fateful. There may have been some who worked with their tongues in their cheeks, and in their hearts hoped for failure ; I have no doubt there were some. But the great majority of those hundreds of representatives of the states of the world made earnest and honest endeavor for agreement. There were indeed few who did not foresee that a failure of the conference would bring about unimaginable evils.

It was patent to any observer that the conditions for the conference were not propitious. Fighting was going on between Japan and China, economic dislocation was widespread, in Germany the Communists and Fascists had just gained enormously in the last elections, in France an extreme Right Government under Tardieu could be expected to make little concession to the moderate Bruening government of Germany. Arthur Henderson, who had been chosen chairman of the conference while Foreign Secretary for Great Britain, not only was out of office, but was a sick, and, as it turned out, a dying man. We knew all these things but we were powerless to stop or postpone the endeavor. The thing ground on with steady deterioration, one could only hope that a miracle would reverse the trend that seemed inevitable. Once or twice it looked as if the miracle was about to happen, but the inexorable destiny that hung over Europe willed it otherwise.

Among the peoples of the world, however, there was no lack of faith and hope. One of the opening days of the conference was devoted to the reception of organizations representing millions of members. Innumerable letters, telegrams and petitions poured in to the chairman and the delegations. All over the world groups of people who saw hope for a better existence through a limitation on arms, implored the conference to work for success. They came from veterans' organizations, from peace groups, from universities. They came from cities, villages and farms. They came from France and Germany, and not only as might have been expected, from the Scandinavian and Anglo-Saxon countries.

It was a universal movement of hope that bore striking resemblance to the longing for a better world which showed itself in the faith in President Wilson in the last months of 1918 and the first months of 1919. Sitting in the hall, listening to these demonstrations, sitting in the Hotel des Bergues, the home of the American delegation, hearing the representatives of millions of earnest American advocates of disarmament, was overwhelmingly impressive. In spite of the factors that I recognized which threatened to wreck the movement, I felt an awakened hope that this mighty pressure of public desire might force a success.

What was the fundamental issue that put the conference on the rocks ? It seemed as plain then as it seems now in the light of experience, and I shall try to state it as tersely as possible, even at the risk of simplifying unduly a complex situation. Germany was disarmed by the Treaty of Versailles ; although the French, and the British, too, had evidence which they claimed proved violation of the treaty, nevertheless they all recognized that Germany was disarmed to an extent which rendered effective combat against a great power unthinkable. France was fully armed. The French were about forty million, Germany seventy million. The French birthrate was falling, Germany's expanding. The Germans were more powerful industrially, not alone in possession of plants but in capability for labor. Therefore, an equality of arms between Germany and France meant domination by Germany.

The French had alliances with the Little Entente and Poland which gave them overwhelming superiority over Germany, certainly on paper. The prestige of France was immense, and its authority on the continent as little challenged as in the most powerful period of Louis XIV. How could the French maintain this position if they disarmed? They proposed numerous guaranties and alliances, they preached the doctrine of security and spoke as if security were a measurable and ponderable factor. They said, "Give us security, we give you reduction. The greater the security, the greater the reduction."

The only nations in a position to give this security were Great Britain and the United States through guaranties for the safety of France if attacked. The public in neither country was ready for such guaranties. Furthermore, the French were never specific as to reductions in the event of specific guaranties; certainly the Anglo-Saxons felt that no guaranty would be sufficient to persuade the French to make a sacrifice that would in any way jeopardize their hegemony on the continent. At a later stage of the conference, a French Government under Herriot came into office which made, I believe, sincere efforts to meet the Germans, recognizing that a greater danger lay in a dissatisfied Germany than in taking some risk of reduction. But with this one exception, I could not escape the conviction that no other government of France had the faintest intention of surrendering or impairing its power to dictate to Germany.

CHAPTER V

The conference opened in great solemnity, with prepared speeches by all the chief delegates ; weeks were occupied by this opening phase. It then broke up into Land, Sea, and Air Committees. The organization of the conference was put into effect in the early stages. The Vice President was M. Politis, Greek Minister to Paris, a man of unusual command of French, a forceful and eloquent speaker. He was a jurist of high reputation and his lucidity was remarkable. His devotion to the French cause was such, however, that the Germans and neutrals had little faith in him. In League of Nations practice, in every conference there is appointed a *rapporteur* whose duty it is to assemble the results of debate and attempt to harmonize them into effective purpose. It can be seen that this duty is most important, and indeed in many conferences the *rapporteur* plays a much more effective role than the chairman.

M. Benes of Czechoslovakia was chosen for this post. His abilities as a conciliator were of a high order, his intelligence unquestioned, but again, as far as Germany was concerned, the choice was unfortunate. Benes represented the most devoted of the nations in the French orbit, a nation whose very existence depended upon a continuance of Germany's weakness. The conference also set up what was called a "bureau," or steering committee, consisting of the chief delegates of certain selected countries, a relatively small body supposed to advise with the chairman for conference planning.

My particular task at this phase was the representation of the American delegation on the land committee. We debated calibers and mobility of guns, size and effectiveness of tanks, value of various types of training in making soldiers. Certainly no one was so indelicate as to suggest numbers of any of these things for a specific country. We made the first effort of many to distinguish between "offensive" and "defensive" weapons. Of course every delegate present felt that his type of weapon was defensive and the other fellow's offensive. To my mind, Madariaga summed up in this debate the genuine differentiation between offensive and defensive weapons when he remarked, "A weapon is either offensive or defensive according to which end of it you are looking at." Even the fixed guns of the Maginot Line, the Germans argued, could cover an assault upon the unfortified Rhineland and hence could be called offensive weapons.

It may be of interest to say something of the American delegation. Hugh Gibson was our chief delegate. Senator Claude Swanson had served for years on the Senate Naval Committee, he knew his subject thoroughly but the European scene was new and strange. I can see him now sitting on the Sea Commission, blowing great clouds of smoke from his cigar and demonstrating in fervid Southern eloquence that battleships were the most defensive of all types of weapons; they became a symbol of the American home and family, they could be given to children to play with as toys, so harmless was their use and purpose.

We had a delegation meeting in the early days of the conference, and at the suggestion of the chief delegate I explained as adequately as I could the French demand that security precede disarmament. Perhaps I presented the case too sympathetically in my endeavor to give a fair picture, for the Senator said, "Mr. Wilson, do you believe that this is a righteous claim?" I replied that as a matter of fact I deplored it for I thought it would wreck the conference, but added that it didn't much matter whether it was righteous or not, the French were powerful enough to insist on it. The Senator eyed me sternly. "Mr. Wilson, I am relieved that you, an American, do not feel that such an unreality constitutes a righteous claim."

Now I find that remark interesting since it illustrates a common American point of view. Our most certain reaction to the stimulus of a piece of news from a foreign land is to judge it "good" or "bad," "righteous" or "unjust." In other words, we instantly assess it by a moral evaluation based on our own standards. Let me give an example : An American will condemn a whole movement of a race or of nations on the ground that such movement is undemocratic. And yet democracy has never prevailed over a great section of the world. Democracy in genuine application has existed only on the northwest fringe of Europe, in France, Switzerland and the Anglo-Saxon countries. And yet we assess a moral condemnation on measurements that are not even accepted as valid in the lands which are condemned.

This tendency to moral condemnation is a relatively new thing, speaking historically. I have heard the theory advanced that late eighteenth century French philosophy adapted the yardstick of reason to the assessment of all human action. Under this measurement, each human act fell into the category of reasonable or unreasonable, and was accepted or rejected on this count. Even this measure is fallible as reason itself is finite. But how much more finite is the moral judgment, which, according to the theory, resulted from the Anglo-Saxons' endeavor to adopt the French philosophy. As this philosophy poured through the filter of the conscience of the Protestant churchman, he unconsciously twisted reason into conscience, and adopted his own conscience as the measure of judgment of all human action, foreign or domestic, without regard to his own limitations to knowledge. Conscience as a means of judging and condemning our own acts is God-given, as a measure for the acts of others it is unjust and it is dangerous.

In recent years I have become more and more aware of our characteristic in this regard, the phenomenon of moral judgment is essentially Anglo-Saxon and essentially what we might call non-conformist Anglo-Saxon. Even the Protestant communities of the European continent, even the Calvinists of Geneva, have a broader attitude and a reluctance to utter moral judgment without full knowledge.

Another delegate was Mr. Norman Davis, later to become chief delegate after Mr. Roosevelt's inauguration. Norman Davis has a deceptive exterior; gentle manner, snow-white hair, mild blue eyes; he speaks with a gentle Southern drawl. He is one of the most lovable personalities I have met, but let no one be deceived by appearance and manner. They hide a shrewdness and cool brain, he is a "horse-trader" of unusual astuteness. In playing golf with Norman, although he is a sound player, we always feel that the moment of greatest peril has passed when we have left the first tee and the discussion about handicap has ended.

The President of Mt. Holyoke College, Miss Mary Woolley, was also a delegate. She is an earnest, intelligent and charming woman ; we all held her in deep affection. She was of genuine value to the delegation since she was respected and followed by the women's clubs of this country, and her common-sense idealism helped us in many a difficult position. She fulfilled a task on the delegation that none of the rest of us could have accomplished.

As I think of that delegation in the light of the intensely political composition of most succeeding delegations to international conferences, it is curious to consider the selection. Mr. Hoover, a Republican President, chose as his representatives to this most fateful meeting two Democrats, Senator Swanson and Mr. Davis ; two non-partisan diplomats, Gibson and myself ; and Miss Woolley, and I don't know to this day how she votes.

In the month of April, 1932, the Secretary of State, Mr. Stimson, came to Geneva to assume chairmanship of the American delegation. He leased the villa of Bessinges, a lovely place a few miles from Geneva, set in a grove of stately trees. Mr. Stimson made one visit only to the building which the Swiss Government had set up for the conference, he took no part in the debates of the committees, nevertheless, his visit brought about one of the few hopeful situations which the conference produced.

Mr. MacDonald came from London, Mr. Bruening from Berlin, Mr. Stimson had had a long conference with Tardieu on coming through Paris. Day after day, MacDonald and Bruening visited Bessinges and there worked out with the Secretary of State a possible basis of agreement. They then set about to bring Tardieu from Paris. First Tardieu declined on the grounds of an imminent election, later on account of sickness.   Bruening and MacDonald returned home and Mr. Stimson sailed for America.   The opportunity had passed.

The committee work had become arid, enthusiasm had departed for the unending discussion of method and type.   A sudden refreshing breeze passed over the proceedings with our introduction of the Hoover Plan.   Not only was the plan itself ingenious but for the first time reality entered the debates through the introduction of figures.   The plan was roughly as follows : for the sea, a flat one-third reduction of existing tonnage for each fleet ; for the air, abolition of bombing planes and prohibition of bombardment ; for the land, abolition of heavy mobile artillery and a force of troops for each nation calculated on a coefficient based on the ratio of the German Army to the German population, but giving an additional force based on overseas possessions for the maintenance of order in colonial territories.   There was a rough justice about this basis since the Allied and Associated Powers had fixed the figure of one hundred thousand men as the minimum force necessary to maintain order in Germany.

We worked our hardest on this plan, not only was it necessary to defend it on the floor from attack and criticism, but we spent hours every day with members of other delegations, demonstrating by charts how the plan would work out for land effectives, and trying to convince them that the plan was a generally acceptable and just basis.   We had rough sledding with the continental powers but a sympathetic hearing ; we had blunt opposition from the British to the proposals for naval reduction.   The British took the position that their need for a navy was absolute and not dependent upon the size of navies of potential enemies.   They argued that the immense extent of the British Empire and the dependence of the British Isles upon imported foodstuffs meant the necessity for a navy of irreducible proportions regardless of what others might have. Even General Temperley, for years military adviser to British delegations at Geneva and a convinced advocate of disarmament, has this to say about the British position on the Hoover Plan :

> On the naval side it was obvious that the cuts would not be accepted. Our standards were not set by another Power but by our absolute needs of guarding trade routes. We could not afford to reduce, even if the Americans and Japanese did so.

The formal presentation of the Hoover Plan gave rise to a dramatic debate in the conference. Immediately following Gibson's speech, Grandi arose. He read the American proposal point by point, at the end of each paragraph he stated in resonant tones, "Italy accepts." Spreading enthusiasm for the project foundered on the rock of Sir John Simon's suavity. He praised the plan and President Hoover, he praised the American people and their chief delegate, but his phraseology had so many "weasel" clauses, that every delegate knew that Great Britain would resist the project.

As I look back at the rare positive efforts in this long and dreary conference, I am convinced that the Hoover Plan represented the fairest proposal, and the one least governed by selfish considerations. It was a just basis for agreement. Even Germany would have accepted at that time had the others done so.

In the summer of 1932 the conference came to a dead end in a blunt disagreement between the French and Germans on the question of Germany's position in the proposed treaty. The French made it clear that Germany was to remain bound by the military terms of Versailles, the Germans as bluntly stated that they would be bound only by the same terms as the rest of the States. They insisted upon what they called *Gleichberechtigung*, equality of treatment, and withdrew from the conference until this should be accorded them.

Lively efforts persisted through the Assembly of that year, and subsequently, to persuade the Germans to return to the Disarmament Conference. Eventually Baron von Neurath, the Foreign Minister, agreed to a further discussion of "equality of rights" during the December Council. The meeting took place in the gaudy salon which the British delegation always took as their meeting place in the Hotel Beau-Rivage. MacDonald and Simon were there for England, Herriot and Paul-Boncour for France, Von Neurath for Germany, Aloisi for Italy, and Norman Davis and myself for the United States.

The discussion was arduous and at times heated. The French had arrived with a formula prepared, apparently already submitted to, and approved by, the French Cabinet. Baron von Neurath was a stubborn debater, a German of the old school, giving away nothing but maintaining a rigidly correct exterior in spite of heightened color and a flash of the eye when irritation mounted. Herriot and Paul-Boncour, eloquent and plausible, showing a sincere purpose for agreement but unable at times to withhold a wounding thrust at German susceptibilities. MacDonald and Davis sat on the side-lines, so to speak, and united in pushing, or soothing, first one side then the other when signs of recalcitrance or irritation were visible. Aloisi took practically no part in the discussion.

We rose from this lengthy struggle exhausted but happy in the knowledge that Germany was to return to the discussions.

In my memory this scene often returns to me, an oval inlaid table, gilded armchairs, and the faces of those men. MacDonald spoke with resonant voice, full of unction, throwing arguments of morality upon the skeptical continentals, Simon with comment of amazing penetration, the greatest intellect of them all, his plausibility made his proposals sound unattackable. Herriot with booming voice and rotund body, insisted upon his point of view with a force of reiteration that was devastating. He held before him on the table his bulging briefcase, the rest of us knew, if Von Neurath did not, that it contained his evidence of German violations of the treaty provisions.

Paul-Boncour with actor's face, musical voice and fluid gesture, poured out his persuasion like honey. Norman Davis spoke softly and insistently, deeply in earnest and showing signs of distress when the argument became heated. Aloisi sat silent, lean, hard, taciturn, he seemed to epitomize the age-old cynicism of the Italian. Von Neurath's granite face showed no emotion save in the ebb and flow of color as temper rose or subsided. His French was difficult and no easy vehicle for the communication of his thought, nevertheless, he persisted in it and doggedly made himself clear. This was the last international act of importance of Republican Germany. Hitler became Chancellor the following February.

Throughout the year of 1932 and the spring months of 1933 the crisis of Manchukuo was ever present, sometimes in active form in meetings of the Council and Assembly, sometimes dormant as when awaiting the results of the investigation of Lord Lytton. The fighting around Shanghai had eased off after the bombardment of the Chapei section by the Japanese and an agreement dealing with this area had been written by the two belligerents under the auspices of the Admirals of the French, British and American fleets in those waters.

During the course of this fighting the Japanese delegation in Geneva made persistent efforts to convince representatives of other nations of the provocation of the Chinese in Shanghai. One day Mr. Matsudaira, at that time chairman of the Japanese delegation, called on Hugh Gibson and myself. There had been heavy fighting in and around Chapei and the fighting had been intensified by the arrival of a Chinese armored train which at first created considerable havoc among the Japanese forces. Mr. Matsudaira, loyal servant of the Japanese Government, explained to us in all solemnity how provocative it was on the part of the Chinese to accelerate the fighting by the utilization of this mechanized weapon. The arrival of the armored train in South Station in Shanghai was, Mr. Matsudaira said, "indiscreet, very indiscreet."

I was, of course, in the closest touch with Sir John Simon, British Secretary of State for Foreign Affairs. Messages were constantly coming and going between Mr. Stimson in Washington and Sir John in Geneva. It was at this period that the incident occurred which has been so much publicized and on account of which the American public is so ready to accuse the British Government of having been unwilling to act vigorously. It will be remembered that Mr. Stimson had embarked upon a campaign to accomplish what he called "a mobilization of public opinion against Japan."

In the course of this procedure Mr. Stimson had written Senator Borah a letter which was a masterly arraignment of Japanese acts in Manchuria. Mr. Stimson and Sir John were in constant telephone communication, and in my frequent encounters with Sir John he would tell me what had taken place over the telephone. I had, of course, no other access to information about such conversations. Furthermore, in as much as I assumed such conversations were recorded in Washington, I made no reports as to what Sir John told me of their tenor.

One day Sir John recounted to me a talk over the telephone which he had had with the Secretary of State in Washington. Sir John was perturbed. Mr. Stimson had suggested taking such vigorous action that Sir John felt that it might lead to the use of the American and British fleets to enforce it. He added that the British public was in no state of mind to support a war in such a remote region and for purposes which they would consider remote. From his reports received from Washington as to the state of mind of the American people he questioned whether the American public would not also be reluctant to assume such a risk.

It became clear subsequently that the Secretary of State in Washington understood that he had met with a definite refusal, or rather with such dilatory co-operation as to constitute a refusal in fact, and considerable acrimony developed later in the press of the two countries on the failure of the British Government to give thoroughgoing assistance to the American Government in a matter of such importance as the established peace of the world. I have never seen the actual record of these telephone conversations so I am unable to quote from them.

However, it seemed to me then as now that the telephone between two responsible statesmen is a method of communication which is fraught with danger. Few men in the world are able to think rapidly enough or accurately enough in matters involving war and peace to take the immediate decisions that a telephone conversation calls for. Messages of this importance should be carefully drafted, experts in both Foreign Offices should go over them thoroughly, they should be so formulated that their meaning is precise and clear and offers no basis for subsequent misunderstanding. The danger of a few hours' delay in sending a written message is incomparably less than the risk of a misunderstanding arising between the Foreign Ministers of two great nations. I have seen cases in public affairs where the transoceanic telephone has been of inestimable service, but those cases have been rare.

It was determined by the Assembly to send a committee of investigation to the Far East to prepare a report on the situation on which the Assembly might eventually act. Lord Lytton of Great Britain, formerly Viceroy of India, was made chairman, and the United States was represented by an extremely competent officer, General Frank McCoy, of the American Army.

In the meantime the doctrine of nonrecognition of changes of territory brought about by force was initiated by Mr. Stimson and became incorporated into League doctrine in the Manchukuo affair, largely at the insistence of the United States. I am going to discuss this doctrine later; at present it is enough to say that I worked enthusiastically to do what I could to persuade the delegates of the virtue of this position.

Lord Lytton's report became available in the late autumn of 1932 and in the early spring of 1933 a meeting of the Assembly was held to take position thereon. Japan, as everybody knows, refused to accept the report and contested the findings of the

Assembly, and in the final session Mr. Matsuoka, now Minister for Foreign Affairs of Japan, finished his speech, summoned his assistants, and brusquely left the Assembly. The report was adopted and Japan withdrew from the League of Nations.

The final session of the Assembly remains indelibly printed on my mind. M. Huysmans of Belgium was in the chair. He was an excellent presiding officer and showed, I felt, a fine sense of discrimination in refusing to permit Wellington Koo, Chinese delegate, to terminate an attack on Japan which he tried to make after Matsuoka had left the Assembly. Matsuoka himself is a hard-bitten businessman with a considerable appearance of frankness. Most of his life has been spent in Manchuria where he has been an official and president of the South Manchurian Railway. His English is good but not flawless. He speaks with vigor and determination and has a fund of reminiscence which he loves to pour out in intimate company. His stories of dealing with the various Tuchuns of China revealed a scope of venality among Chinese leaders which was equalled only in the Balkans in the years preceding the Great War.

Matsuoka's speech on that day in the Assembly was delivered with a passionate conviction far removed from his usual businesslike manner. He pointed out the danger of pillorying a great nation. He warned that the Assembly was driving Japan from its friendship with the West toward an inevitable development of a self-sustaining, uniquely Eastern position. He terminated by saying that as Christ was crucified on the Cross, so was Japan being crucified by the nations of the League.

I said earlier that I would try to be scrupulously honest while making comment on events, to distinguish between my attitude at the moment and my attitude on subsequent reflection.   In the case in point, when I listened to Matsuoka, for the first time the gravest doubts arose as to the wisdom of the course which the Assembly and my country were pursuing.   I began to have a conception of the rancor and resentment that public condemnation could bring upon a proud and powerful people, and I began to question, and still do question, whether such treatment is wise.

If the nations of the world feel strongly enough to condemn, they should feel strongly enough to use force, if necessary, to rectify a situation which they find so deplorable.   To condemn only merely intensifies the heat.   Condemnation creates a community of the damned who are forced outside the pale, who have nothing to lose by the violation of all laws of order and international good faith.   It is exasperating without being efficacious.   If it were only exasperating that would be bad enough, but it is worse, it is profoundly dangerous.   The community of the damned can bring together unnatural allies, allies who in their hearts despise one another but who can unite in their hatred of the smug and respectable nations.

Japan was the first great nation to be condemned ; it was followed by other instances, and in no single case has the condemnation brought forth good fruit ; in every case deplorable consequences have flowed from it.   A domestic court may arraign and castigate a prisoner because it has the power to inflict punishment and because the laws of domestic society have provided sanctions which may restrain the bitterness arising from the arraignment.   Not so in international law ; there is no force other than war, or risk of war through economic sanctions, which can be brought to bear, hence the arraignment leaves a sullen resentment which no sanction of society yet invented can curb.

I left the Assembly that spring afternoon of 1933 troubled in spirit as I have seldom been. Not only did such doubts regarding arraignment arise in me, but for the first time I began to question the nonrecognition policy. More and more as I thought it over I became conscious that we had entered a dead-end street. I could see no way out of this situation with dignity for either side. A declaration of nonrecognition means that eventually one side or another will find itself in a position where it must "eat crow." If it were in any way a deterrent to the use of force one could, of course, admit its value. I doubted then if it would prove such a deterrent, and the past few years have more than justified such doubt. I once talked with M. Avenol, Secretary General of the League, about this matter. He made a brief remark which epitomized my thoughts on the policy. In speaking of the Assembly he said, "They are pitting their finite wills against infinite fact." In the long run it can be the fact only which prevails.

We in the United States existed well over a century with a totally different conception of recognition. In the long series of wars which occurred in the world between 1789 and 1914, recognition meant exactly what the word indicates, we saw that a thing existed and so stated. Recognition came as a result of observation of the facts. This was conscious policy and had been stated definitely by President Monroe as part of what we call the Monroe Doctrine. The Doctrine is set forth in two paragraphs of his message to Congress of December 2, 1823, and the sentence pertinent to my argument reads as follows :

Our policy in regard to Europe, which was adopted at an early stage of the wars which have so long agitated that quarter of the globe, nevertheless remains the same, which is, not to interfere in the internal concerns of any of its powers ; *to consider the government de facto as the legitimate government for us* ; to cultivate friendly relations with it, and to preserve those relations by a frank, firm, and manly policy, meeting, in all instances, the just claims of every power ; submitting to injuries from none.

It was President Wilson who launched the new phase of recognition when he announced that in our relations with the states of the American hemisphere we would be governed by the rule that we would not recognize régimes in those lands which came into being by methods in violation of their constitutions. In other words, we shall appoint ourselves the judge of the legality of a situation of purely domestic concern to the nation in question. Further, as a result of our judgment, if it is favorable, we issue a sort of blessing on the régime, a princely gesture from a people of superior virtue. Thus recognition has come to have a moral quality in the minds of the American people, and many a good citizen suffers in his conscience because his country has accorded, and still accords, recognition to ruthless rulers of large sections of the earth's territory and population.

If we desire to be involved in every squabble on the surface of the globe, let us by all means retain this moral conception of recognition. If, however, we are of the opinion that the Lord has given us exceptional blessings by separating us from the troubles of most of the world by wide seas on the east and west, then let us return to the ideas of President Monroe, who merely set forth the wisdom of his contemporaries.

President Wilson's new policy immediately encountered a hard fact, and that fact was a stout and ruthless individual,

President Huerta of Mexico. Our ideology prevailed, but at the expense of some years of tumult for Mexico, years which threatened to involve us in a senseless war. The Republican Administration succeeding President Wilson's had not learned its lesson. It instigated, in 1923, certain treaties among the Central American Republics by which the latter agreed among themselves to apply the principle of nonrecognition. While we did not sign these documents, we announced that we would be guided by this policy. Hard fact again intervened; in 1931, we encountered a situation in Salvador which made it advisable to recognize a revolutionary government. We denounced our policy of collaboration with the 1923 treaties and duly accorded recognition. We no longer maintain the doctrine in fact for our own hemisphere, whatever our theoretical stand, but we have maintained it rigidly for eight long years in respect to the remote province of Manchuria. Our policy has been, and is today, one of the principal factors which poison our relations with Japan.

I do not say we could negotiate our difficulties with that country even if we accepted the humiliation of according recognition to Manchukuo, I do not believe we could at the moment, but I do say that the maintenance of nonrecognition stultifies in advance any attempt to better our relations. If we as a people prefer a sentiment of righteousness, flowing from our refusal to deal with a nation which we in our judgment have condemned, to the possibility of having friendly rather than hostile powers in the world, then let us hold fast to our doctrine.

One thing further in regard to this policy, namely, that when in 1935 to 1936 the states of the League applied sanctions against Italy and even risked the possibility of warlike activity, no state urged that the doctrine of non-recognition be applied to the Ethiopian conquest. In the short space of three years the futility of the policy had become evident.

On March 4, 1933, I shared an experience which millions of Americans will remember. Major Goetz, our Military Attaché, and his wife invited the delegation staff to dinner to hear on a short-wave radio the inaugural address of our new President, Mr. Roosevelt. The country was in the depths. A week before I had received a letter from a friend of mine which had analyzed the situation and closed with these words : "I fear it's the end of our old Republic. Our economic life seems so desperate as to be beyond human wisdom for its salvation." Then flowed from the radio a beautiful voice which poured courage and faith into the hearts of all listeners. There was a man unperturbed by the magnitude of the task which confronted him. Courageous and buoyant himself, he was able to pour his faith into the entire nation. When the voice ceased, we silently drank a toast to the President with tears in our eyes. It must have been one of the most fateful speeches in the history of the nation.

In the spring of 1933 the Disarmament Conference resumed its activities. It had been apparent from the attitude of the press and other indications that the French were going to make a supreme effort to persuade the conference to accept their ideas of security. Norman Davis had been made chairman of the delegation by the new Administration and was shortly due to arrive. The logicians of the continent were able always to devise schemes of mutual assistance and methods of resisting aggression ; nevertheless, they were always shaky when they came to the point of eventual British participation.

Whether or not the British in their turn regarded the American attitude as of supreme importance, nevertheless their reply to any suggestion for collective security through the use of sanctions or force was that it was impossible for them to make a commitment as to what they would do unless they in their turn knew what the United States would do.

For example, they said : "Let us suppose that members of the League of Nations agree to establish a blockade on an aggressor continental country, and that the United States insists upon its neutral rights, declines to recognize the blockade, and continues to trade with the aggressor. In this event Great Britain would risk a war with the United States, and such a risk is out of the question."

In the days preceding Norman Davis' arrival, Fred Mayer, Counselor of the Legation, and I turned our thoughts to devising some method which would alleviate British anxiety in respect to our eventual attitude and at the same time not commit the United States to any positive act in support of the sanctions policy. We felt that if we could arrive at such a formula not only might we break the deadlock so that the Continental States would be free to work out their own problems of security and collective action, but at the same time such a declaration would put a definite limitation on our own cooperation in the event of trouble. There would be no ground, in the event of sanctions, for the European States to call on us to participate, establish a blockade ourselves, or to adopt other than a purely negative attitude.

We eventually hit upon a formula by which the United States would undertake — if and when the States members of the League agreed upon collective action against an aggressor, and if we ourselves felt that the State in question was in fact an aggressor — no action which would tend to nullify the collective action of the other States, nor would we protect our citizens if they themselves undertook acts which would tend to nullify the collective action of the States members of the League. I then proceeded to Paris with a carefully prepared brief explaining this formula. After consultation with Norman Davis and Allen Dulles, who had accompanied him, we submitted the formula to Washington and received approval for its use.

In a meeting of the General Commission of the Conference on May 22, Mr. Davis made a pronouncement of American policy in respect to collective security. I quote the formula which we were ready to undertake in the event that a general disarmament treaty came into being.

Excerpt from Minutes of the General Commission,
Geneva, May 24, 1933

As the delegates were aware, the United States Government proposed to set forth its policy in the matter of consultation in neutral rights by unilateral declaration. As an illustration and without committing himself at the moment to the exact words, this declaration would be in some such form as the following — that was to say, assuming that the form which Sir John Simon had drafted was accepted by the General Commission :

"Recognizing that any breach or threat of breach of the Pact of Paris (the Briand-Kellogg Pact) is a matter of concern to all the signatories thereto, the Government of the United States of America declares that, in the event of a breach or threat of breach of this Pact, it will be prepared to confer with a view to the maintenance of peace in the event that consultation for such purpose is arranged pursuant to Articles . . . and . . . of Part I of the Disarmament Convention. In the event that a decision is taken by a conference of the Powers in consultation in determining the aggressor with which, on the basis of its independent judgment, the Government of the United States agreed, the Government of the United States will undertake to refrain from any action and to withhold protection from its citizens if engaged in activities which would tend to defeat the collective effort which the States in consultation might have decided upon against the aggressor."

This declaration would be drafted in final form previous to signature of the Disarmament Convention, and would be made at the time of the United States' deposit of ratification of that Convention.

Our proposal was received with great rejoicing by most of the Continental States, although the Germans were somewhat derisive on the subject, stating that they had waited a year and a half to hear numbers mentioned for men and guns and could not regard as an epoch-making achievement a formula on security, however important it might seem to the other States.

It is impossible to know whether this formula would have met with the approval of the people of the United States if a disarmament treaty had been written. A disarmament treaty might have brought about such an alleviation of tension throughout the world that the United States might have felt that this self-denying rule was a small price to pay for universal betterment. Such criticism as arose over the pronouncement arose after the situation in Europe had deteriorated still further and after all real hope for a disarmament treaty had vanished. Certainly the formula alone, and without a disarmament treaty, would never have stood the test of our public opinion. However, it was not proposed as a unilateral act, but rather as complementary to much broader obligations by the other states of the world, the formula merely anticipated the policy eventually incorporated in our Neutrality Act. In any case the declaration in question marked the high point of

American collaboration in the attempts of the States of Europe to work out a system for their own protection, and while we collaborated in subsequent efforts at collective security, we collaborated later by unilateral, and not consultative, policy.

Another comprehensive attempt at a general plan was made, in 1933, by the British this time. Mr. MacDonald came from London, accompanied by Sir John Simon and Anthony Eden, determined to make a supreme effort to write a treaty. Eden had come to Geneva a few times before but it was on this visit and during the course of the debates which followed, that I grew to know him well. His appearance is familiar to every American, through pictures if not through personal contact on his visit to the United States two years ago. The characteristic "Foreign Office" black felt hat, the immaculate costume, the handsome face and carriage can be reproduced by photograph. There is a charm of manner, however, coupled with intelligence and determination, which only personal acquaintance brings out. The foreign delegates began by liking this young man, though I often heard doubts expressed as to whether anyone so young and handsome could be fit for serious work. The delegates soon found however, that there was genuine force behind the pleasing personality. In the years that followed it was Eden's character we grew to appreciate, its stability, dependability, and its idealism ; qualities that the British public has clung to instinctively in the man, whether in office or out of office.

Under the direction and impetus of Mr. MacDonald the British delegation not only wrote a complete treaty but had the courage to insert figures for armies, thus making their project a reality. General Temperley goes into detail of the

British Plan in *The Whispering Gallery of Europe*; it is needless to recapitulate its points. We in the American delegation had some feeling that the plan dealt amply with everything but British interests, nevertheless, we were so glad to see something concrete that we gave the plan our most enthusiastic and wholehearted backing. It failed, as other efforts had failed, under the completely irreconcilable opposition of the German and French contentions.

In the summer of 1933 there were numerous meetings between the British, French and American delegations in an attempt to devise some sort of a project which might be acceptable to all. The meetings culminated in the Quai d'Orsay of Paris. There were present M. Paul-Boncour for France, Simon and Eden for England, Davis and myself for the United States. Technically we seemed to be making progress. The French were willing to entertain the idea of two stages : during the first stage there was to be no increase in armament, during the second stage general curtailment of armament was to begin.

On the other hand, there was decided divergence of opinion on what I might call the spirit of the proposals presented. The French regarded the first stage as a "probationary period." During this stage, they candidly stated, they would see whether Germany lived up to its agreement, and, if not, decline to go further in the second stage. The British and ourselves, on the other hand, wished the second stage to follow the first automatically as we knew that no nation would accept the humiliation involved in undergoing a probationary period.

As I look back on these negotiations I am struck by the fact that the leading delegates of the three countries seemed to have believed sincerely that they had reached a measure of agreement, when that understanding was split by a vast chasm. It was certainly apparent to Cadogan, Massigli and myself who were put to work by the three chief delegates to draft phraseology of the "agreement." No one of us three was under any disillusion as to the importance of our divergencies.

CHAPTER VI

The Assembly of the League of Nations of 1933 was of unusual interest in that it marked the first and only appearance of one of the leading Nazis in Geneva. Dr. Goebbels accompanied Baron von Neurath as representatives of Germany to the Assembly. From the talks which I had with both men in the early days of the gathering it appeared to me that Goebbels had come with the intention of telling the Assembly all about the achievements of the revolution and of what the leaders of National Socialism expected to accomplish for the people of Germany.

Enthusiasm for the dissemination of such information, however, quickly evaporated before the series of hostile assaults upon National Socialism in the Assembly. Speaker after speaker criticized Nazi methods and Nazi objectives in pointed, and, in some instances, even in derisive form. The result was that Goebbels departed from Geneva with a feeling of bitter resentment toward the League of Nations, resentment directed not only against the League but against all form of international collaboration. I have no doubt that the reception accorded to Goebbels prepared the ground for Germany's eventual withdrawal from the League and that this man of high intelligence was, by this experience, converted into an implacable enemy of the institution.

On this occasion and subsequent ones I have never failed to find Goebbels an interesting and stimulating conversationalist.

Among the leading men of the Nazi Party there is none who, at least from the foreigner's point of view, is so well able to expound the Nazi doctrine, or so competent to meet the foreigner upon his own ground. He is intelligent enough to use his own argument, and not to depend alone on quotation from authoritative Nazi doctrine, a habit only too prevalent among his colleagues.

One occasion of meeting Dr. Goebbels I remember well because of a curious incident which happened to my wife and me. I have spoken before of Alix Barton and of the entertainments which she gave with the purpose of bringing together persons of conflicting opinion in the life of the League. Her house on the edge of Lake Geneva, the Villa Lammamuir, lies in the midst of a spacious garden, the only entrance through a grilled gateway. I was driving my own car, and as I approached the gateway I heard behind me the raucous cry of a klaxon. I gave way, and allowed an enormous car bearing the German swastika to enter the gate before me.

As I swung back into line, another horn began to scream, but having given way once I declined to do so again, and went through the gate. I pulled up behind the first car, the second klaxon still screaming behind me, and saw Baron von Neurath and Dr. Goebbels descend. At that moment my own car, with my wife and myself in it, was completely surrounded by members of the German police in plain clothes, every man of the guard bulging at the hips with heavy caliber revolvers. They held the handles of the doors of my car until Dr. Goebbels and Baron von Neurath had entered the house and until we had been recognized by the butler.

At the luncheon, Alix Barton and my wife were the only

women.   In addition to the Germans there were present Sir
John Simon and Cadogan, Norman Davis and myself.   The
English-speaking members of the luncheon made the mistake,
I think, of trying to talk to Dr. Goebbels through Baron von
Neurath as interpreter.   Not only was the latter irritated at
having this task thrust upon him, but at several points in the
conversation he replied brusquely to a question from Simon
or Davis, that he had already explained the German point of
view and that it was needless to inquire further from the Minister of Propaganda.   The luncheon, like the entire visit of
Goebbels to Geneva, was far from a success.

It had been determined that the project elaborated by the
British, French and American delegations should be presented
not before the Conference for Disarmament itself but before
the Steering Committee.   The date of this meeting was set for
October, after the Assembly terminated its work.   It was a
clear cool autumn afternoon when I walked with Eden to
attend the meeting.   We had just been lunching together
with Simon and Davis at the house of Baron Rothschild and
had sampled some of the priceless vintages of his cellar.   We
needed more than that to put any optimism in our hearts.   We
felt that there was a chance of continuing the work with Germany on the technical basis provided in the project of the
Three Powers, but we were apprehensive lest Paul-Boncour,
the French representative, should insist upon his "probationary
period" and destroy the chance.

Sir John Simon presented the proposal.   It was not a bad
proposal, indeed it contained a high measure of satisfaction to
Germany from a technical standpoint.   He spoke of the two
succeeding periods, and of course avoided any suggestion as

to the probationary nature thereof. He was followed by Norman Davis in the same sense. Then came Paul-Boncour. He spoke of the Germans as if he were dealing with a group of not very bright and rather recalcitrant schoolboys. He emphasized not only once but repeatedly that the first period was to be a period of probation during which Germany's behavior would be carefully scrutinized and he said in so many words that the reductions provided in the second period would only be carried out if Germany's behavior justified them.

Before the German delegate, Baron von Rheinbaben, had risen to his feet, we knew what was coming. He made a very brief declaration to the effect that the course of the negotiations was such that Germany had no recourse but to withdraw from the discussions on disarmament. I hurried around the table to von Rheinbaben when the meeting adjourned and asked him whether he and his government fully realized the technical advantages offered by the proposal, the opportunity offered Germany to create a modern army under the same conditions as other nations. He replied that these considerations were secondary to the idea of probation and that he had received decisive instructions from Hitler that Germany was to leave the conference if the probationary scheme was offered.

Immediately following this meeting of the Bureau there occurred one of those phenomena in the relation of the United States to Europe which have repeatedly taken place within my lifetime. Whenever a situation so develops that it appears that the United States is about to align itself decisively with one or another side in the European struggles, a spontaneous outburst of opposition has arisen in this country, particularly in the Mississippi Valley. In the ten days following the meeting of the Bureau there was hardly a newspaper in the United States that did not point out the danger of the American delegation's aligning itself with France and Great Britain against Germany and the editorials usually closed with the words, "Bring Davis home." With his customary sagacity, Mr. Davis anticipated the rising storm and departed for home a few days after the session.

In the meantime the French press had adopted an ominous tone. The editorials took the position strongly that a treaty should be written which provided the relations in armament between the other States, that Germany should be invited to return, but that whether it returned or not its place in the disarmament scheme should be provided by a treaty, and that Germany should be forced to accept it. Paul-Boncour desired a meeting of the British and Americans to discuss this phase of the problem. That meeting in the Beau Rivage Hotel was small in number, Paul-Boncour and Massigli, Sir John Simon and Cadogan, myself and the Counselor of Legation, Fred Mayer. It was one of the most tense of the many similar meetings I have witnessed. The lobby was packed with newspapermen, the French press was hammering in a tone daily more arrogant and ominous, the American press was making equal noise in the opposite direction.

The British press had not taken a decisive position, and Sir John's hands were probably freer than those of either Paul-Boncour or myself. Paul-Boncour addressed this meeting of six men as if he were addressing a constitutional assembly. In an impassioned speech of long duration he developed the French thesis, and it differed very little with the point of view of the French press. Sir John replied brusquely and tersely to the effect that in his mind it was madness to attempt to write a treaty dealing with armament without the presence among the negotiators of a representative of potentially the most powerful military nation on the continent. I stated that I agreed with Sir John but that whether I agreed with him or not, there was not the remotest chance, with our public opinion as it was, of an American representative writing with any other nations a treaty which was to be imposed on Germany.

I have a personal reason to remember this meeting well. It had become the habit to issue joint communiqués after private meetings in Geneva in which the press had shown an interest, and since the press was omnipresent, the city small, and the political importance of these meetings great, it was almost impossible to hold a meeting of which the press was unaware. I had had numerous experiences of issuing communiqués with the French with the implied understanding that the communiqué would be the full revelation of what had happened and that no further discussion with the press would take place. Time after time, however, we had read in the French press the following morning detailed and often distorted accounts of what had taken place at the meeting.

In this instance, then, when it was suggested that we write a communiqué, I dissented. I told of our previous experience and said that I would prefer to be free to give such an account as I saw fit, as long as the other delegates present felt they were free in spite of communiqués. I added that the only condition under which I would join in a communiqué would be if Paul-Boncour gave me his personal word that neither he nor any other member of the French delegation would even speak to the press on this subject after issuing the communiqué. He did so, and the communiqué was issued. That time it worked.

Early in 1934, if I remember rightly, during a meeting of the Council, Fred Mayer and I had a conversation with Anthony Eden which might well have led to valuable results. It was a period in which, as usual, French and German conceptions of disarmament procedure were diametrically opposed. The French had been attempting to negotiate both with the British, Italians, and ourselves, and various combinations of these three ; in no case had they attempted direct negotiations with the Germans.

I urged upon Eden that the time had come for an attempt by a Great Power to negotiate direct with the Germans. I added that that Power could only be Great Britain, that the French were not only temperamentally unfitted but were so tied by their Continental alliances that they would not have a free hand to negotiate. I pointed out that in the years of the conference no Great Power had yet dealt with the Germans on a footing of equality ; the whole effort until that date had been predicated on writing a treaty of disarmament for the world in general, and then to attack the problem of how the States disarmed by the peace treaties could be fitted in. I remember saying that the sudden and violent awakening of national pride under the Nazi régime might be usefully played upon by a British representative, if he visited Germany to negotiate an arrangement by which Germany could participate in a disarmament treaty.

At that time Eden, although a Cabinet Minister with a special portfolio relating to matters of the League of Nations, was not Secretary of State for Foreign Affairs. He stated, however, that he found himself in hearty agreement with my point of view and that he would gladly accept the risk of failure involved in a visit to Berlin if he could assure himself thereby that he had covered every possible means of negotiating with Germany ; he would find it necessary, of course, to discuss the project with Sir John Simon and probably with the Cabinet, but he would do his best to win these gentlemen to his point of view.

He visited Berlin in February, 1934, and the result of that visit was an offer by Hitler to the British Government by which Germany agreed to limit its standing Army to three hundred thousand men, or even to two hundred and fifty thousand men, its aviation to one-third the combined strength of its neighbors, and the caliber of its mobile artillery to approximately six inches. It was the best offer that was ever made by Nazi Germany ; it was an offer which the French would have rejoiced to take two years later, after the opportunity for doing so had been lost. No one can know whether an obligation of such a nature by Germany at that time would have been observed ; on the other hand, nobody can demonstrate convincingly that it would not have been observed.

Eden returned to Geneva shortly after the receipt of this offer, and stated that the British were about to send a communication formally to the French Government and to ask them, using this offer as a basis, to signify their conditions as to their own acceptance. "I imagine," said Eden, "it must give you a curious sensation to watch His Majesty's Government carrying out Hugh Wilson's policy."

The communication was duly made to the French Government but encountered no better fate than a brusque rejection, on April 17, at the hands of Barthou. Barthou was engaged at the time in the first of many endeavors by the French to bring the Soviet Union into the system of automatic and effective help against possible aggression by Germany. He felt that he was making good progress along this line ; and that, therefore there was no necessity for conciliating German opinion, in view of the ring of force which he felt competent to build around Germany.

Among the many political figures in French public life that I have known, Barthou was one of the most interesting and distinctive. A small nervous man, pugnacious in manner, violently argumentative ; in social interchange he exercised an uncommon charm. He gave a small dinner one evening at Geneva, half a dozen of his compatriots, Eden, and myself were present. The talk turned to Shakespeare, and the Anglo-Saxon guests quickly realized that the Frenchman Barthou was discussing the Anglo-Saxon poet with a breadth of knowledge, understanding and admiration which we could not hope to master without years of study.

Barthou met a tragic end ; he was assassinated at Marseilles driving in an automobile with the King of Yugoslavia, who lost his life at the same moment. Barthou was a figure of virile power ; to me, however, he was what the French call *néfaste*, a figure destined for tragedy, a figure who in spite of his intelligence followed a course dangerous for his nation and dangerous for the peace of Europe.

The final sessions of the meeting of the Disarmament Conference, in the spring of 1934, were marked by a display of acerbity on the part of Barthou. He made a venomous attack not only upon the Secretariat of the League of Nations but upon Mr. Arthur Henderson, the President of the conference, whom he accused of partiality and of continuously favoring the thesis which England proposed. M. Barthou, the French delegation members explained to me, was a man who had been bred in the rough and tumble of political life, who had not learned the amenities of international discussion. In this case he met his match. Arthur Henderson had learned the amenities of international discussion, but he had been bred in the fierce political arena of British trade-unionism. For this moment he laid aside his acquired amenities and destroyed M. Barthou in a crushing and devastating revelation of the continuous dilatory and obstructive policy of the French in relation to disarmament.

"Uncle Arthur" Henderson, as he was known to the British Foreign Office, was a figure on whom I like to reflect. He started as a puddler in an iron mill, he gained control of the trade-union movement of Great Britain, he became His Majesty's Principal Secretary of State for Foreign Affairs, he was President of the World Disarmament Conference; he remained the simple, religious, nonconformist figure that he was born. His honesty was so apparent that I never heard even the Continental representatives question it. His English phraseology and diction revealed the humbleness of his origin, but on the day that he assailed Barthou he was an Old Testament Man of God aroused in wrath.

On a July morning of that year the citizens of every country of Europe read their morning papers with a sense of shock and horror. The "blood purge" had taken place in Germany the day before. Roehm and General von Schleicher had been done to death, scores of others followed. It was the first and most public demonstration since the Nazi Party had come to power, of the ruthless and violent steps they were willing to use to retain their position and accomplish their ends. The purge affected profoundly the attitude toward Germany of every man of politics in Europe and of most of them in our own country. The temper of Europe toward Germany changed from indignation and exasperation to fear and horror.

The Government at Washington was deeply distressed when the last hope of disarmament agreement faded, and consulted me as to whether there was nothing that might be salvaged of the wreck of our hope. For some weeks prior to this inquiry I had been exploring with the delegation whether the measure of agreement already attained on the restricted subject of the manufacture of and trade in arms was such as to warrant an attempt to conventionalize an agreement in treaty form. This was one of the few subjects on which practically all the nations had been in agreement, and, while certain reservations had been made in the course of the discussions on manufacture and trade, no explicit opposition had developed. Texts had been written on appropriate articles and the method of supervision had been explored thoroughly. This subject, then, might be one which would offer at least a chance of salvaging something from the Conference. I suggested this in my reply to Washington and was told to come home and work it out.

My work on the trip home was necessarily highly technical and of no general interest. The only episode which might be so termed was a visit that I paid to the Italian Chief of State on my way back to Switzerland. Since Mussolini's representative in Geneva had expressed some doubts on the application of control in the manufacture of arms, it seemed well to do what I might to bring about a greater degree of co-operation on the part of the Italians.

Mussolini received me in the Venetian Palace and in the huge room which has been described by a hundred interviewers. I am not going to describe it, but I am going to state that Mussolini was courtesy itself, he arose from his desk, met me at the door, and escorted me back. I cannot but feel that the air of ominousness which the magazine writers have encountered is put on for their benefit with a carefully accurate knowledge of the theatrical effect.

I stated my case to Signor Mussolini. He asked me a number of shrewd questions, but gave me no inkling of what his decision would be. He told me he desired to reflect upon the matter and consult the members of his delegation. He then said abruptly :

"Mr. Wilson, this plan of yours, which I understand is also a League of Nations plan, will demand an element of faith between nations in spite of the utmost thoroughness of your proposed inspection. You have dealt for years in international meetings ; do you believe that a nation can have any faith in the pledged word of another ?"

I have no record of this conversation so my quotations must embody an approximation of memory rather than of verbatim statements. I replied :

"Unless I were convinced that a nation may have faith in the pledged word of another I could not continue this type of work. Without such faith no document is worth the writing, and, however much history has proved that faith is unjustified, an absence of faith would make international relations still more intolerable."

I remember the Chief of State rose to his feet, went to the window and looked out. Turning back, he said :

"You know history is against you. By and large, faith between nations is unjustified, nevertheless I agree with you. If we are not to have faith in each other, then all of our international acts are futile, and this I refuse to believe."

It was a stimulating experience being received by Mussolini. He is one of those rare people who makes you speak better and more convincingly than you know how to speak, who forces you to use your own mind to its maximum, and who in the intensity of intellectual interchange exercises a genuine charm on his listeners. I regretted exceedingly when our interview came to an end ; I would like to have taken him out to dinner and gone on talking.

Before proceeding with the account of the negotiations on traffic in arms, it may be of interest to examine briefly the state of Europe in that autumn of 1934, both because it adds to the comprehension of the profound and disturbing changes which occurred in the succeeding year and because it is interesting and even tragic to note the contrast between the type of thought prevailing then and now.

I have re-read my letters to the Secretary of State Mr. Cordell Hull during this period and find that I took French policy as the point of departure for the examination of Europe. Bear in mind that the French Army was still overwhelmingly predominant, hence French policy was the focal point about which the policies of the other States shifted and eddied.

The basic consideration in France was, as always, Germany. They were apprehensive regarding increasing German construction of guns and tanks but, curiously enough, seemed rather less troubled than did the British about the signs of an increased air force. A German of my acquaintance, cognizant of these two attitudes, said that there was a very simple explanation of why the British were especially troubled about aircraft construction and not about tanks : "Tanks can't swim," he said.

In any event, Barthou was so hopeful of his policy toward Russia that the French were now specifically rejecting that "equality of rights" with Germany which had been agreed upon in December, 1932.

The Poles, of course, were in a state of considerable exasperation with France. The French endeavors to bring Russia specifically into the French orbit of resistance to Germany, frightened and exasperated the Poles. It is curious to note now that at that time the Poles stated vigorously that they were sufficiently strong to carry on independently and to maintain their position between Germany and Russia by the force of their own right arms. This confidence on the part of the Poles had given rise to numerous claims for rectifications of boundaries, and vague dreams were stirring their consciousness. To such an extent were they giving expression to their aspirations that at that time we aligned Poland in the group of "revisionist countries," namely, those not satisfied with the status quo of the peace treaties.

The Austrian question seemed to be drawing Italian and French policy closely together. Italy had mobilized on the Brenner, it will be remembered, to prevent German entry into Austria. France and Italy were making repeated attempts to solve their African difficulties, and the French had reason to congratulate themselves that their position in respect to Italy was better than it had been for some years.

The French were critical of, and irritated at the British, but consoled themselves for this coolness by their hopes for Russian support and their closer relations with Italy. In any case, they were frank in saying that whatever their relations with Great Britain, if hostilities broke out and France were threatened, Great Britain would be obliged in its own interests to come to their assistance. Hence, to their logic, the ephemeral relationships between Great Britain and France were of considerably less importance than the relation of France to those countries which might find themselves in the other camp.

As I said before, it is interesting and tragic to contrast such a state with the present. A few months later, a series of events caused steady deterioration from the French point of view. Potent new factors clamored for attention, and France's role of predominant power on the Continent began to disappear, perhaps forever.

Now to return to the limitation of armament. At a meeting of the Steering Committee of the Disarmament Conference held after the close of the Assembly in 1934, I presented on behalf of the American Government a project on the manufacture of and trade in arms, coupled with a project for the setting up of a Permanent Disarmament Commission with adequate powers for the control of production of and trade in arms. The members of the Steering Committee voted to summon a Special Committee to discuss this American project after the first of the coming year, 1935. Although the project which I submitted was generally known as an American plan, nevertheless, it was based on articles — almost textually reproduced

— which had been elaborated in various committees of the Disarmament Conference, and represented not so much an American project as a recapitulation of points on which there had seemed to be general accord.

Discussions of the American project for the control of the manufacture of and trade in arms began in the Special Commission called for the purpose in the early days of 1935. My talks with Lord Stanhope, who had come from London to represent Great Britain in the discussions, showed immediately that there was no hope of bringing the meeting to a successful conclusion. The project that we had drafted had been submitted to the British Cabinet, and the Cabinet had determined that it could not accept the convention. The British were in the first stages of their own rearmament program and explained that they could not permit such detailed control and publicity of their rearmament efforts. We were obliged to go through with discussions with the certainty of not reaching an agreement. We knew the gravity of the developments in Europe, so that our main effort was devoted to preventing a disclosure of the depth of the divergencies between us. I was deeply disappointed when Lord Stanhope explained his position, since I had kept in close touch with the British throughout the development of our project. Eden had been careful to explain to me that he could not give the project his approbation until the Cabinet had passed on it, but I had had no reason to anticipate such an entirely negative decision on their part.

These sessions of the Special Committee represented the last endeavor of the States of Europe to bring about an agreement in respect to arms. The effort had been foreseen in the Treaty of Versailles, in 1919 ; the first discussions had taken place, in

1923 ; and this, the final effort, terminated twelve years later, in April, 1935. From that time on, overwhelming events on the European stage thrust ideas of disarmament into the background. Month by month, German armament was accelerated, and the Allies, as well, turned to the task of increasing the strength of their own positions.

I cannot close this account of the attempt to limit armament, without mentioning some of the men who worked with me, and worked with unabated devotion through months of increasing discouragement. I have mentioned Fred Mayer, the Counselor of Legation. He and his delightful wife, Katie, had a most attractive house on the edge of the lake where we were as much at home as in our own. Fred had energy and intelligence, a mind fertile in new ideas. He became subsequently Minister to Haiti and has just retired from that post.

Colonel, now General George Strong, lived through the battle of Geneva from beginning to end. Year after year he attended Commissions on Disarmament and attained a grasp of the subject which made him almost unique among the experts. General Strong has recently become widely known to the American people through the radio and newspapers. He was sent to England on a special mission and on his return gave a reassuring account of what he saw in that country, and of the determinations and valor of the British.

In the later years Colonel, now General John Magruder, became Military Attaché to the Legation. His ability to win friends is outstanding, his mentality alert and penetrating, his energy indomitable. As a collaborator, he was of the highest value.

CHAPTER VII

Europe in the early months of 1935 was tense with apprehension. It was known that German rearmament was proceeding feverishly; added to this was the knowledge, which gradually came to light, of the enormous preparations that Mussolini was making for an expedition into Abyssinia. That these preparations were being made was first revealed to me in a talk with Sir John Simon and Eden late in February. They both expressed the greatest apprehension, particularly as they had already instructed Sir Eric Drummond, British Ambassador to Italy, to discuss the preparations with Mussolini, and Sir Eric had been unable to get any satisfactory assurances as to their purpose.

In April came the formal announcement from Germany that it intended to scrap the clauses of the Treaty of Versailles which restricted the organization and size of the German Army, and to build up an army based on universal service. The declaration was followed by a meeting of the Council which issued a vigorously worded condemnation of Germany for its violation of the treaty. This meeting was followed by a further meeting in Stresa in which was built up what became known as the "Stresa front" against Germany.

Some weeks after the condemnation, the British negotiated a naval agreement with Germany by which the fleet of the latter country was not to exceed one-third of the total tonnage of the British fleet. I had heard rumors of the negotiations, nevertheless, I was surprised at the sudden shift of British policy.   I wrote to a friend at the time :

I have been beguiled the last few days by the spectacle of the British.   They sponsor and force a declaration from the Council condemning Germany for its "unilateral violation of the treaty" ; six weeks later they make an agreement with Germany on relative naval strengths which is essentially and inescapably a "unilateral abandonment of the treaty."   The English are unique.   I would like to be able to stand up and not only say but feel that such action was entirely consistent and that doubtless God Himself had inspired it !   They are a wonderful race, but regardless of this and other strange contradictions they generally work out sound results.   More power to them !

The meeting of the Council in April, 1935, followed by the meeting at Stresa, indicated a sharp turning in British foreign policy.   Up to that time the British had taken the position, perhaps somewhat complacent in view of their presumed invulnerability, that there was no peace to be found in Europe until Germany was a willing partner in the affairs of Europe, and a partner on an equal footing.   In these two meetings, however, the British swung to an approximation of the French policy, namely, to acts which tended to brand Germany as the enemy and to align the States of Europe in resistance thereto.

Roughly speaking the British Government adopted a policy which had been advocated by the permanent staff of the Foreign Office.   This policy only differed from the French in that French thought tended to believe that war with Germany at some time was inevitable, while the British Foreign Office officials still hoped that a determined and united front against Germany would bring about in that country a frame of mind capable of negotiation and of peaceful relationship.

My recollection of the futility of the condemnation of Japan in the Manchurian episode gave me grave concern as I listened to the condemnation of Germany at Geneva, a condemnation which, like that of Japan, was not backed up by a show of force but remained in the realm of phrases.

Among the speakers of the Council there was apparently only one man who shared my view, the Danish Minister for Foreign Affairs, Peter Munch. He spoke as follows: "I should like, however, to express the hope that events will prove that the three Great Powers who have put forward this proposal are right in their view of the effects which will follow from the adoption of this resolution, and I should like also to add the hope that they will succeed in bringing about an agreement between all the Great Powers of Europe, and thus give effect to the common aspiration entertained by all the peoples of Europe, namely, an aspiration for their happiness which depends upon peace." The careful phraseology of the Danish Minister shows, I think, that same skepticism which I felt as to beneficial results flowing from the condemnation of a great people.

In May again the Council met in session and achieved the objective of establishing the interest of the Council in the Ethiopian dispute with Italy. Mussolini's representative acquiesced in League jurisdiction after considerable opposition, and only did so under vigorous pressure by Great Britain first, and France in second line.

My reports and letters after this meeting show the emergence of Great Britain as the dominating factor on the Continent, for the first time over-shadowing the influence of France in that area. They show, as well, a growing apprehension in my mind lest Italy was working itself, and being shoved by the others, into a position from which it could have no escape save by throwing in its lot with Germany.

I remember feeling at that time a certain satisfaction that Great Britain was beginning to play a dominant role on the Continent and to supersede the influence of France. The British attitude toward the League seemed to me comparable to that of its attitude toward law in general as exemplified by the use of common law. The French attitude, on the other hand, seemed to typify the legal conceptions of the Code Napoléon, that is to say, the French tended to regard the Covenant of the League as fixed and unalterable ; violation of the Covenant should be punished, but punished after the fact. The British, on the other hand, tended to regard the Covenant more as a live organism, to be modified when necessary to meet existing conditions, and their effort seemed to be directed more specifically to the warding off of violation rather than toward punishment for violation.

There was no indication that Mussolini had abandoned his intention of invading Ethiopia. We were all aware that we were enjoying a respite only due to the summer rainy season in Ethiopia when military operations were impracticable.

It was, therefore, with the most passionate interest that I followed these developments. For the first time there seemed a possibility that the great military states of the world might be ready in advance of the fact to take steps to forestall aggression. There emerged the vision of perhaps a better and more orderly world in which all states would realize that the cost of such adventure was out of all proportion to the ends gained.

The summer of 1935 passed without incident, although there

was growing realization of the enormous increase in the force of Germany and of the intensity of Mussolini's concentration against Abyssinia. On the other hand, a new factor became recognized on the Continent. The League of Nations Union in Great Britain had taken a widespread ballot, and they reported that eleven million British voters had expressed themselves in favor of the use of the punitive articles of the Covenant of the League in case of aggression.

When the Council and Assembly met in September there was a pause for some days during which the various delegates endeavored to assess the genuine readiness of each other to adopt punitive measures under Article 16 of the Covenant in case of Italian aggression. Since the failure of the League machinery to deal with Japan in respect of Manchuria, there had been considerable skepticism as to measures of collective security, particularly if adopted against a Great Power. Nevertheless there were a number of men in this Assembly who earnestly desired to see the machinery put into effect, some because they were convinced adherents of the League system and believed that proof of its efficacy would establish a more permanent and durable relationship of peace between the states; others — the majority, I think, — desired to put the machinery into effect because of the influence that a successful operation might have upon Hitler.

In their minds Germany was the menace, not Italy; but if one dictator could be forced to bow before the will of the League members, the other dictator would surely hesitate, they argued, from risking such concerted action. To their minds the establishment of League predominance in the question of Ethiopia would be a sort of dress rehearsal for what they would do to Germany if that nation attempted to fulfill the ominous promises that it was making.

These men were, I think, surprised to find how wide-spread was the desire in the Assembly to test out the League machinery. When they were finally assured by Sir Samuel Hoare on behalf of England, and by Laval on behalf of France of their determination to invoke that machinery, there was overwhelming and ready assent on the part of the members of the Assembly.

Scarcely had the Assembly closed when Mussolini launched his attack and the Council and Assembly were re-convoked early in October 1935.

Not only did the delegates come back under the impression of the meeting just past, but they were further heartened by the news from the United States. Without waiting for the Assembly to act, President Roosevelt had declared a state of war to be existing within the meaning of our legislation, and had established an embargo of arms on both parties. Furthermore, the President had taken a position in respect to neutral rights which opened the way for economic sanctions as far as we were concerned if the States of the League chose to apply them against Italy.

The Council acted promptly, found that "Italy had had recourse to war in violation of its obligations." The Assembly ratified these findings, immediately set up a committee to discuss sanction measures. Before the Assembly even adjourned, certain sanctions had been put into effect.

The behavior of the Council and Assembly in this instance was a revelation to me. For years I had been watching the affairs of the League of Nations and had noted unfailingly small progress accompanied by the clanking of ill-fitting machinery. In this particular instance, however, the Assembly acted with speed and decision. For one of the few times in the history of the institution, the two chief Powers — Great Britain and France — were throwing their weight in the same direction and Great Britain was exercising its power to an extent never before seen in Geneva.

I find from my papers that at the time I was considering also the problem of American neutrality both in respect to the President's unilateral acts relating to the Italian-Ethiopian dispute and also with respect to the endeavor to pass legislation on the subject in our Congress. I find a copy of an undated letter to the Secretary of State which from internal evidence must have been written during November 1935, and I am reproducing portions of it herewith since it deals with what is known as the "spirit" of neutrality and not with its technical aspects. It seems to me as true today, in the light of our experience in the present war, as it was of the day that I wrote it.

Yesterday I drafted a letter to you concerning certain phases of the neutrality question. As I wrote the letter my mind kept turning to what I might call the philosophical conception of neutrality, but I excluded such consideration in that draft in the fear that it might not immediately concern the question of the powers of the President in a crisis, however much it may indirectly bear upon it.

Such criticism of our present policy as I have read and heard has been based on the spirit in which that policy was conceived rather than on its material results. To cite the opposing views: ardent enthusiasts for the League of Nations both at home and abroad reproach the United States for having acted in a manner which they claim shows at least a blunted moral conception in that the American Government has taken no official cognizance of the fact that a manifest aggression has been perpetrated. On the other extreme, criticism arises from the fact that the present neutrality bears infinitely more heavily upon one belligerent than upon the other and consists essentially in discrimination against Italy.

I believe, and this is what I should like to emphasize, that criticism from both extremes springs from a misconception as to neutrality. Neutrality is a legal status. Its rules are provided by legislation and practice. It is recognized in our courts. It is the means by which our Government formulates its official policy toward a state of war, and by which it hopes so to curtail its action and that of other governments as to minimize the risk that we should be involved in war. It has nothing to do with "impartiality" in thought. That is where the misconception occurs. Neutrality implies impartiality in conduct with respect to the belligerent powers. There impartiality ends. Misunderstanding occurs in the prevalent assumption that "neutrality" and "impartiality" are synonymous. Such is not the case.

Millis in the *Road to War* reproaches the Administration of Mr. Wilson and particularly Colonel House and Mr. Page with an "unneutral" attitude while under the law of neutrality. The latter were not unneutral; they were undeniably partial. President Wilson urged the American people, if I remember the phrase correctly, "to be neutral in thought as well as deed." Had he urged them to be "impartial in thought and neutral in deed" his meaning would have been clear. I remember vividly the confusion created by this statement in the Middle West, my part of the world, when people busily shipping munitions to the Allies were urged to be neutral in thought. It caused real distress as to their duty. They knew they could not be impartial; they did not see how they could be neutral in thought.

Further, the conception of impartiality in the practical results of neutrality cannot, I feel, ever be achieved. In the Great War, in the present war and I think in any conceivable war, there can be no neutrality that is impartial in its ultimate effects. Accidents of geography, or the existence of a strong navy on the part of one of the belligerents, will to a large measure do away with any impartiality that lies in neutrality. One belligerent will be affected more than the other by whatever restrictions our neutrality imposes.

Thus it seems well to face the fact that we cannot legislate impartiality into human beings, and that no acts mandatory upon the President in all situations will affect the belligerents impartially. Neutrality legislation can bring about impartiality neither subjectively nor objectively.

A curious little episode involved me personally to some extent in the Ethiopian dispute. Early in November the League Committee was discussing the application of sanctions to Italy and the French delegate raised the possibility of establishing a rationing system for commodities of those States which did not join in the sanctions. It was reported to me by a member of the Committee that the League members were not concerned with the attitude of the United States since Mr. Roosevelt was already taking adequate measures in respect to sanctions, but that their concern was lest Germany, not being bound by the League, should pour unrestricted quantities of sanctioned material into Italy. On the same day that this information came to me the German Consul in Geneva called at my office and asked me whether I had any news of the discussions in the Committee.

My information had not been given me under an obligation of secrecy. Accordingly, I told Mr. Krauel of what was taking place. He felt immediate concern, returned to his office, telephoned Berlin and received instructions to inform the Secretariat of the League that Germany would ship into Italy only "normal quantities" of various commodities. I had forgotten the episode when some weeks later I received a letter from the State Department informing me that the Italian Ambassador, my good friend Rosso, had left a protest, under instructions from his Government, against my "pro-League attitude" in this episode. I replied to the Department giving the facts of the case and suggesting that they say to Rosso in respect of my "pro-League attitude" that the Italian representative in Geneva was the only representative of any Great Power who took no interest whatsoever in what the American representative was doing or thinking about League matters, and that hence in this Ethiopian dispute all my information was coming from anti-Italian sources. The suggestion worked beautifully. From that time on, few days went by without one or the other of the Italian representatives coming in and discussing things.

For two months, the Committee of Coordination, as it was called, elaborated and maintained economic sanctions against Italy. As the discussions progressed and consideration arose of embargoes on materials essential to the Italian prosecution of the war — notably petroleum — reluctance began to develop among the States members of the League to the adoption of steps which might drive Mussolini to some desperate act. I was told by both the British and French in explicit terms that neither nation was ready to take any steps which in their opinion could cause war. The British fleet had been sent to the Mediterranean, the new arm of air power had unknown possibilities, particularly on vessels operating in narrow seas. Great Britain had hardly begun its rebuilding program, and the combination made them recoil from pushing the sanctions to the point where they could be genuinely efficacious.

In December a bombshell burst on an astonished world. By means of a carefully calculated revelation on the part of the French journalist Mme. Geneviève Tabouis, the whole ac-

count was published of a secret arrangement between Sir
Samuel Hoare, then British Secretary of State for Foreign Affairs, and M. Laval under the terms of which a wide sweep of
Ethiopian territory was to be ceded to Italy and a rump State
only was to be left.   Astonishment and indignation were wide-
spread, particularly in England. The storm assumed such
proportions that Sir Samuel had to be released from the Cabinet. Eden was made Foreign Minister, and Mr. Baldwin felt
obliged to make an exceedingly lame excuse for his own
position.

In Geneva there was universal indignation against Great
Britain ; from adulation arose universal condemnation. The
League members could see no mitigating circumstances, and
regarded the episode as a sinister maneuver of a Conservative
British Government which had won its recently held election
on lip service to the League, and once that election over, had
come out in its true colors of imperialistic conservatism and
sympathy for the Fascists. This explanation seemed unduly
simple to me. I could not believe that the British Government
would deliberately and cynically alienate a large section of its
own public, as well as a strong portion of the Continent, without what it considered a good and valid reason, and I set myself to the task of trying to ascertain that reason.

I had numerous conversations with Anthony Eden and other
Britishers in Geneva. I collected opinions from the French,
the Italians and other nationals, and tried to evaluate the result.
An explanation finally emerged in my mind, and while it gave
satisfaction from the point of view of pure logic, it never convinced me that Sir Samuel Hoare was justified in taking the
political risk that he did.

I submit my explanation of this matter. It was an explanation evolved in the middle of December 1935. The published explanations from authoritative sources are still unconvincing ; perhaps some day we shall learn the full truth of this extraordinary piece of diplomacy.

I believe that some members of the British Cabinet were impressed with the continued reports from Italy that Mussolini and the Italian people were in a frame of mind to assault Great Britain if the League adopted the petroleum embargo which was then under discussion. Even those members of the Cabinet who did not so believe were unable to guarantee that this was not the fact. The British had found that in spite of the assurances given by the French Government, the French people could not be relied on to take a stand against Italy.

To the French people the possibility of hostilities with Italy over a question of a remote land in Africa, when they had a really dangerous neighbor in Germany, was merely foolish. Whatever their Government might do, they themselves were not prepared to carry through a serious war other than against Germany. They would not proceed merely for the preservation of the principles of collective security and to give satisfaction to the British. Furthermore, the British had not yet obtained satisfactory assurances from the Mediterranean States as to their attitude in case of conflict and as to the use of their ports and facilities.

The British Cabinet suddenly realized that Great Britain and Great Britain alone was bearing the burden of the hatred of the Italian people and that unless they were willing to risk war immediately, something had to be done about it. Sir Samuel Hoare may well have argued that under these circumstances what could be better than a conciliatory gesture to Mussolini ? If the League States would not accept this idea and insisted on further embargoes, then Great Britain would be in a position to insist that it should not bear the risk alone.   The French public would be more ready to accept responsibility if Mussolini refused their conciliatory offer, and the League States, if they extended their embargo, could only do so by spreading the risk, so to speak, instead of the risk being concentrated as at that time on Great Britain.

I said before, and I repeat, that while such may well have been the type of argument in the mind of Sir Samuel Hoare ; nevertheless, it is hard to conceive how this genuinely intelligent statesman could have supposed that such a document would be accepted by his own people, particularly after the enthusiasm that the British public had shown for collective security and the trust they had reposed in the Government because of its alleged devotion to this principle.

The sanctions were maintained but not increased through January, 1936.   More and more the conviction was born in my mind that with the possible exception of Great Britain this whole punitive endeavor against Italy was the dress rehearsal, as I have called it before, for subsequent dealing with Germany.   The Germans in Geneva told us of rumors of an occupation of the Rhineland in the near future, of enormous German military preparations.   For the first time, reports of an overwhelming air force reached persons outside of Germany.   These Germans were under no delusions as to the fact that the sanctions against Italy had as their primary purpose the desire to overawe Germany.   Even those of liberal tendencies, however, made no secret of their fear lest the League activity should have an opposite effect, deepen the hostility of Germany to any form of international co-operation, drive Italy into Germany's arms, and provoke Hitler into violent action.

CHAPTER VIII

One evening late in January, 1936, I had a telephone call from
Paris and I heard with astonishment the voice of Colonel William Donovan, "Fighting Bill" Donovan, as he was known in
our Army. Bill told me over the phone that he had just been
to Ethiopia and asked whether I would like him to fly down
and tell me about it. Since Ethiopia was the one subject that
was present with us day and night, I accepted enthusiastically,
and Bill duly arrived the next day.

He told a story which I shall endeavor to set down as closely
as I can in the way it was related to me. As most people in
the United States know, Colonel Donovan has played an active part in American political life and is one of the leading
lawyers of the country, but he has a hobby and that hobby is
war. Bill is not happy if there is a war on the face of the earth
and he has not had a look at it. He was contemplating a trip
to Europe in the autumn of 1935 so he proceeded to Washington where he asked the Italian Ambassador Rosso whether
it was possible for him to go and see their war in Ethiopia.
Rosso replied that no doubt it was possible but that only Mussolini could authorize such an expedition. Rosso suggested to
Bill that the latter proceed via Rome and ask the Duce for permission.

In Rome the interview was most successful; Mussolini offered not only to let Bill see anything he wanted to see, but
gave orders that all forms of transportation — horse, mule,

camel, or airplane — should be made available to him.   All this under the one condition that Colonel Donovan promise to return straight to Rome and tell him (Mussolini) what he thought of the show.   This Bill undertook to do.

I don't need to go into the full details of Bill's account of what he saw.   Suffice it to say that from a technical point of view the Italian effort was magnificent, the road construction was superlative, the health of the Army something that had never been seen when Westerners were fighting in tropic conditions.   Bill told me that a great advance was being organized, that it would not be launched until it was ready but that when it was launched it would be irresistible ; we could count with certainty on the Italians' entry into Addis Ababa in good season before the rain commenced.

The press of Europe at that time was filled with articles by military experts all of an opposite tenor, namely, that Mussolini's expedition had bogged down, that all forms of tropic diseases were wasting the Army away, that rains would soon come which would so flood the country that no advance could be made, that sanctions were crippling Italy's effort.   To such an extent were these views repeated and believed that even the Italians in Geneva were in the depths of despair and were already discounting an Italian defeat.

The news brought by Donovan was of overwhelming importance ; the whole of the League policy and, especially, British policy was predicated on the effectiveness of the sanctions in preventing an Italian victory.   If the sanctions had no such effect it was obviously the part of wisdom to alter radically the policy which depended on sanctions for success.   Bill's story carried absolute conviction to me.   I knew he was a competent observer, I knew he was completely unprejudiced, and I knew he submitted me his observations only because he was convinced of their complete soundness.

The next morning I met Anthony Eden and we walked along the edge of the lake to the Council session in the old Disarmament Building. In the brief time at my disposal I told him about Colonel Donovan and gave him some of the information. I also told him of my conviction that the Colonel's evidence must be believed. Eden was deeply perturbed. He recognized the importance of the report and asked me to send Donovan to see him at six o'clock that evening. It was perhaps five o'clock when Eden rang on the telephone ; he explained that news had just arrived of the death of King George, that he and the rest of the British delegates were obliged to return at once by airplane to London, hence he could not receive Colonel Donovan but desired to know when the latter would be in London and his address there. This information I gave him.

Colonel Donovan proceeded to London and in accordance with arrangement notified Eden's private secretary of his address. Unfortunately, the ceremonies brought about by the death of the King and the installation of a new Cabinet were such that Eden never received my friend. I visited London some two weeks later. At dinners at various houses I heard repeatedly the story of the Wild Irishman who had been to Ethiopia and who had had the temerity to question the judgment of the best military opinion on the Continent.

It was a lamentable fate that prevented a talk between Eden and Donovan. The advance of the Italians, the fall of Addis Ababa, the flight of the Emperor, all took place within a few weeks. The realization that these events were about to occur might well have brought about a shift of British policy that would have kept Italy in the League and prevented the birth of the axis between Rome and Berlin. The history of mankind is the history of men. Sudden unpredictable decisions sometimes dictated by nothing more serious than indigestion have changed the fate of history. In this case an infinitely more serious factor, true, the death of a king, may have been that fortuitous event which kept Europe on the steady path to disaster.

It was about this period that I closed my house in Geneva and made my headquarters again in Berne. The breakdown of disarmament negotiations had brought about a position in which the representative of the United States no longer had a role to play as negotiator. Furthermore the evidences of the failure of sanctions against Italy were an indication that work of a political nature in the League would soon become a thing of the past. I was distressed to leave our dwelling in Geneva since few houses among the many which we have occupied gave my wife and me the same measure of satisfaction. Most of Geneva, while gay and bright with the sun sparkling on the lake and beautiful trees and gardens, has, nevertheless, little of interest or little that is particularly characteristic.

The old part of the city, however, crowded all together on a narrow hilltop, possesses to a degree the characteristics which the rest of the city lacks. In the center of the little *cité* is the cathedral, before the main entrance of the cathedral is a small deserted square, cobblestones, with three enormous chestnut trees. It was on this Cour St. Pierre that we found a dwelling directly opposite the cathedral entrance. In the midst of the city we lived in a silence that was broken only by the carillon across the square. We lived in an old house, the floors were warped and the walls undulated, but the woodwork and brasswork were lovely, and a glimpse from the windows was warranted to restore peace of mind.

From those windows once each year at the end of November we could witness a memorable scene. Citizens of Geneva celebrate what they call the Escalade in memory of their repulse of an attack by the King of Savoy. In commemoration of the event a band of citizens dress up each year in medieval armor, mount horses, proceed to the Cour St. Pierre and re-enact the scene of the announcement by the Geneva Government of the repulse of the Savoyards. The procession takes place at night, it winds up the steep streets of the *cité*, the citizens assemble about a huge bonfire under the chestnut trees. All artificial lighting is turned off and the scene has a brilliance and an otherworldliness that is seldom achieved in these attempts at reconstruction.

Early in April Germany moved again. This time the German forces went into the Rhineland and Europe trembled on the brink of war. In the light of history this was obviously the time when the Great Powers of Europe should have called a halt. It was the first overt act in violation of the Treaty of Versailles; even the announcement of a standing army did not constitute such a flagrant violation. It was a violation of all the Locarno Pacts, pacts to which Hitler himself had confirmed Germany's adherence. Germany had not had time to build defenses in the Rhineland, its war preparations were still embryonic; it was obviously the moment to halt. This seems clear as crystal today ; it was not so clear in April, 1936. A silent but intense struggle went on among the members of the French Government and among the members of the French General Staff as well. Whether or not, as the French now claim, the determining factor in their decision was England's negative position, I cannot confirm. In any case, they failed to act, and the last moment for successful preventive action passed.

Through March and April, 1936, enthusiasm for sanctions was waning perceptibly. The French, shaken as they were by the German occupation of the Rhineland, began to make desperate attempts to draw Italy again into the community of the States which might offer resistance to Germany, back into what was known as the "Stresa front." The tremendous advance of the Italian forces in Ethiopia began. The Emperor fled on May 2, and Addis Ababa was captured.

The attempt to establish collective security by means of sanctions provided under Article 16 of the Covenant of the League of Nations had definitely and probably finally failed. It seemed to me then, and it still seems to me, that there was only one course of wisdom for the British to pursue at that moment. Their game was lost, the loss should have been acknowledged, the past wiped out, and every effort should have been made to bring Italy back into the ranks of the respectable powers. Such a policy would have demanded ruthlessness.

It would have been necessary to refuse entry to the Ethiopian delegation to League discussions, to lift the sanctions immediately, and to undertake at once close collaboration with Mussolini in view of the German menace. Such steps would have been bitter and humiliating to British opinion, nevertheless, they were the steps I am convinced that wise statesmanship called for.

I so stated my conviction in no uncertain terms to members of the British delegation during the Council meeting in May, 1936. Unfortunately, the British were convinced that the Cabinet could not survive such an admission of defeat. The Council's session was without leadership, and was far from edifying. The blow to the League structure and to League prestige was such that the members of the Council failed to recover rapidly enough to take decisive steps. The Ethiopian delegation remained at the table, and the sanctions were not lifted.

I took a trip home in the summer of 1936 which was memorable to me in that it was the first time since 1919 that I had come home for a real vacation in my own country. We brought a motor with us, and my wife, my boy and I crossed the Continent as far as Colorado where we spent some weeks in the mountains fishing and riding. In spite of the fact that we made the trip in a heat so intense that it has become a record in the Middle West, I enjoyed the experience greatly.

It was during a Presidential campaign, and every filling station and corner drug store was the scene of a political discussion. I had never before seen Kate seated on a counter stool gesticulating with a doughnut and discoursing on the merits of Landon and Roosevelt. I was struck again, as I had been before, by the kindly friendliness of our people. Everybody wanted to talk, everybody wanted to be helpful. It is a self-respecting courtesy not to be found in other parts of the world ;

there is a readiness to like the stranger which other places do not share.

I went farther west and attended both the High and Low Jinks of Bohemian Grove outside of San Francisco. This, let me state, is an experience that should be seized upon by every American who has the opportunity. The Bohemian Grove is unique in any land. Members of the Bohemian Club in San Francisco years ago had the foresight to purchase a huge valley full of enormous redwoods; now that the timber has been cut through the entire area, it stands alone as a monument of the majesty and antiquity of those glorious trees. Members of the club have built camps on this property and for two weeks in the summer live in the camps in reunion. Open-air theaters, of which the redwoods form the background, are filled every night by the members who listen to music by such singers as John Charles Thomas, such quartets as the Pro-Arte; or to lectures by men known throughout the United States for their ability.

The scene is full of majesty, the life is full of gaiety and beauty, the spirit is full of amusement. It is a unique adventure.

I returned to Geneva only in September so did not attend the special meeting of the Assembly in July, 1936. At that meeting sanctions against Italy were finally terminated, but when it came to the question of bringing Italy back into normal relationships, the members of the League preferred to salve their consciences by retaining the Abyssinian delegation in the Assembly. This gesture could do no conceivable good to the Abyssinian cause, indeed that cause no longer existed, except juridically. The gesture might, however, and I believe did, do serious injury to the cause of the peace of Europe. It was the last moment, I think, in which there was even a possibility of bringing Mussolini back, and from then on his course tended irrevocably and uninterruptedly to the formation of the Axis.

That closes the story of the Ethiopian struggle at Geneva, as I saw it. I had watched developments with deep interest and much sympathy, even if with a tinge of skepticism. The attempt of the nations of the world to work out some sort of orderly procedure to replace the anarchy of unbridled nationalism, could not fail to be interesting, nor could it fail, I think, to arouse one's sympathy. Imagination kindled at the thought of a better existence for us all, a world in which it would be too costly to assault one's neighbor, but a world in which at the same time an opportunity would be presented to right injustices by peaceful means. It seemed to me in certain stages of the struggle that that sort of an organization might be about to arise.

But it was also clear, even at that time, that the machinery of sanctions had to be applied ruthlessly, if applied at all. Clearly there were risks involved, not only of trade losses, but of actual hostilities with Italy. The beginning of sanctions implied both these risks, and to the logical mind the States embarking upon the path should have been determined to carry it through. There should be no illusion on this point, measures short of war are war measures, or at least may readily become so if the State to which they are applied finds them intolerable.

The statesmen of Europe, however, had not carried through this thought to its inevitable conclusion. Time and again I was told that sanctions applied to Italy must be such as not to drive that nation to desperation, not to push it to a point where it would assault the States applying the pressure. The statesmen apparently believed sincerely that they could walk a tight-rope, that they could so conduct the pressure that it would be sufficient to spoil the chance for a successful operation against Ethiopia, but at the same time not be sufficient to drive Mussolini into a desperate assault, let us say, against the British fleet in the Mediterranean. The result, of course, was a series of half-way measures, measures intensely exasperating to the Italians without being effective.

The analogy is striking between this experience and the treatment of Germany after the war. In both cases a ruthless course might have been effective, in both cases half-hearted courses were adopted, and in both cases disastrous results followed.

The results of the Ethiopian experience are widely known, the Italians, condemned by the respectable, joined the community of the damned. They made friends with Germany, the Axis was born, and when the test came in the spring of 1938 and Germany seized Austria, the circle had been completed, and Mussolini aided and abetted the very move which he had mobilized his armies to prevent a few years before. A further result, the States of Europe became convinced that the theory of collective action was a fallacy. It had been tried and found wanting. The small States in particular realized that they had accepted grave risks only to find that the great States would not accept the ultimate risk involved in the practice of sanctions. By the summer of 1936, if not earlier, the idea of collective security had perished, the small States of Europe faced the troubled future with no better consolation than the catchword, "every man for himself."

From the particular to the general, I submit that we can draw certain conclusions. The first and most striking : that in the present development of civilization States will not accept grave risks for the maintenance of abstract justice, they will only accept such risks when their own existence or vital interests are involved. Another conclusion : that economic pressure is a form of warfare which can and probably will turn rapidly into military warfare if severe enough. Those who advocate economic sanctions are between the devil and the deep blue sea. Ineffective sanctions are merely exasperating and tend to confirm rather than to break the determination of the people on whom they are applied. Effective sanctions, on the other hand are acts of war, and any proud people would rather go down fighting, even against overwhelming odds, than to submit tamely to be crushed. If civilization ever reaches a point where the welfare of one is the responsibility of all, then every nation will be ready to use its armed forces against an aggressor, with the full realization that measures short of this will be futile and worse than useless.

As I think over ten years of intimate association with the League of Nations, I ask myself whether I am glad or sorry that the people of the United States repudiated the Treaty of Versailles and the League. One has heard the assertion a thousand times, both here and abroad, that if the United States had been a member of the League the whole story of post-war Europe would have been different, and the League would have functioned efficiently and effectively. To this day, I am not sure whether our abstention was for the best or not, but I am inclined to believe that on the whole it was better for Europe and for ourselves that we stayed out. The agenda of the Council and Assembly meetings dealt overwhelmingly with European affairs, our representatives would have been constantly voting on matters of local and regional interest in Europe.

Suppose the point at issue a question of Polish minorities. We would have had mass meetings on the west side of Chicago and other centers of Polish immigration. Pressure would have been brought to bear on the Administration, and the position we took might well have been dictated by the fear of the Polish vote rather than the welfare of the United States or of Europe at large. A racially homogeneous folk could act effectively under these circumstances, we in the United States would have had a minor European war within our own territory over every squabble in Europe.

I recognize the force of the argument that an American member of the Reparations Committee would have prevented the assessment of fabulous sums against Germany, sums beyond the ability of Europe as a whole to pay in foreign exchange. In all probability an American on that committee would have prevented Poincaré's occupation of the Ruhr, in 1923. I recognize the probability that Americans in the Council and Assembly would have exerted a moderating influence, our distance from most of the conflicts would probably have made us dispassionate. But when I hear it stated that if Americans had been there, use would have been made of Article XIX, the peaceful revision article, there I cannot agree. I do not believe that the full weight of our authority could have brought about peaceful revision in a League where one dissenting voice could block any movement, and in a Europe in which the armies of France and its Allies were the only visible factor of power. I think our efforts would have failed, just as those of Great Britain failed, and we would have recoiled even farther from the obligations of the Covenant, just as Great Britain recoiled from a literal interpretation of Article X which guarantees the territorial integrity of every State, and from the Protocol of 1924, which provided for automatic aid against an aggressor.

Again I reflect on the type of people we are. Not only are we of every race, every creed and every blood, not only are we peculiarly unable through our mixed ancestry, to judge dispassionately in disputes in Europe. But, further, we are not accustomed to the day-by-day participation in diplomatic struggle. The British people, for example, accustomed to imperial interests, recognize that the British Foreign Office must take an active interest in any problem arising in any quarter of the globe. Our people, on the contrary, will show intense interest in foreign matters for a brief period only and then ignore them. The past twenty years have shown that we displayed the deepest interest when there was any chance of our being caught up in a European struggle on one side or the other. Then our interest was to get us out of it.

Had we been on the Council when Nazi Germany began to emerge and Europe began its war alignment, I am not sure that we would not have severed connection with the League at that moment. Those who believe that the United States should have been on the League argue about the influence we could exert, as if the United States were unanimously in favor of acceptance of responsibility abroad. If we were such people, if we had even a large majority in favor of continuing and persistent effort in world affairs, and if we were willing to accept the risk involved, then, I think, I should have been in favor of our membership. We might then have exerted a genuinely useful influence. But until we become such people, I doubt whether we can collaborate effectively and usefully in any such organization.

In the paragraphs which I have just written, I am dealing, of course, only with the political aspects of the League. The League has performed a vast number of useful services over the past twenty years, services which are not dramatic, which do not get into the press. The work on public health, narcotics, sociological problems and various technical questions has been beyond praise and of lasting benefit to the world, whatever kind of a world we have to face. On these phases of international effort, this country should and undoubtedly will, continue its collaboration when collaboration in some form becomes practicable again.

I have written of the sort of people we are, that is, we Americans. Suppose we think for a moment of people in general. It is only about a hundred years ago that the first of those incredible inventions was made by which the mechanical world was revolutionized. The world, that is the visible world, has been more changed in the past century than in perhaps any thousand preceding years in the history of the human race. Steam engines, electric light, motor transportation, flying, wireless, radio, to mention only a few, have altered life and its economic problems out of all recognition. Human thought and character have not kept pace, however, with the mechanical changes. It is inconceivable that they could. Our minds have taken millions of years to develop, the evolution has been exceedingly slow, but I believe that there has been evolution.

How can we expect a change of a perceptible nature in one hundred years? One hundred years ago, our own grandfathers were living and in their maturity many of them! In this briefest of spans, it would be folly to suppose that human thoughts and human hearts the world over have been remodeled, and have been purged of the provincialism and selfishness that wrecked this first comprehensive attempt at international co-operation. In the realm of the spirit, certainly, we must count on evolution and not revolution, and the machinery which may be worked out for future co-operation must take into account our actual state of ethical development and international consciousness, and not be framed to fit a human nature which has not yet come into existence.

CHAPTER IX

The attempt to prevent aggression by sanctions had failed, and my visits to Geneva after the failure became rare and reluctant. The Secretariat had moved into their vast new building on a ridge above the lake. It was a beautiful edifice, but to me, after these years of intense activity, it seemed the shell of a departed spirit ; the most devoted adherents to the League could not bring reality back to the meetings of that body. The war in Spain was the subject of repeated debates in the Council, but conversations behind the scene revealed that practically all the Great Powers were doing their utmost to minimize the public debate at Geneva and to hold the direction of affairs in the hands of the Non-Intervention Committee at London. The center of interest had not only shifted definitely from Geneva, but it had been shifted purposefully. Both the British and the French recognized that the Geneva institution was regarded in both Germany and Italy with such hostility that it would be provocative and dangerous to attempt decisive action there.

I found that life in Berne without the stimulus of the activity of Geneva hung heavily upon my hands. Physically, it could not have been more agreeable ; I could make expeditions on skis whenever I desired, a day's run by motor could bring me to the Riviera, Paris, Milan, or Munich. I took frequent trips and profited by this unusual opportunity when I had so little to occupy me.

But the change from intense work to the serenity of Berne became increasingly irksome, and I cast about for some occupation in which I could become engrossed. After much reflection I determined to give myself the task of writing a book, and through the early months of 1937 and, indeed, through July of that year, I worked on the story, which eventually was published under the title of *The Education of a Diplomat*. To anyone who finds the days tedious, I strongly recommend this method of filling them. It was engrossing and it was amusing. I wrote about the early years of my diplomatic life and I found as I lived them over again a joy and amusement that was perhaps sharper than the actual experience had been. Youth as it is lived is full of perplexities and worries; youth as you look back at it is full of gaiety and friendship. I finished the book in St. Jean de Luz, whither I had gone for the month of July. Mr. Claude Bowers, the American Ambassador to Spain, had his headquarters in St. Jean de Luz. He became interested in my manuscript, made valuable criticism, and eventually wrote the introduction to the book.

In the late spring the Secretary of State informed me that the President was desirous of naming me an Assistant Secretary of State. I was not filled with any undue elation at the suggested appointment; my own experience had taught me that I was happier in the field abroad representing the United States than I was participating in the administrative machinery of the Government. Nevertheless, I had been ten years in Switzerland; a change was more than due, and I accepted the assignment.

I finished my first book with a half promise to write a second chapter. I added, however, that the second chapter would be a different kind of a story and of a different person. As I read this manuscript, I believe that this statement has come true. It is a different sort of a story and it is of a different person ; the first was a book of youth, this is a book of maturity. When it became known that I was leaving Berne, M. Pilet-Golaz one of the Federal Councilors came to see me. After the usual courtesies deploring my departure from Switzerland, he said : "You are going back into your Foreign Office, you are going to be caught up in the big affairs of your nation, you are going to forget how to laugh." Perhaps I have forgotten. In any case, the third chapter of my story if I write it will be still further removed from the tone and spirit of the first.

INDEX

341